ACCULTURATION AND ITS DISCONTENTS
The Italian Jewish Experience between Exclusion and Inclusion

Edited by David N. Myers, Massimo Ciavolella,
Peter H. Reill, and Geoffrey Symcox

Exploring the fascinating cross-cultural influences between Jews and Christians in Italy from the Renaissance to the twentieth century, *Acculturation and Its Discontents* assembles essays by leading historians, literary scholars, and musicologists to present a well-rounded history of Italian Jewry.

The contributors offer rich portraits of the many vibrant forms of cultural and artistic expression that Italian Jews contributed to, but this volume also pays close attention to the ways in which Italian Jews – both freely and under pressure – creatively adapted to the social, cultural, and legal norms of the surrounding society. Tracing both the triumphs and tragedies of Jewish communities within Italy over a broad span of time, *Acculturation and Its Discontents* challenges conventional assumptions about assimilation and state intervention and, in the process, charts the complex process of cultural exchange that left such a distinctive imprint not only on Italian Jewry but also on Italian society itself.

This collection of rigorous and thought-provoking essays makes a major contribution to the history of Italian culture and the cultural influence and significance of European Jews.

DAVID N. MYERS is a professor in the Department of History and director of the Center for Jewish Studies at the University of California, Los Angeles.

MASSIMO CIAVOLELLA is a professor in the Department of Italian at the University of California, Los Angeles.

PETER H. REILL is a professor in the Department of History at the University of California, Los Angeles.

GEOFFREY SYMCOX is a professor in the Department of History at the University of California, Los Angeles.

ACCULTURATION AND ITS DISCONTENTS

THE ITALIAN JEWISH EXPERIENCE BETWEEN EXCLUSION AND INCLUSION

Edited by David N. Myers, Massimo Ciavolella, Peter H. Reill, and Geoffrey Symcox

Published by the University of Toronto Press in association with the UCLA Center for Seventeenth- and Eighteenth-Century Studies and the William Andrews Clark Memorial Library

© The Regents of the University of California Press 2008
Toronto Buffalo London
utorontopress.com

Reprinted in paperback 2021

ISBN 978-0-8020-9851-1 (cloth)
ISBN 978-1-4875-2620-7 (paper)

UCLA Center / Clark Series 10

Library and Archives Canada Cataloguing in Publication

Title: Acculturation and its discontents : the Italian Jewish experience between exclusion and inclusion / edited by David N. Myers, Massimo Ciavolella, Peter H. Reill, and Geoffrey Symcox.

Other titles: Italian Jewish experience between exclusion and inclusion | Acculturation & its discontents

Names: Myers, David N., editor. | Ciavolella, Massimo, 1942- editor. | Reill, Peter Hanns, editor. | Symcox, Geoffrey, editor. | University of California, Los Angeles. Center for 17th- & 18th-Century Studies, issuing body. | William Andrews Clark Memorial Library, issuing body.

Series: UCLA Clark Memorial Library series ; 10.

Description: Series statement: UCLA Center / Clark studies ; 10 | Paperback reprint. Originally published in 2008. | Includes bibliographical references and index.

Identifiers: Canadiana 20210201975 | ISBN 9781487526207 (softcover)

Subjects: LCSH: Jews – Italy – History. | LCSH: Jews – Cultural assimilation – Italy. | LCSH: Jews – Italy – Social conditions. | LCSH: Italy – Ethnic relations.

Classification: LCC DS135.I8 A24 2021 | DDC 945.00492/4–dc23

This book has been published with the help of a grant from the UCLA Center for Seventeenth- and Eighteenth-Century Studies.

University of Toronto Press acknowledges the financial assistance to its publishing program of the Canada Council for the Arts and the Ontario Arts Council, an agency of the Government of Ontario.

Contents

Contributors vii

Introduction 3
DAVID N. MYERS

PART I: RENAISSANCE REVERBERATIONS

1 How 'Other' Really Was the Jewish Other? The Evidence from Venice   19
BENJAMIN RAVID

2 Emotion and Acculturation: Masquerading Emotion in the Roman Ghetto   56
KENNETH STOW

3 Between Exclusion and Inclusion: Jews as Portrayed in Italian Music from the Late Fifteenth to the Early Seventeenth Centuries   72
DON HARRÁN

4 Can Fundamentalism Be Modern? The Case of Avraham Portaleone (1542–1612)   99
ALESSANDRO GUETTA

PART II: INTO MODERNITY

5 Jewish Women, Marriage Law, and Emancipation: The Civil Divorce of Rachele Morschene in Late Eighteenth-Century Trieste   119
LOIS C. DUBIN

6 The Jews of Italy in the *Triennio Giacobino*, 1796–1799   148
GEOFFREY SYMCOX

7 Singing Modernity: Synagogue Music in Nineteenth- and Early Twentieth-Century Italy   164
EDWIN SEROUSSI

8 'Their *True* Tongue': History, Memory, Language, and the Jews of Italy   183
SIMON LEVIS SULLAM

9 Growing Up Jewish in Ferrara: The Fiction of Giorgio Bassani   203
GUIDO FINK

Index   211

Contributors

MASSIMO CIAVOLELLA is Professor of Italian Studies at the University of California, Los Angeles.

LOIS C. DUBIN is Professor of Religious Studies at Smith College.

GUIDO FINK is Professor of English at the University of Florence.

ALESSANDRO GUETTA is Professor of Jewish Thought at the Institut National des Langues et Civilisations Orientales, Paris.

DON HARRÁN is Artur Rubinstein Professor Rmeritus of Musicology at Hebrew University.

SIMON LEVIS SULLAM is currently a Max Weber Postdoctoral Fellow at the European University Institute in Florence.

DAVID N. MYERS is Professor of History and Director of the Center for Jewish Studies at the University of California, Los Angeles.

BENJAMIN RAVID is Professor of Early Modern Jewish History at Brandeis University.

PETER H. REILL is Professor of History and Director of the Center for Seventeenth- and Eighteenth-Century Studies at the University of California, Los Angeles.

EDWIN SEROUSSI is Emmanuel Alexandre Professor of Musicology at Hebrew University.

KENNETH STOW is Professor Emeritus of Jewish History at the University of Haifa.

GEOFFREY SYMCOX is Professor of History at the University of California, Los Angeles.

ACCULTURATION AND ITS DISCONTENTS

Introduction

DAVID N. MYERS

Even the casual observer of the annals of the Jews recognizes the familiar cultural images of Ashkenaz and Sefarad, represented by noble pietists and aristocratic courtiers respectively. These cultural images, born in the Middle Ages and burnished by later historians, survived well into the twentieth century, particularly in the State of Israel where the Jewish population was often (and not always accurately) divided into these two groups.

While the story of Ashkenazim and Sefardim does indeed account for a good deal of the Jewish historical experience prior to the modern age, it also reduces that experience to a cultural dichotomy that can be exclusionary. For example, the important and diverse paths of Middle Eastern Jews – in Baghdad, Sana, or Cairo – are often marginalized or neglected in accounts whose central focus is the two European monoliths. And within the received narrative of European Jewish history, the more familiar annals of Ashkenazic and Sephardic history easily overwhelms the historical experience of the community that stands at the centre of our volume: the Jews of Italy.

Raw numbers play a role here. With a premodern population of some 30,000 souls, Italian Jews were dwarfed by their Iberian and northern co-religionists. Not only was the Italian Jewish population much smaller than its Ashkenazic and Sephardic counterparts. It was hardly a concentrated community in any meaningful sense. That is, Jews were dispersed over scores of Italian cities and towns, extending from Trieste in the north to Sicily in the south, with the most ancient of them, Rome, in the centre. Customs and religious ritual varied widely from community to community. The arrival of Ashkenazic and Sephardic Jews in the fourteenth through sixteenth centuries introduced new ritual rites that competed with customs whose origins were properly Italian (and which came to be collected under the name *minhag italki* – the Italian rite – despite shades of local difference among them).

Indeed, the Jewish experience in Italy is marked by a rich diversity – ethnic, regional, culinary, and even religious (e.g., the presence of Jewish women slaughterers in Piedmont). And it is this diversity that raises an important question of a more general nature. Can one speak of a single Italian Jewish history? Does the local variation among Jewish communities in Livorno, Modena, Siena, Florence, or Naples permit us to speak of a cohesive Jewish experience? At one level, we should not rush to surrender the historian's mandate to study each historical phenomenon – for example, each community – in its own discrete context. At another level, though, we can hardly avoid the pull of generalization – in this case, by imposing a degree of unity onto Italian Jewish history. Have not generations of historians, from Cecil Roth on, operated under the assumption of unity in writing of Italian Jews? Have they not noticed something distinctly Italian, and rightly so, relative to other Jewish histories – a lustrous range of activities (literary, musical, theatrical, culinary, and recreational) that is noteworthy in the Jewish historical experience?

But it is precisely in this sense, as an artifice of unity, that Italian Jewish history is a microcosm of the larger Jewish historical experience. Scholars often speak of Jewish history as a relatively coherent unit, mindful of the shared historical consciousness and religious practices of Jews while suspending awareness, at least temporarily, of the divergences developed over time and space. The challenge of this volume is to extract the conceptual gain from the premise of historical coherence without ignoring the diversity and tensions in the Italian Jewish experience. To this end, the chapters in this book seek to reveal the dialectical relationship between commonality and divergence in Italian Jewish life, as well as between Italian Jews and their non-Jewish Italian environment.

What particularly interests us is the way in which Italian Jewish history, especially in its famous 'Renaissance' phase, is *exemplary*, in both literal and popular senses. That is, it is *extraordinary* by virtue of its endurance – as the longest-standing continuous Jewish community in Europe – and its dazzling cultural repertoire. And it is *typical* (although a bit *avant la lettre*) by exhibiting a set of social dynamics that seem classically modern to our eyes. In this latter regard, we should recall that the great Jewish historian, Salo Baron, argued that early modern Italian Jews adumbrated both the Enlightenment and *Wissenschaft des Judentums*.[1] We renew this claim here, at the risk of treacherous historical comparison, but with a different twist. Our attention is less geared to the proto-Enlightenment quality of Italian culture than to the fact that the Italian Jewish experience, particularly in early modern times, anticipates the problematic of acculturation that animates much of subsequent Jewish history in the modern West.

What that experience in sixteenth-century Venice or Rome offers is a window into a complex dynamic by which a minority group, armed with its own competing desires, encounters a surrounding society simultaneously open and hostile to it. The mix of cultural seduction, fear of assimilation, economic utility, and lingering group prejudice that accompanied Italian Jews made for an interesting laboratory of social experimentation. It was not simply a matter of Jews craving entrance into the broader Christian ambience and being rebuffed or welcomed. As the essays in this volume show, the currents of cultural exchange in early modern Italy were multidirectional, moving back and forth between Jewish and Christian communities. One result was undeniably an expansion of the Jewish cultural appetite. But there was also a new awareness, interest, and perhaps even tolerance on the part of Italian Christians towards Jews.

To complicate matters even further, the distinguished historian Robert Bonfil has advanced the claim that there were powerful centripetal currents within Italian Jewry in this very same period.[2] Partly stimulated by the animus of the host society (e.g., the imposition of a ghetto in Venice in 1516) and partly by 'immanent' Jewish processes, these currents, according to Bonfil represented an inward turn towards more introspective and insular pursuits (e.g., mysticism). Bonfil's work poses a conscious and forceful challenge to the rosy portraits that his predecessors, especially Cecil Roth, drew of the Golden Age of Italian Jewish history.[3] In writing of Roth's view, Bonfil observes with a trace of sarcasm: 'Persecutions, blood-libels, expulsions, the perennial precariousness of living on the terms of a *condotta* – all this was nothing more than a small cloud in a vast blue sky stretching over the heads of jolly people laughing and singing and drinking in the streets!" Meanwhile, Bonfil's American foil, David Ruderman, seeks not only to salvage Roth's reputation by arguing that he was not as uncritical about the travails of Jews in Renaissance Italy as Bonfil suggested. He also challenges Bonfil's internalist or centripetal corrective to Roth, according to which Italian Jewish creativity emerged as much within the narrow confines of a ghetto community as through open and free contact with the non-Jewish world. The juxtaposition of these competing views makes clear how instructive Italian Jewish history is, both in its own right and for understanding the dynamics of Jewish cultural formation beyond Italy. That history cannot be reduced either to a story of outright toleration or unrelenting discrimination, nor to self-imposed insularity or unrestrained interaction. Rather, it manifests a mixture of competing tendencies, often in the same compact period, that prompts the scholar to rethink the very oppositions – for example, between internalist and externalist perspectives – common in narrating the Jewish past.[4] To wit, Alessandro Guetta argues in this volume that fundamentalist and modern sensibilities coexisted in a well-known early modern Italian Jewish text. To be sure, such competing impulses have been presented at other points in Jewish history (e.g., the ancient Greek empire, medieval Spain). Moreover, they have affected other minority groups existing within larger majority cultures. But there is a particular pungency to the unique cultural expressions – liturgical, mystical, poetic, recreational – that emerged from the Italian Jewish environment.

How might the typical Venetian Jew in 1520 have made sense of the multiple social and cultural layers of his existence? On the one hand, he was now confined at night behind the locked gates of the ghetto. Even if the intention, in the most benign case, was to protect rather than to punish, ghettoization was perceived not only as an act of constriction, but at some level, as an insult. Nonetheless, the ghetto walls did not prevent him from crossing over to Gentile society during the day and engaging in regular economic, social, and cultural exchange. For some Jews, the appetite for that exchange may have only increased as a result of the new restrictions. For others, however, ghettoization may have induced, *pace* Bonfil, a new interiority that pushed our Venetian Jew to deepen his own sense of commitment to and engagement with Jewish tradition and culture.

Of course, the allures of the surrounding society were still open to him, at least during daylight hours. And they were destined to change the face of Jewish culture in his day. In the same year that the ghetto was imposed in Venice, the first edition of the Talmud, the foundation of the Jewish Oral Law, was published in Venice. It is true that less than four decades later, the Talmud would be consigned to the flames in the heat of the Counter Reformation. But the emergence of a print culture in early sixteenth-century Italy led to an efflorescence of Jewish letters that had few parallels in the history of the Jews.

The imposition of the ghetto and the publication of the Talmud in 1516 stand for us as the symbolic poles between which Venetian Jews forged their collective identity. They mark both the limits and potential of that cultural moment for Jews. But in a more enduring sense, these poles mark off the borders of the process of acculturation for Italian Jews. The term *acculturation*, we may recall, was most definitively introduced into the American sociological lexicon by Milton Gordon in 1964 to describe a form of absorption of mainstream cultural norms by a minority group.[5] This absorption *did not* entail the loss of distinctive features by a minority group usually associated with the term *assimilation.*

Others, most notably Gerson Cohen, have argued that the term assimilation need not be equated with self-abnegation – that, in fact, the kind of cultural interaction that has often been labelled as 'assimilation' is, surprisingly, indispensable to Jewish survival.[6] While much taken by this claim, we have nonetheless chosen acculturation as the more fitting term to capture the inevitable, vitalizing, and yet at times debilitating processes of cultural exchange in which Jews engaged in Italy.[7] It captures well the multifaceted process of cultural absorption from the non-Jewish milieu, but lacks the hint of a total surrender of particular identity that 'assimilation' bears.

The 'discontents' of acculturation here (with obvious Freudian echoes) refer to obstacles, both external and self-imposed, that prevented Jews from passing unhindered into Italian society and disappearing, in the words of a later Jewish convert, 'like a river into the ocean.' Many observers have noted the discontents of acculturation in modern Jews, principally focusing on the German cultural sphere which has often been seen as the chief testing ground of 'the project of modernity' – or, to borrow again from Gerson Cohen, as the very 'mirror of modernity.'[8] The innovation of this book rests on two interrelated features. First, it shifts the focus from central to southern Europe as an important site of Jewish acculturation. This in itself is not a novel move, as Todd Endelman and David Ruderman have advocated and then demonstrated a move from a German-centric emphasis in their work on England.[9] But second, the focus of this book is not restricted to one or two centuries. Rather, it ranges over five. This wider lens offers a *longue durée* perspective on the Italian Jewish past and the dynamics of acculturation that is rare. Indeed, a number of excellent collections of scholarship have recently been published on one or another aspect of the Italian Jewish experience, ranging from Ruderman's and Giuseppe Veltri's *Cultural Intermediaries: Jewish Intellectuals in Early Modern Italy* (2004) to Joshua Zimmerman's *The Jews in Italy under Fascist and Nazi Rule* (2005).[10] The current volume frames a somewhat wider canvas, one that contains the most vivid colours of the Renaissance age as well as the more solemn tones of the Fascist era. This resulting picture provides us with a nuanced understanding of Italian Jews as cultural actors – at once extraordinary and yet typical in both their Italianness and their Jewishness.

Each of the chapters that follows is a rich case study that reveals the diversity of the Italian Jewish experience. To be sure, these essays do not – indeed, cannot – encompass the entire range of cultural expression found among Italian Jews. Such a systematic and massive undertaking would include appropriately detailed discussion of Italian Jewish innovations in the realms of mysticism, poetry, historical scholarship, and music, among other pursuits. It would also include treatment of the composition, demography, and demise of Jewish communities in that geographic entity (and terminological anachronism) – Italy – that lacked political coherence until the agitation of Mazzini and Garibaldi began to assume concrete form. And yet, our aim here has not been to offer such a comprehensive sweep. Rather, it has been to disentangle and analyse distinct strands of the Italian Jewish acculturation process over time, noting both triumphs and failings. In doing so, we seek to mark off that space between insularity and integration in which Italian Jews have dwelt throughout much of their millennia-old history.

Part I commences this exploration by exposing the ruptures of acculturation in the early modern period. Thus, Benjamin Ravid takes note at the outset of his essay of the formal legal restrictions placed upon Jews by the City of Venice, including and especially through the imposition of the ghetto. But Ravid also shows, following Brian Pullan and others, that these restrictions were neither unique to, nor uniquely onerous upon, the Jews. Moreover, the physical isolation intended by the creation of the ghetto hardly prevented economic, social, and cultural exchange between Jews and Christians. Not only did Jews leave the ghetto behind to engage in a wide range of daily activities, but non-Jews regularly made their way to Jewish merchants, teachers, even synagogues to buy, learn, listen, and compare.

Whether this interaction rises to the level of 'tolerance' by modern standards is a different matter. If there was a Renaissance-era tolerance at all, it surely rested, as Simone Luzzatto understood well in crafting his apology for the Jews from 1638, on economic utility more than on philosophical principle or altruism. But if a fully articulated tolerance was not necessarily present in this age (and overrated in its later form anyway, according to various modern critics), there was an ongoing and often robust cultural exchange – and, as Kenneth Stow shows, a subtle process of cultural mimesis – between Jews and Christians in early modern Italy. Stow's chapter points out the presence of a political instinct found among the Jews of Rome, and refined in the wake of the imposition of a ghetto in that city in 1555, to create a 'virtual Jewish state.' This instinct drew upon the incipient state-building in the Italian peninsula and Europe of the day and prompted Jews to assert their own quasi-autonomous public space in parallel. Stow argues that this impulse and the attendant 'publicity' of Roman Jewry were brought to life through notarial acts recorded by and for the Jewish community. It was not merely that political and legal deeds were preserved in these acts. It is also that the acts served as a conduit – a 'masque' in Stow's reading – through which individual and collective emotions were bared but also contained. The unrestrained expression of emotion was both unbecoming and potentially dangerous to Jews; consequently, a coded language of emotions was introduced into notarial acts that described a wide range of social interactions involving Jews and non-Jews in Rome. By analysing the coded language in these acts, Stow seeks to demonstrate a link among politics, publicity, and the articulation of emotion in Roman Jewish life. More broadly, he attempts to uncover an early manifestation of what David Sorkin called in the context of nineteenth-century Germany a 'subculture' – that is, a collection of Jews who live adjacent to, but in constant interaction with, non-Jews, drawing upon cultural values from the larger community and recrafting them in their own idiom.[11]

A similar attempt, although in a different key, as it were, comes in Don Harrán's study of *ebraiche* from the fifteenth to the seventeenth centuries – songs about Jews written by Christians that were both satirical and yet reflective of the mix of familiarity and disregard with which Jews were held. On the basis of his close reading of the music and accompanying lyrics of the ebraiche, Harrán attempts to mediate between two historiographical poles to which we alluded earlier in order to trace the shifting and often evanescent boundary between Jews and non-Jews: the pole of celebratory triumphalism associated with Cecil Roth and the more darkly hued perspective of Robert Bonfil. Thus, Harrán notes that in the theatrical world of the Renaissance, Jews were hardly the only group to merit satirical branding. Alongside the Turks, French, German, and English, Jews were saddled with negative, although often humorous, qualities. Jews in turn harboured condescending views of non-Jews. All of this rampant stereotyping did not prevent a high degree of cultural exchange, and even intimacy between Jews and Christians in Italy. The payoff of Harrán's essay is to use the analysis of musical texts to measure anew the competing forces of inclusion and exclusion that figure so prominently in the Italian Jewish experience.

A related set of oppositions informs Alessandro Guetta's essay on Avraham Portaleone, the sixteenth-century Jewish physician and savant from Mantua. Guetta juxtaposes the two main books that Portaleone wrote in order to highlight a set of competing impulses in his intellectual personality, which Guetta somewhat provocatively refers to as 'modern' and 'fundamentalist.' The earlier book, *De Auro dialogi tres* (Venice 1584), was a Latin treatise on the scientific properties of gold, which afforded Portaleone the opportunity to discuss, in good Renaissance polymath fashion, 'Greek, Latin, and Italian literature, mythology and a host of other disciplines.' The second book, written after a sudden illness (and thus prompting the author's attempt at repentance), was *Shilte ha-Giborim* (The Shields of the Mighty), a fascinating and wide-ranging Hebrew text from 1612. Portaleone not only 'returned' to the Hebrew language in this book, but also made his way back to Jewish antiquity. *Shilte ha-Giborim* revels in the glories of the Holy Temple and its age, as Portaleone provides lavish detail on topics such as the garments of the priestly class, musical norms of the Temple, and even the art of ancient Jewish warfare. At one level, the text could be read as Portaleone's 'fundamentalist' return to Judaism after deep immersion in the sea of Gentile culture (as in his first book). But Guetta pushes to another level by noting that the erudite physician not only refers back – and without disdain or remorse – to his earlier scientific pursuits, but maintains a rather 'modern' notion of historical time in his recounting of the Holy Temple. Animated by distinct, often competing, and yet coexistent desires, Portaleone then comes to embody the very complex – and complexity – of acculturation.

The second part of this volume moves from the well-known era of Renaissance Jewish life to the less-known eighteenth and nineteenth centuries. The essays here trace important shifts in the political and legal status of Italian Jews at a time when the very notion of Italian statehood was being forged – indeed, when the Italian peninsula was moving from a collection of city-states that marked its medieval and Renaissance history into a centralized national polity in the modern era. Thus, Lois Dubin offers a detailed and illuminating report of the divorce case of one Rachele Luzzato Morschene in late eighteenth-century Trieste. By appealing to the civil court for dissolution of her marriage in 1795, Rachele was abandoning the traditional Jewish courts in which such matters of personal status were to be adjudicated. And in granting the divorce, in part by consulting with rabbis as experts, the civil court of Trieste was diluting the authority of rabbis to pass judgment on such matters. In addition to offering a textured view of social and sexual norms among Jews at a vital moment of transition in European history, Dubin compels us to recall that the Italian Jewish experience (even under Habsburg rule) merits attention alongside the more renowned French case. It was at the Paris Sanhedrin of 1807, the gathering of rabbis and lay leaders summoned by Napoleon, that Jews were essentially forced to acknowledge the coexistence and even primacy of the state in matters of marriage and divorce. Dubin demonstrates that this development occurred earlier and in less formal fashion in Italy, partly impelled by Jews seeking to shake off the shackles of rabbinic power. She further asserts that one of the important effects of state intervention into the formerly rabbinic domain of marriage was to herald a new measure of liberty, particularly for the Jewish woman.

The next chapter in this section, Geoffrey Symcox's essay on the *Triennio Giacobino*, offers a different angle on this theme of liberty. Symcox focuses on the attempts by Napoleonic forces between 1796 and 1799 to gain a foothold on Italian soil. Where they did succeed in conquering territory from 1796, they introduced Jacobinian principles on democracy, equality, and anti-clericalism that spelled new freedom for Jews. Thus, in 1798, the gates of the Roman ghetto were opened, and the Pope was deposed and then imprisoned. These events were hardly greeted with unanimous praise. Symcox traces the hostile response of Italian peasant forces to the French conquest, which they regarded as repugnant as much for the spread of dangerous ideas as for the surrender of territory. He also speculates at the end that this curious Jacobinian phase in Italian history may have induced 'a mixture of joy and foreboding' among Jews themselves, as they contemplated a world without the restrictions of the past, but also without the familiar Italian brand of acculturation to order their universe.

Moving from the intersection of law and politics, the next three chapters illuminate various aspects of musical, literary, and scholarly creativity among modern Italian Jews. With a nod to Don Hárran's earlier piece, Edwin Seroussi explores the role of and transformation in liturgy in Italian synagogues at the dawn of the modern age. Similar to others here, he portrays an interesting mix of cultural conservatism and openness in Italian Jews in the late eighteenth and early nineteenth centuries. Not all, he reminds us, were enthusiastic about the prospect of Napoleonic reform; many Venetian Jews, for example, cheered the advances of the Austrian army against the very French forces that brought down their ghetto's walls in 1797. And to be sure, not all were enthusiastic about the prospect of German-style religious reform in the second decade of the nineteenth century; the denunciation by Italian rabbis of the Hamburg reformers in 1819 was fierce. And yet, Seroussi shows that those seeking to stem the tide of political or religious innovation also manifested a distinctively Italian openness in the cultural, and more particularly musical, realm – for instance, by welcoming a choir and musical instrumentation in the synagogue in advance of more self-conscious religious reformers in Germany. Seroussi then goes on to trace a shift in cultural and social disposition around mid-century that prompted the creation of new works of liturgical music under the rubric of 'musica sacra.' The emergence of this body of music signalled a new moment in Italian Jewish life – a degree of distance from the religious and liturgical norms of old – while at the same time it underscored the continuity of a largely a-religious aesthetic strand in Italian Jewish culture (reflected in the love of opera). Throughout, Seroussi recalls the simple but valuable point that Italian Jewish culture is not a monolith, but rather a patchwork of local and regional cultures woven into the surrounding environments.

The final essays in this volume mark a shift from the realm of music to the realm of literature. Simon Levis Sullam's chapter seeks to excavate traces of Italian Jewish dialects that survived into the age of assimilation, well after the ghetto walls came down. His field of exploration includes Italian Jewish scholars of language (e.g., Ascoli, Terracini) and writers (Ginzburg, Saba, Bassani, Levi) among whom he discovers linguistic shards of an Italian Jewish past – words and expressions drawn from the repository of Italian Jewish dialects. The fact that his protagonists clung to these shards, even as they surrendered more formal bonds of Jewish identification, allows Levis Sullam to investigate what Amos Funkenstein called 'the dialectics of assimilation.' In similar fashion, his study of these largely twentieth-century figures makes clear how the process of acculturation that we have been following here was inverted over time. That is, in the Renaissance era, we are often surprised, given the powerful symbol and structure of the ghetto, by the extent to which Jews actually shared in the culture of the broader milieu. But by the nineteenth and early twentieth centuries, we are surprised when we find any trace of traditional customs, practices, and dialects in otherwise highly assimilated Italian Jews. Indeed, by this point, the unrestrained (because unconscious) discarding of most remaining vestiges of Jewish culture was as much a discontent of assimilation as was the unwillingness of Gentiles to embrace the Jew.

Of course, that statement could hold true only until 1938, the year in which the racial laws were introduced in Fascist Italy. Guido Fink's concluding chapter brings us to that *terminus ad quo* in the Italian Jewish experience, and reveals yet another turn in the process of acculturation: just as the Jews were beginning to disappear 'like a river in the ocean' of Italian society, the Gentile recalled for them what they themselves had forgotten, their Jewishness. Fink demonstrates this turn by analysing the writing of Giorgio Bassani, the renowned author of *The Garden of the Finzi Continis*. He evokes Bassani's textured and at times melancholic depiction of assimilated Jewish life over three generations in the sleepy city of Ferrara, noting the faint connection to traditional Jewish culture and yet the unmistakable social code developed by and among Jews, especially during the dark years of Fascist rule. Throughout his analysis, Fink pushes to the surface the autobiographical feature of Bassani's writing, before concluding with an intriguing autobiographical twist of his own.

This final essay, in a sense, brings us full circle. The advent of the Fascist era, with its overt anti-Jewish hostility and earnest Jewish desire for integration, reminds us of the year 1516, when the ghetto was introduced in Venice and the Talmud was published. To be sure, the Fascists' collaboration with Nazism entailed a far more sinister and murderous outcome than the Venetian ghetto. Indeed, it pushed well beyond the cycle of cultural integration and social exclusion, as symbolized by these Venetian developments, that the broader Italian Jewish experience played out for more than five centuries. The task of this volume has been to illuminate the wide spectrum of activity between these poles with fine chromatic range and thematic control. The essays included here expose the breadth of cultural creativity, spontaneous and ever-evolving, in Italian Jewish life, while also recognizing the presence of a strain of social exclusion that reached final form in the Fascist age.

By exploring this defining tension between exclusion and integration, this volume is less a summation than an opening to further study of Italian Jewish history. Indeed, Italy's significance as a laboratory of Jewish cultural transformation far exceeds the size of its Jewish community (or more accurately, communities). There is a growing body of scholarship in Italy, Europe more generally, and Israel that stands in acknowledgment of this significance. Slowly, the point is beginning to be understood in the field of Jewish studies in North America.[12] Those who gathered at the University of California, Los Angeles, in April 2003, for a conference on 'Acculturation and Its Discontents: The Jews of Italy from Early Modern to Modern Times' – on which this volume is based – provided an important impetus to deeper engagement with the Italian Jewish experience that has now assumed institutional form. In 2005, UCLA inaugurated a new pilot program in Italian Jewish studies, thanks to the vision and generosity of the Viterbi Family Foundation. That pilot program has become, as of 2008, the Viterbi Program in Mediterranean Jewish Studies, the first endowed program of its kind in North America and perhaps the world. Profound thanks are owed to Andrew and Erna Viterbi, whose deep personal interest in the Italian Jewish experience reveals the best and most noble in that tradition. One can only hope that their inspired example in support of Italian Jewish studies will be replicated by other institutions in the coming years.

Thanks are also due to the Cini Foundation of Venice and its former director, Gino Benzoni, for supporting the original conference on 'Acculturation and its Discontents.' The conference was held at UCLA under the auspices of the Center for 17th- and 18th-Century Studies at the Clark Library in Los Angeles. Peter Reill, director of both the Center and the Clark Library, presided over the conference with his customary intelligence and grace. Another UCLA colleague and friend, Massimo Ciavolella, was a key planner of the conference and paved the way towards publication through his connection with the University of Toronto Press. Yet another conference co-planner, Geoffrey Symcox, contributed his invaluable scholarly and literary common sense to this volume. Stephanie Chasin cast her fine editorial eye over the text and assured a more readable book. The fine professionals at the University of Toronto Press have made the production of this book a pleasure, especially editor-in-chief emeritus Ron Schoeffel, assistant managing editor Richard Ratzlaff, and our excellent copy editor, Kate Baltais. We also thank the Indiana University Press for allowing us to reprint Lois Dubin's article, based on her conference lecture, 'Jewish Women, Marriage Law, and Emancipation: The Civil Divorce of Rachelle Luzzatto Morschene in Late Eighteenth-Century Trieste,' *Jewish Social Studies* n.s. 13:2 (Winter 2007). We owe thanks as well to the editors of *Judaism* for permission to republish Guido Fink's essay, 'Growing Up Jewish in Ferrara,' which first appeared in *Judaism* 53 (Summer-Fall 2004). Final thanks are due to the staff of the UCLA Center for Jewish Studies, especially Vivian Holenbeck and David Wu, for their constant efforts above and beyond the call of duty.

Notes

1 See Salo W. Baron, *A Social and Religious History of the Jews*, vol. 2 (New York 1937), 205, 218.

2 See Robert Bonfil, *Jewish Life in Renaissance Italy* (Berkeley 1994).
3 See Cecil Roth, *The Jews in the Renaissance* (New York 1959), and Bonfil's critique in 'How Golden Was the Age of the Renaissance in Jewish Historiography?' *History and Theory* 27 (1988), 78–102.
4 Kenneth Stow, e.g., has argued that social and legal interaction between Jews and Christians in early modern Rome was a 'two-way street.' See his *Theater of Acculturation: The Roman Ghetto in the 16th Century* (Seattle 2001), 69.
5 Milton Gordon, *Assimilation in American Life: The Role of Race, Religion, and National Origins* (New York 1964).
6 See Gerson Cohen, *The Blessing of Assimilation in Jewish History*, Commencement Address at Boston Hebrew College, June 1966, published in *Great Jewish Speeches Throughout History*, ed. Steve Israel and Seth Forman. (Northvale NJ 1994), 183–91.
7 See, e.g., my essay, '"The Blessing of Assimilation" Reconsidered: An Inquiry into Jewish Cultural Studies,' *From Ghetto to Emancipation: Historical and Contemporary Reconsiderations of the Jewish Community*, eds., D.N. Myers and W.V. Rowe (Scranton PA 1997), 17–35.
8 Cohen, 'German Jewry as Mirror of Modernity,' *The Twentieth Leo Baeck Memorial Lecture* (New York 1975).
9 See, e.g., Todd Endelman, *The Jews of Georgian England: Tradition and Change in a Liberal Society* (Philadelphia 1979), and David B. Ruderman, *Jewish Enlightenment in an English Key: Anglo-Jewry's Construction of Modern Jewish Thought* (Princeton 2000).
10 Zimmerman's introduction merits special mention for its excellent survey of historiography on Italian Fascism and the Jews.
11 David Sorkin, *The Transformation of German Jewry, 1780–1840* (New York 1987).
12 Growing awareness of Italian Jewry and its relationship to the Catholic Church and the Fascist regime of Mussolini has risen considerably over the past decade and a half owing to a spate of outstanding works that extend well beyond the narrow monograph. These include David Kertzer, *The Popes against the Jews* (New York 2001) and *The Kidnapping of Edgardo Mortara* (New York 1997), Alexander Stille, *Benevolence and Betrayal: Five Italian Jewish Families under Fascism* (New York 1991), and Susan Zuccotti, *The Italians under the Holocaust: Persecution, Rescue, and Survival* (New York 1987) and *Under His Very Windows: The Vatican and the Holocaust in Italy* (New Haven 2000). Mention should also be made of the recent translation into English of Michele Sarfatti's *The Jews in Mussolini's Italy: From Equality to Persecution* (Madison 2006).

PART I

RENAISSANCE REVERBERATIONS

chapter one

How 'Other' Really Was the Jewish Other? The Evidence from Venice

BENJAMIN RAVID

It is certainly neither original nor profound to assert that the Jew constituted the Other – even the Other par excellence – in pre-emancipation Christian Europe. Indeed, that assertion is often invoked as a short-hand abbreviation to allude to the status of the Jew or adduced as a supposedly self-evident explanation for specific lachrymose manifestations of the Jewish experience. However, the situation requires closer examination. What did Jewish Otherness really entail in both theory and practice, and what better location in which to examine it than the city which, as Robert Bonfil so aptly formulated it, 'retains the "copyright" for the semantically innovative term *ghetto*,'[1] certainly one of the outstanding visible manifestations of the status of the Jew as the Other.

Let us begin, however, not by considering that most visible manifestation of Otherness, but rather by examining the legal status of the Jews in Venice. By law, native Venetians were divided into three categories: nobles, native citizens by birth (*cittadini originarii*), and commoners. The status of nobility was limited to descendants of those who had been members of the Great Council after the process of the 'Serrata' or closing which took place during the last years of the thirteenth century and the first quarter of the fourteenth,[2] although financial straits compelled the Venetian government to expand the ranks of the nobility by admitting more families in the second half of the seventeenth century and the early eighteenth in return for substantial payments. Below the nobles were the *cittadini originarii*, the native citizens by birth, who, in the formulation of Brian Pullan, constituted 'the frozen middle class.'[3]

These two categories of nobles and native citizens by birth possessed the right to engage in the lucrative trade between Venice and the Levant, a very important privilege that since the fourteenth century had been denied to all non-Venetians. An exception came to be made for Ottoman subjects, to whom it had to be granted out of considerations of reciprocity, and of course that category included visiting Ottoman Jewish merchants who were known as Levantine Jews, although after the end of the fifteenth century an increasing number of them were actually of Iberian origin or descent.[4] Additionally, non-Venetians could acquire Venetian citizenship of two types. The first, and more limited, was that of citizenship *de intus*, which conferred rights within the city of Venice. For this, according to the revised citizenship law of 1552, a foreigner could apply after residing in Venice with family as a taxpayer for fifteen consecutive years, shortened to eight if he married a Venetian woman. The second, and more extensive, category of acquired citizenship was called citizenship *de intus et de extra*. It additionally conferred the coveted right to engage in trade between Venice and the Levant and to pay the lower customs rate established for Venetian citizens, but could be applied for only after residing in Venice with family as a taxpayer for twenty-five consecutive years.[5] The nobles, native citizens by birth, and citizens *de intus et de extra* combined – the only Venetians who could legally engage in the Levant trade, generally constituted not more than 10 per cent of the population of the city of Venice.[6]

As for the Jews, all Jews initially residing in the city and their descendents came to be called by the Venetian government Tedeschi (i.e., German) Jews because many were ultimately of Germanic origin, even though their families might have lived on the Italian peninsula – including territory under the rule of Venice – for generations, in order to differentiate them from the Jewish merchants, and they were considered collectively as constituting the *università degl'Ebrei*, the community of the Jews. Their presence in the city was authorized by charters (*condotte*) that permitted them to reside in the city for a specified length of time, after 1548 always for five-year periods. Additionally, the charter set forth the laws governing their residence in the city and especially their pawnbroking, usually referred to somewhat misleadingly as moneylending since the full Italian name for the establishment in which the transactions took place was *banco* (plural: *banchi*) *di pegni* (bank of pawns), which became shortened to just *banco* or *banchi*, with the result that understandably their owners and managers were often referred to as *banchieri* (bankers) rather than *prestatori* or *feneratori* (moneylenders).[7] The provisions of the charters were supplemented by many additional laws enacted by the major legislative councils of the Venetian government and regulations established by its numerous administrative bodies. Meanwhile, starting in 1573, the Portuguese-born Jewish entrepreneur Daniel Rodriga sought from the

Venetian government privileges in Venice for both Levantine Jewish merchants and also New Christian merchants living on the Iberian peninsula, who were referred to as Ponentine Jews, that is, western, from the Italian *ponente*, referring to the setting of the sun in the west, parallel to *levante*, the east, where the sun rose. The designation 'Ponentine Jews' constituted a neutral circumlocution, indeed euphemism, possibly formulated by Rodriga and accepted by the Venetian government in order to avoid any specific alternatives that might allude to their New Christian status.[8]

Finally, in 1589, utilitarian considerations of commercial *raison d'état* induced the Venetian government to depart from its long-standing protectionist policy of limiting the right to engage in trade between Venice and the Levant only to the nobles, the native citizens by birth, and the citizens *de intus et de extra*. The city faced serious difficulties in maintaining the entrepôt nature of the Venetian marketplace in the face of the shift in maritime trade from the Mediterranean to the Atlantic, the increased presence of the ships of England, France, and Spain for the remaining goods coming to the Eastern Mediterranean ports, and the tendency of native Venetians to withdraw from trade, which combined to cause a decline in the volume of merchandise coming to the city and consequently also in the customs revenue. As a result of the persistent lobbying of Rodriga, the government decided that the least objectionable way of remedying the situation without opening trade between Venice and the Levant to all foreigners who sought it would be to issue a charter inviting Iberian New Christian merchants to settle in the Venetian state, with the privilege of engaging in trade between Venice and the Levant immediately without any waiting period and paying the same customs rates as the native and naturalized Venetian merchants. However, to avoid religious ambiguity and confusion and the precedent of allowing non-native Christians to engage in trade between Venice and the Levant without a lengthy waiting period, the Iberian New Christians were required, upon their arrival in Venice, to assume Judaism and go directly to reside in the ghetto under the designation of Ponentine Jews. At the same time, this charter also invited Levantine Jewish merchants, who previously had been supposed to stay in the city on their own only briefly in order to complete their commercial business, to settle in it with their families with the same commercial privileges as the Ponentine Jews. This charter, although issued for a limited ten-year period, was to be renewed periodically down to 1711, and its provisions were to remain in effect until the end of the Venetian Republic in 1797.

Allowing – let alone requiring – New Christians who had been born on the Iberian peninsula and there baptised as Christians to revert to Judaism constituted a clear rejection of the new hostile Counter-Reformation papal policy. While doctrinally a loyal Catholic state which generally accepted the Catholic position on the Jews, nevertheless Venice was ready to challenge the papacy whenever it perceived that its vital self-interests were involved, and here the most basic vital self-interest of commercial *raison d'état* was indeed at stake. Consequently, the Venetians went their way and, as could well be anticipated, the papacy sharply condemned and challenged the Venetian policy towards Iberian New Christians for decades.[9] Furthermore, understandably, non-Venetian Christians resented having to reside in the city for twenty-five years before they could become citizens *de intus et de extra* and acquire the privilege of engaging in trade between Venice and the Levant. Accordingly, they sought on more than one occasion to obtain that privilege without any waiting period, citing in support the precedent of the Jews, but the Venetian government rebuffed all such requests. Thus the Levantine Jews and the former New Christians retained their privilege of being the only individuals who could become instant merchants of Venice.

It would appear that down to the last quarter of the eighteenth century, twenty years before the end of the Venetian Republic, the Venetian government never formally defined the status of the Jews of Venice, but rather generally considered them to be in the category of Venetian subjects. The eventual determination of the status of the Jews was set forth in the ten-year charter issued for the Jews of the Venetian state in 1777. Among its ninety-six clauses was the provision that the Jews could never claim or enjoy any right of *sudditanza* (i.e., of being a Venetian subject), nor at any time or in any place enjoy any privilege reserved only for Venetian subjects, and consequently were never anywhere to be regarded as such.[10] But then followed a remarkable modifying provision that reflected a compromise intended to resolve the tension between the Venetian religiously motivated anti-Jewish orientation and the rational Venetian sense of *raison d'état*. It was stipulated that in the exercise of their trade the Jews were to enjoy the protection and support of the magistracy of the Cinque Savii alla Mercanzia (which, as its name implied, was concerned with mercantile matters) in Venice, of the public representatives throughout the state, of the ambassador (*bailo*) in Constantinople, and of the Venetian consuls in the ports, so that their property and business would be protected and assisted as was that of Venetian subjects.

Most of the basic conditions under which the Jews were permitted to reside in Venice were clearly formulated in the charters of the Tedeschi

Jews who had been the original group of Jews in the city, while the later charters of the Levantine and Ponentine Jewish merchants dealt primarily with specific mercantile issues, and additional matters were spelled out in further legislation and administrative rulings. All the Jews were required to live in the ghetto, the gates of which were closed in the evening, usually one hour after sunset in the summer and two hours after sunset in the winter when it got dark earlier. They opened again at dawn when the marangona bell sounded, summoning the arsenal workers to their jobs. Only Jewish doctors and merchants were routinely allowed outside after curfew time, while permission to do so was occasionally granted upon special request to other individuals, but almost never – with the exception primarily of a few doctors – was a Jew authorized to stay outside all night.[11] Moreover, in accordance with the Catholic policy established by the Fourth Lateran Council of 1215 that Jews were to be distinguishable by a special mark on their clothing, Jewish males were required to wear at all times a special identifying sign, originally instituted in 1397 as a yellow circle on their outer-garments and then in order to make evasion more difficult, changed in 1496 to a yellow head-covering, which eventually became red for all non-Levantine Jews.[12] Penalties were established both for being outside the ghetto after hours and also for not wearing the prescribed head-covering; indeed often the two were linked together, presumably out of concern that unidentified Jews might have sexual relations with Christian women.[13]

Economic restrictions were generally expressed not by specifying what was prohibited but rather by affirming what was permitted. Most basic was the activity for which the Tedeschi Jews had initially been invited to the city, pawnbroking. Since eventually the Jews were not allowed to refuse to lend sums of up to three ducats at 5 per cent if given an adequate pledge, over time the nature of their pawnbroking changed from a private profit-making enterprise to the equivalent of a Monte di Pietà subsidized by the Jewish community, which assumed responsibility for its operation and granted the individuals who operated the pawnshops a subsidy by augmenting the economically unviable 5 per cent interest rate in order to make lending profitable.[14] Also explicitly permitted was the sale of second-hand goods, known as *strazzaria*, literally rags but, by extension, second-hand clothing and other used items, especially household furnishings which, prior to the industrial revolution when relatively inexpensive mass-produced items first became available, were sought by a large part of the population, as well as foreign diplomats and visitors to the city, and even the government itself for state occasions. Additionally, the Jews were allowed to make and sell veils and coifs. Later, after the Levantine and Ponentine Jewish merchants were invited to settle in the city, they were allowed only to engage in wholesale maritime importing and exporting. On the negative side, the Jews were specifically forbidden to engage in tailoring for themselves or on behalf of others, or to print and publish books, apparently as a result of pressure from the guild of Christian printers on the government at a time when it was trying to regulate the printing trade of the city.[15] Although the range of economic activities in which the Jews of Venice could legally engage was very limited, obviously such comprehensive restrictions were not always effectively enforced, and indeed could not be, and in practice Jews engaged in a host of other activities, both within the ghetto and also outside it, thereby augmenting the ghetto economy.[16]

Notwithstanding its generally restrictive legislation vis-à-vis the Jews, in order to attract Jews, and especially Jewish merchants, to Venice and to retain them in the city, the Venetian government had to assure them that they could practise their religion freely. Thus, initially the legislation establishing the ghetto in 1516 had asserted that it was shameful and a very bad example that all over the city the Jews had synagogues to which Christian men and women came, and provided that the Jews were not to have synagogues anywhere in the city, even in the ghetto.[17] However, the charter of 1528 provided that the Jews could live in Venice according to their rites and customs (*possano ... star et habitar in questa città secondo il rito et costume loro*) and twenty years later, the charter of 1548 specifically gave them permission to have synagogues 'according to custom.'[18] In its heyday, the ghetto contained five major synagogues and at least three minor ones, and no attempt seems ever to have been made to limit the number of synagogues in the ghetto in accordance with the terms of the papal bull *Cum Nimis Absurdum* of 1555.[19]

The charters also contained several other provisions resulting from the permission to live according to Jewish rites and customs.[20] The charters of the Tedeschi Jewish moneylenders allowed them to bury their dead on the Lido. Also, it was stipulated that the butchers were to provide the Jews with kosher meat at the same price as that at which they sold meat to others. Furthermore, the Jews were assured that they could not be compelled to engage in moneylending or to be summoned to court on the Sabbath and on their holidays, or forced to do anything against their rites and customs. Indeed, respect for the right of the Jews to observe the Sabbath led at least once to a change in the laws. Starting with the charter of 1618, it was provided that all cases involving converts, their relatives, and other Jews were to be decided by all three of the Avogadori di Comune. By the early eighteenth century this was causing a problem, because the three Avogadori only met twice a week, on Wednesday and Saturday – which meant that Jews could only come once a week, on Wednesdays – and then had much business to transact. Accordingly, to facilitate matters, in 1727 the Senate legislated that in order not to compel the Jews to come to the Avogadori on Saturdays, cases involving Jews could be dealt with by only one of the Avogadori, that is, also on those days of the week on which all three did not meet together.[21]

The charters of the Levantine and Ponentine Jewish merchants provided that they too could observe their 'rites, precepts and ceremonies' (*li loro riti, precetti e ceremonie*) and have synagogues according to their custom. Additionally, they were to be secure from molestation for religious reasons by any magistracy, certainly a very necessary provision needed to reassure former New Christians who had assumed the religion of their ancestors and were living openly as Jews in the ghetto.

The favourable approach of the Venetian government extended also to other matters. It opposed the baptism of Jewish minors under the age of fourteen without the consent of their parents, in accordance with a clause in a charter granted to Jewish pawnbrokers in Mestre in 1503 and eventually introduced into clause 68 of the charter of the Jews of Venice of 1777.[22] Indeed, the fear that the perceived danger of the forced baptism of their minor children might cause Jewish merchants to leave Venice to the detriment of its commerce was adduced as a reason for respecting the policy of opposing such conversion.[23] Furthermore, compulsory conversionary sermons were never introduced in Venice, and indeed a clause prohibiting forcing Jews to attend them was incorporated into clause 68 of the charter of 1777.[24] Additionally, provisions were made for Jews to take oaths in court according to a special formula acceptable to them. Apparently, the purpose of this oath was not to humiliate the Jews but rather to enable them to avoid pronouncing the tetragrammaton, for when an attempt was made to change the oath in 1687, the Jews related in a petition to the Venetian government that some rabbis considered it less of an evil to change their country than to change their religious rites and others were thinking of leaving, while none were coming to Venice out of fear of that change and 'greater things.' In response, the Venetian Senate provided that the Jews could not be required to take any oath other than the usual one,[25] and this provision was also incorporated into clause 68 of the charter of 1777. Finally, two eighteenth-century reports (*consulti*) written by the legal advisers of the Venetian government, the *consultori in iure*, related that, among other provisions enabling the Jews to observe their own laws, when it had been necessary to subject corpses to autopsies, the Council of Ten had ruled that Jewish corpses were to be exempted, since autopsies were not permitted by Jewish law.[26]

Moreover, in accordance with the assurance that the Jews could live according to their own laws, the Venetian government most remarkably adjudicated cases involving the financial aspects of dowries, divorces, and inheritances according to Jewish law, especially, it seems, when individuals who had converted to Christianity were concerned. This led to the preservation of numerous Italian translations of passages from traditional Jewish sources, including the Talmud, the *Mishneh Torah* of Maimonides, and the *Shulhan Arukh* of Joseph Karo, as well as of contemporary wedding contracts and wills, often undertaken by the official Translator of the Hebrew Language (*Interprete della Lingua Ebrea*), whose position had been created for that purpose. Remarkably, on occasion these translations were even printed, along with other relevant documents, in booklets, presumably for the benefit of the Venetian officials who had to adjudicate the matter at hand.[27]

To comprehend further the situation of the Jews, it is illuminating to compare the Venetian treatment of Judaism with its treatment of other non-Catholic religions.[28] Most basically, the Venetian situation confirms the view that in Christian Europe it was generally better to be a Jewish infidel than to be a Christian heretic, whose experiences were even more lachrymose than those of the Jews since heretics did not have the right to observe their religious rites. As Brian Pullan has observed, 'the Jews were more highly privileged than any other community of religious aliens, with the sole exception of Greeks adhering to the Union of Florence,' while Protestants 'could expect only liberty of conscience, as distinct from freedom of public worship, and seize the chance to attend an embassy chapel.'[29] On the other hand, Jews were permitted to have synagogues that Christians could and did visit.[30]

The Greek Orthodox in Venice were initially not allowed to build a church in Venice because the Venetian government suspected their religious loyalty to Catholicism and the Papacy, and their clerics were only allowed to lead services in one designated chapel. When the Greeks petitioned for the right to build a church in 1511, they expressed their confidence that 'your lordships will grant it, both because you are men of honour and devotion, and to show us that in your eyes we are no worse than the Armenian heretics and the Jewish infidels who here and in other parts of your lordships' dominions have synagogues and mosques for worshipping God in their own misguided way.'[31] In 1514, the permission was granted with the approval of the Pope, who placed the Greeks directly under his supervision. However, the Venetians still suspected that the Greeks might revert back to their previous schismatic practice, and the Venetian patriarch Girolamo Querini generally considered the schismatic Greeks to be worse than the Jews. Their church, whose construction commenced in 1539, was completed only in 1573.[32]

As for the Protestants, only in 1657 did the Protestant merchants from the Germanic lands who were residing in the Fondaco dei Tedeschi finally receive permission to hold private services in the Fondaco and they brought in pastors from Germany.[33] Still, as Frederick Lane noted, 'no organized Protestant propaganda was permitted, and Protestantism was tolerated only marginally as an intellectual plaything of a few sceptics and as the religious custom of a few foreigners: the German merchants in their Fondaco, a flourishing colony of German bakers, and the many German students at Padua.'[34]

Certainly, the Moslem Turks, who were generally perceived as a real political threat as well as religiously undesirable, were viewed with more antipathy than were the Jews. After the Turkish merchants had been interned as enemy aliens during the Venetian-Ottoman war of 1570–73, they requested from the Venetian government 'for the convenience of trade, a place of their own, as the Jews have their ghetto,' but it was not granted.[35] An anonymous memorandum addressed to the Venetian government in 1602, which may have only constituted a literary exercise, urged the Senate not to give the Turks a Fondaco of their own. Among other things, it pointed out that doing so would lead to the erection of mosques and to the worship of Mohammed, with a scandal greater than that caused by the Jews and the Protestant Germans. Also, a Fondaco would further the political aims of the Turks who, headed by one Sultan and possessing great naval power, were in a position to harm Venice more than were the Jews, who were without any head or prince and everywhere repressed.[36] Only in 1621 were the Turkish merchants finally given a building of their own, subsequently known as the Fondaco dei Turchi. There, they lived segregated, subject to many restrictive provisions similar to those in effect for the ghetto, and not allowed to have a mosque.[37]

Summarizing the situation in the late seventeenth century, Maximilien Misson observed that in Venice, the Greeks, Armenians, and Jews were allowed the public exercise of their religion, while all other sects or religions were tolerated, but one pretended not to know about their meetings, which were held in so secret and discreet a manner that the Senate did not have any reason to complain about any abuse or indiscretion. Further, in the course of asserting that Protestants could be buried in the churches if their relatives desired it because one ignored that there were Protestants in Venice, Misson claimed that all those who were neither Jews nor Greeks nor Armenians were deemed to be Catholics.[38] As Frederic Lane concluded, 'Venice was far from being any champion of freedom of thought in principle ... But men of a great variety of views succeeded one way or another in living in Venice pretty much as they pleased, and thinking as they pleased, so long as they did not attack the government.'[39] Marino Berengo further characterized the Venetian attitude towards non-Catholic religions as one of indifference and not of official toleration. It did not proclaim the freedom and equality of religions, but rather gave tacit consent for foreigners privately to practise their own religion without harming Catholicism because of the necessity to have foreign merchants in the city, but strictly forbade both proselytism on behalf of the tolerated denominations as well as anti-Catholic propaganda.[40]

Obviously the nature of the Otherness of the Jew cannot be reconstructed only on the basis of laws and administrative promulgations and regulations, which to a great extent reflected general Catholic policy towards the Jews and were not unique to Venice. Rather, a discussion of those factors serves as the necessary background for the exploration of the everyday local dynamics. Very illuminating insight into the nature and extent of relations between Christians and Jews can be obtained from the autobiography of Leon Modena, a unique and invaluable document currently conveniently available in three languages,[41] which testifies to continual close contact of all sorts. A further indication of the contact that could occur between Jews and Christians on the upper level of the socio-economic and intellectual ladder is the perhaps even more remarkable – and certainly even more unrepresentative – life of Sara Coppio Sullam (ca. 1592–1641).[42] Born into a prominent Venetian Jewish family, she received a secular humanistic education and married Jacob Sullam, also a prominent member of the Jewish community of Venice. In May 1618, after reading *L'Ester*, a verse epic by the Genoese monk Ansaldo Cebà (1565–1623), Coppio Sullam wrote to Cebà expressing her admiration and spiritual love for him and informing him that she carried his book with her at all times and slept with it under her pillow at night. A correspondence ensued, which became increasingly personal, as they exchanged sonnets in Italian and Spanish, gifts, and even portraits. Cebà asked for permission to pray for her conversion, to which she responded by requesting permission to pray for his. Despite his monastic status, he nevertheless pointed out to her that the fact that her middle name, Coppio, meaning 'couple,' was spelled with two letter p's indicated that they could form a Christian couple. Thereupon, Coppio Sullam immediately removed one of the two p's from her name, henceforth spelling it as Copio or Copia.

While corresponding with Cebà, Coppio Sullam attracted to her dwelling in the ghetto Christian men of letters, who gave her academic lessons in return for her financial backing, intellectual conversation, and salon environment. Gradually, however, many of them turned against her. In 1621, Baldassare Bonifaccio, a priest, poet, and legal scholar, published a treatise on the immortality of the soul, in which he claimed that two years earlier, Coppio Sullam had told him that she did not believe in that doctrine, which was a fundamental aspect of both Judaism and Christianity and therefore denying it could render her liable to the charge of heresy from the Jewish and Christian vantage points alike. Coppio Sullam wrote a strong defence of her position, in which she denied that she rejected the immortality of the soul, and castigated Bonifaccio for using her as a foil for his ill-conceived arguments, upbraiding his character, logic, and style, and chastising him for attacking a woman who, although educated, was not a professional scholar. Bonifaccio in turn rebutted her charges by asserting that her *Manifesto* actually had been written by a rabbi whom he did not name; if Coppio Sullam indeed had any help from a rabbi, it was probably from her friend Leon Modena, who was a member of her circle, dedicated his play *Ester* to her, and wrote her tombstone inscription. Clearly, Bonifaccio, like Cebà, found the conduct of Coppio Sullam very uncharacteristic for a Jew.

Around this time, Coppio Sullam's teacher, a syphilitic Roman writer and poet named Numidio Paluzzi, left her, taking with him a substantial amount of money that he had borrowed from her, including a three-month advance on his salary. Some six months later, he returned to Venice and was welcomed back by Coppio Sullam. Meanwhile, two of Coppio Sullam's servants, her black Marrano maid and her Christian laundress, were stealing from her and blaming the thefts on spirits, and upon his return, Paluzzi joined them, using his position as Coppio Sullam's teacher to encourage her predilection for magic, which was characteristic of the times. Paluzzi was unable to stand up because of his syphilitic condition and accordingly another member of Coppio Sullam's circle who was also a close friend of his, the Roman painter and poet Allesandro Berardelli, was hired to bring him his meals, and soon joined in the exploitation of Coppio Sullam. He and Paluzzi told her about an alleged French admirer who had heard of her and the magical activities of her maid and wanted to correspond with her. They then fabricated alleged letters of his to her which led to costly gifts that ended up in the nearby room of Paluzzi. They even enticed Coppio Sullam to commission Berardelli to paint her picture for the Frenchman for a fee of over one hundred ducats. Eventually she discovered the truth, dismissed Paluzzi, and brought charges against Berardelli in one of the Venetian courts. Thereupon, the two men retaliated by asserting, in two works that have not survived, that Coppio Sullam had appropriated writings of Paluzzi as her own.

Interestingly, several contemporaries referred to the close relationship that existed between some Jews and members of the Venetian nobility, which presumably was based at least initially on common economic and commercial interests. For example, the convert Giulio Morosini, who was born in Venice sometime between 1608 and 1612 and resided there until his conversion in 1649, in his conversionist work *Via della fede* (1683), which generally has to be taken with some caution because of its polemical anti-Jewish nature, asserted that in Venice Jewish merchants were so close and important to the Christian nobles (*hanno gran familiarità gli Ebrei mercanti e riguardevoli con i Christiani nobili*) that sometimes the nobles would give the Jews the keys to their dwellings.[43] This relationship was confirmed by various travel accounts, which may not be completely independent of each other and certainly exaggerated the position of the Jews. The Englishman John Clenche, who toured Italy in 1675, related that the Jews 'for their reputed secrecy are very much cherished by the nobility, there not being one but has his Jew for his confidant, nor Jew without his protector.'[44] Likewise, his contemporary, the French traveller Alexandre-Toussaint Limojon de Saint-Didier observed that 'at Venice every Noble Family hath an Intimate and Confident Jew; for as they are esteem'd to be men of Secrecy, so this good Quality gets them many Protectors among the Nobility, who have divers ways of employing them.'[45] His fellow countryman Maximilien Misson related that the Jews 'are generally a Sort of People that never refuse any Kind of Employment, and are made Use of on several Occasions, especially by the Nobles, who are a very great Support to them.'[46] The French consul in Venice, in the course of commenting on the weddings of wealthy Jews in the city in a report written in 1709, related that it was acceptable for 'honourable people' to attend and usually one saw there noblewomen wearing masks. Moreover, at a recent wedding of a daughter of Levi del Banco, 'there was a large crowd, among whom were some foreign Ministers.'[47] Most remarkably, in a recent book dealing with the course of events that led Simone Luzzatto to write his *Discorso sopra il stato degl'Hebrei et in particolar dimoranti nel'inclita città di Venetia* (Discourse on the State of the Jews and in Particular Those Living in the Illustrious City of Venice; Venice, 1638),[48] Gaetano Cozzi demonstrated that certain Jews, because of their close relationships with members of the Venetian nobility, were able to act as brokers or intermediaries in affecting the course of justice in the highest Venetian courts by means of bribes.[49]

Jewish religious observances attracted the attention of Christians, clearly demonstrating Christian interest in Judaism without any necessary personal relationship and certainly without any economic or commercial component. Although as noted above, the legislation establishing the ghetto in 1516 had provided that the Jews were not to have synagogues even in the ghetto because it was shameful and a very bad example that the Jews had synagogues all over the city to which Christian men and women came, after they were granted permission to have synagogues, native Venetian Christians, as well as Christian visitors, Catholic and Protestant alike, to the city, continued over the decades to attend the services in the ghetto synagogues and to listen to the sermons, which were delivered in Italian.[50] To cite one prominent example, Leon Modena related in his autobiography that at a sermon which he gave on 28 April 1629, 'in attendance were the brother of the King of France [presumably Gaston, Duke of Orleans, brother of Louis XIII], who was accompanied by some French noblemen and by five of the most important Christian preachers who gave sermons that Pentecost. God put such learned words into my mouth that all were very pleased, including many other Christians who were present ... Both before and afterward, noblemen and other great men came to hear my sermons, notably Duke Candale and Duke Rohan [the Protestant leader who had been defeated at La Rochelle in 1628] among others.'[51]

Further testimony to the attendance of native Venetians in the synagogues of the ghetto is to be found in the *Via della fede* of Morosini. Morosini related that on the evening of Simhat Torah, which he characterized as a semi-carnival, many male and female members of the Christian nobility came to the synagogues, 'almost more than on other holidays,' to see the magnificence of the illuminated synagogues and what he termed the foolish gaiety of the Jews, with the result that the ghetto guards had to open the gates long after curfew time to let the Christians out of the ghetto. Furthermore, he added that since on that day many Christians came to the synagogue out of curiosity, when the cantor recited the usual prayer for the Venetian government in Italian, he would mention the Doge and the Serenissima in as loud a voice as possible.[52] The continued interest of Christians in Jewish sermons is attested to by the comment in the diary of the eighteenth-century Venetian Pietro Gradenigo that numerous Christians attended a certain sermon in 1752.[53] Moreover, the music of twelve of the first fifty biblical psalms that were set to music by Benedetto Marcello in his *L'estro poetico armonico* was based on Jewish liturgical melodies that Marcello had heard in the synagogues of Venice.[54] Despite the request of the patriarch of Venice, Lorenzo Cardinal Priuli, in 1596–97, to have a prohibition against the Jews admitting any Christians into their synagogues added to the charter of the Tedeschi Jews, the Venetian government did not take any action on the matter at that time or at any other.[55]

The interest of Christians in events in the ghetto was not limited to synagogue services. Marino Sanuto related in his voluminous diary that on the night of 4 March 1531, the Jews were granted permission to perform a *bellissima comedia* (Purim play?) which ended at the eighth hour of the night, but by order of the Council of Ten, no Christian could attend.[56]

In a wider context, music appears to have constituted a significant area of interaction between Jews and Christians in Venice. A perusal of the record books of the Cattaveri, a minor Venetian magistracy that had been given substantial jurisdiction over the Jews and the ghetto, dealing with the Jews during the later years of the sixteenth century and early seventeenth, reveals that many of the permissions that it issued for Jews to be outside the ghetto after the closing of its gates involved dancing or engaging in a musical performance, especially during carnival time. Often such permissions were valid only until a specified hour and sometimes it was stipulated that the privileged individuals were limited only to specific places or generally to homes of respectable people and were not to sleep outside the ghetto, and only rarely were they exempted from wearing the specially coloured identifying Jewish head-covering.[57]

Detailed information has been preserved regarding Rachel *hebrea can-*

tarina and her father Jacob and brother Marco, who had been given permission to go out at night into homes of Christians. Subsequently, secret reports from allegedly reliable persons had revealed that, under pretext of going to sing in homes of 'nobles, citizens, and other honourable persons,' they were staying in homes of common persons, eating, drinking, and behaving dishonestly with Christians. Therefore, on 26 September 1609 the Cattaveri decided that in order to eliminate what they called a great scandal offensive to God and a bad example to all, henceforth those Jews were not to be allowed out at night unless the permission were granted by all three Cattaveri, and should one or two of them be absent, then their place was to be filled by certain other specified officials to assure that the permission was signed by three people. However, three and a half months later, on 1 January 1610, the Cattaveri had to moderate their stance. Noting that the substitute provision in its ruling regarding permission for Jews to stay outside the ghetto after curfew time was invalid since only the *Maggior Conseglio* or Senate could authorize substitutions, the Cattaveri now ruled that if all three Cattaveri were present, the approval of two would be sufficient; should two be present, then both would have to give their consent, while if only one were present, his approval would suffice, but in any case permission could only be granted for one evening.[58] Shortly afterward, on 21 January 1610, the Cattaveri returned to their original stance of 26 September 1609 by forbidding Rachel from staying outside the ghetto after the stipulated hours without a permit signed by all three of them, subject to whatever penalty they should consider suitable.[59] However, Rachel apparently continued to disobey the regulations, for in June 1613 the Cattaveri forbade her to continue to go singing around the city at night by gondola without permission, subject to a fine and other penalties.[60]

An interesting earlier relationship involving dancing came to light as a result of an inquisitorial investigation in 1585. It turned out that Giuseppe, a Jewish dancing teacher from Mantua, taught Christian children, including the eight-year-old Paulin whom he instructed for two years at his pupil's dwelling, where he often ate, sometimes once or twice a week. Paulin also visited him in the ghetto to dance, without however ever eating there. Indeed, Giuseppe was on such good terms with the boy's parents that they asked him to take Paulin with him on a trip to Mantua to introduce their son to the *primecerio* of the Church of Sant' Andrea and on that trip the two had eaten and stayed overnight together. Apparently alarmed by the danger that such frequent contact with Jews could pose for Christian children, in 1585 the Inquisition ordered Giuseppe not to teach dancing to Christian children under the age of twelve and especially not to have any more contact with Paulin and his young and pretty mother, subject to three years at the oars in the galleys.[61]

Naturally, the wider question arises as to why Jewish musicians and dancing teachers were sought after in Venice; indeed, legislation of 1443, a time when Jews as a group were not authorized to reside in Venice and only a few were to be found in the city, had expressly forbidden Jews from operating schools of games, *arte, dottrine,* dancing, singing, instrument playing, or 'anything else,'[62] and apparently this legislation was later interpreted as also forbidding Jews to teach such subjects in the homes of Christians. Did Christian Venice not have enough singers and musicians, or did the Jews have different musical traditions that certain skilled individuals could present in an attractive manner, or perhaps in certain circles it was considered fashionable to employ the services of Jewish singers and dancers? In any case, presumably a few Jews were unusually capable performers and the Jewish community was well aware of the Christian appreciation of music performed by Jews, for in January 1611 the Small Assembly of the Jewish Community made provisions to please the Doge by performing a ballet or 'something similar.'[63]

Further glimpses of contact between Jews and Christians at the upper end of the social scale emerge from inquisitorial processes edited by Pier Cesare Ioly Zorattini. It should always be kept in mind that the Inquisition in Venice, as all Inquisitions on the Italian peninsula, was established not to deal with a New Christian–Crypto-Jewish problem, as had been the case on the Iberian peninsula, but rather to prevent Protestantism from gaining a foothold in the land of the papacy. Accordingly, the concern of Italian Inquisitions with New Christians or individuals of New Christian origin reverting to Judaism varied greatly by time and place. In Venice, the majority of inquisitorial cases preserved for the years from 1541 to 1600 dealt with Lutheranism (51.3 per cent) and witchcraft (12.71 per cent), while only 4.7 per cent involved matters relating to judaizing.[64] David Pas, who lived in the Ghetto Vecchio, supposedly 'kept a salon not disdained by Venetian patricians and Christians "of most ancient lineage,"' and was accused of having sexual relations with a Christian employee who lived in his dwelling.[65] Moreover, the New Christian Joao Ribeiro married a young Jewish woman according to Jewish law in the dwelling of a Venetian nobleman on the island of Murano,[66] although of course the complex case of Joao Ribeiro and his father Gasparo cannot be considered as typical, for any discussion of social relationships between Jews and Christians must differentiate between Old Christians, on the one hand, and on the other, New Christians, who were more likely to interact with professing Jews because of their awareness of their own Jewish descent or family relationships.

One of the hardest areas in which to control and minimize contact between Christians and Jews was that of economic relations. The approximately fifteen hundred to three thousand Jews in the ghetto, who generally constituted somewhere between 1 and 2 per cent of the total population of the city of Venice,[67] represented potential employers for numerous Christian workers, especially in those extensive areas in which the Jews were forbidden to engage by law or by guild restrictions or were unable for other reasons to acquire the necessary skills.[68] Many Christians, male and female alike, were willing to improve their economic circumstances in the urban environment of the metropolis by serving the Jews in a wide range of activities, both on a casual basis and also more regularly in relationships that could lead to varying degrees of familiarity. Consequently, maintaining the centuries-old church policy of carefully controlling Jewish employment of Christians, and especially of Christian women as servants, was of very great concern to the Venetian government, which was reluctantly willing to tolerate some such contact in order to provide a living for its poor, marginal, and unskilled Christian inhabitants, but tried to limit interaction to the necessary minimum, as it opposed opportunities for lengthy contact between Jewish employers and Christian employees, especially women. In keeping with one of the provisions of the papal bull *Cum Nimis Absurdum* of Paul IV of 1555 which expressed the new Counter Reformation attitude of the papacy towards the Jews, the Venetian government introduced into the charter renewal of 1566 a new prohibition for Jews to keep Christians in their dwellings as servants or in any other capacity and especially to employ Christian women as wet-nurses, subject to a fine of 100 ducats and three years at the oars in irons in the galley for each offence, while the Christian involved was to be banished from the city for two years.[69]

In late 1602 or early 1603, the government asked the Cinque Savii alla Mercanzia about those women whom they had approved to work for the Levantine and Ponentine merchants, presumably with the intention of restricting their employment.[70] The Savii related that the previous charter of the merchants in 1598 had provided that the Savii were, among other things, to provide the Jews with servants, and accordingly they had permitted some Christian women to work for the Jews in the Ghetto Vecchio. However, the Savii continued, if the government wished, it could order that the permission not be put into effect, for they too did not consider it proper that the Jews should employ those women in their dwellings, and especially to nurse their children or to perform services that could be carried out by men and porters. Therefore, they recommended that in the future permissions to work for the Jews should be granted to those porters and others who would be requested by the Jews in accordance with their privileges in order to avoid the scandal that could result to the harm of religion.

Apparently, a certain laxity continued in the granting of permissions for Christians to work for Jews, for in February 1616 the three Cattaveri, observing that such permissions usually were granted only by one of them and possibly often against the wishes of the other two, agreed that henceforth no permissions were to be granted for any woman to be a servant or wet-nurse in the ghetto nor for the Jews to take their children to nurse outside the ghetto[71] without the permission of all three of them. Accordingly, the notary of the Cattaveri was not to issue any permit unless approved and signed by all three, subject to a fine of twenty-five ducats for each violation, and all permissions previously issued were to be cancelled.[72] Continuous contact between Jews and Christians was also cited by the Cattaveri as a reason for rejecting the request of the Jews in 1634 to be allowed to engage in printing Hebrew books and to employ Christians in their print shops.[73]

In the eighteenth century, the government clamped down on the employment of Christians by Jews and eventually even on the very presence of Christian minors in the ghetto. A ruling of the Essecutori contro la Bestemmia of 22 March 1703 prohibited Christian porters from entering the ghetto and engaging in any sort of service for the Jews on Christian festive days since they were to observe those days with acts of Christian piety.[74] Also, no Christian children under the age of seventeen were to enter the dwelling of a Jew, nor could any Jew at any time under any pretext employ them in any conceivable service in the ghetto, subject to the most rigorous physical and monetary penalties. Similarly, the parents or guardians of the Christian child were to be subject to such penalties should they have permitted the child to perform any service in the dwelling of a Jew, and additionally not only were they to keep their children away from the dwelling of the Jews but also from all other places in the ghetto. Likewise, girls and Christian women were forbidden to stay overnight in the ghetto and also to engage in any service for any Jewish man or woman. The guardians of the ghetto were strictly enjoined, subject to severe penalties, to watch out for transgressors and report them to the authorities. Finally, to assure the observance of their ruling, the Essecutori provided that it was to be announced in the ghetto on the first Sunday of every month at the time and in the place where the most people would hear it, and also posted on the ghetto gates.

This ruling was followed thirteen years later, in 1716, by much more severe regulations of the Cattaveri, likewise required to be announced and posted in the ghetto. Claiming that the Jews scandalously were constantly introducing into the ghetto numerous Christian men and women of all ages, many of whom stayed day and night in the homes of Jews, eating, drinking, and doing other things most contrary to the religious public decrees and terms of the charter, it was reiterated that no Jews were under any pretext to keep in their service in their dwellings any Christian man, woman, or child for any purpose whatsoever. Moreover, since it was most scandalous to see Christian minors frequenting the ghetto, no Christians under the age of eighteen were to enter the ghetto under any pretext, and should they even be found at its gates, they could be arrested, jailed, and next morning irremissibly placed in the stocks for half an hour. Additionally, should they be found in, or reported to have been in, the dwelling of a Jew, then that Jew was to pay a fine of 100 ducats and serve three years in the galleys, while any Christian servants or others living in the dwelling of a Jew were to spend a month in a small cell, with parents, relatives, or guardians serving in place of their children. Also, since Christian piety required that the obligatory Christian holidays be observed, on those days no Christian porter could be employed in the ghetto for any conceivable reason in the service of the Jews, subject to the same penalty for him as well as for the Jew who employed him. A similar sentence was to be meted out to gondoliers who undertook to work or to stay in the dwelling of a Jew under the pretext of gondola service. Finally, to assure implementation of these provisions, the guards of the ghetto gates were to submit weekly a list of all Christians in the above-mentioned categories who entered in the morning and left in the evening, as well as of all those Jews who entered and left at prohibited hours, subject to deprivation of office and other punishments to be determined.[75]

Apparently abuses still continued, for when in January 1739, the Cattaveri ordered the reprinting and posting of an earlier proclamation of 1736 dealing with the enforcement of the special Jewish head-covering, they added a reiteration of the prohibition against Christian minors being employed in the domestic service of Jews and provided for the punishment of any heads of Christian families who permitted such activities.[76]

The charter of 1760 permitted the Jews to use Christian men only to provide light and fire on Jewish festive days – presumably including the Sabbath – as well as for those needs of trade that could not be delayed.[77] These provisions were reiterated in the subsequent charter of 1777, and when in the following year the Cattaveri were asked by the Senate to report on the observance of those terms that were under their jurisdiction, they related that the prohibition against employing Christians was being fully observed in the city of Venice, especially after the strong reprimand issued to some Jews who had been denounced for violating it. Also, they continued, its observance could be demonstrated by the recent number of Christian women of advanced age who had been accustomed to earn their living by serving the Jews and therefore had requested permission to continue but, in accordance with the law, were strongly turned down with indignation and the threat of punishment if they continued.[78]

Cases preserved in inquisitional dossiers validate the concern of the Venetian government regarding the potential influence of contact between Christians and Jews, and presumably the written evidence is representative of a far greater range and number of cases of interaction that have not left any trace in the official records.

Most interestingly, the inquisitional records reveal cases in which Christian employees expressed to their Jewish employers not a negative attitude towards Judaism but rather a neutral or even favourable attitude, which of course was viewed unfavourably by the Inquisition. To cite a few examples, around 1566 a certain Battista de Leone, son of a schoolmaster and himself a bookbinder, worked for the Jewish merchant and communal leader Chaim Saruc in the ghetto for several months. He was suspected of having been the source of certain shocking opinions expressed by one of his father's former pupils, but he denied anything other than a purely business relationship with Saruc and other Jews.[79] Remarkably, in 1580, Antonio, a Christian goldsmith working in a dwelling in the ghetto on two 'pyramids' to place on the top of the rollers of the Torah scroll, allegedly stated that one did not know whether the Jews or the Christians would be saved (*non se sa anchora qual si sia quelli che debbono esser salvi o Hebrei o veramente noi*), and in support related the well-known parable of the father who gave a ring to each of his three sons, each of whom thought that only he possessed the 'good one.'[80]

The widow Valeria Brugnalesco or Brunalesco, who had been engaged to teach Jewish children to read and write Italian, was accused, among other things, of forming very close friendships with Jews and engaging in magic with one of them, of living in the ghetto and eating the same food as the Jews did on Fridays and Saturdays, and also of allegedly asserting that Judaism was better than Christianity and pleased her more because the Jews observed Judaism more than the Christians observed their own religion. In her defence, Valeria admitted that after the death of her husband, a physician, she had lived with her daughter in the ghetto for two years, teaching Italian to around seventy to eighty Jewish girls, but claimed that she had never eaten Jewish bread or meat but only wine, fruit, fried fish, and unleavened bread. She had used an Italian Bible in her lessons, and when she came to passages concerning the Virgin Mary (presumably verses in the Old Testament predicting the coming of Jesus according to the Christian interpretation), she told her students not to dwell upon the subject, for it could cause pains similar to those caused by giving birth. Eventually, when her parish priests would not give her absolution after she confessed, she left the ghetto for the dwelling of her daughter, where she invited a Jew to perform certain magical rituals.[81]

Detailed information is available regarding Giorgio Moretti, whom Brian Pullan has characterized as 'Venice's most serious, or unfortunate, offender.'[82] Several accusations were levelled against him: that he had attended at least two Jewish weddings during Lent[83] and had behaved as did the Jews, inviting guests and receiving them; on three occasions he had eaten meat during Lent; he had joined in the celebration of circumcisions and danced at them; he also supposedly ate unleavened bread and was wounded by some Christians for refusing to share it with them; he had been in the ghetto at all hours of the night and disturbed the Christian guards by demanding with blasphemous curses that they let him out. Finally, when he was accused of courting a Jewish woman named Rachel – incidentally, against the very strong objection of her family – he claimed that he had intended to persuade her to convert to Christianity and then to marry her. The Inquisition was very dubious, and forbade Moretti to enter the ghetto or to approach its gates subject to three years at the oars in the galleys. However, around two months later, he was again seen in the ghetto and also going around the city wearing the yellow Jewish head-covering. This time, neither his explanation that he had put on the head-covering as a prank nor his claim that he had been drunk when he and a few Christian friends had walked through the ghetto was accepted by the Inquisition and the threatened punishment of three years at the oars in the galleys was indeed imposed upon him.

Further evidence of the alleged pernicious effect upon Christians of contact with the Jews is provided by the case of a young Christian, Giovanni Battista Capponi. Capponi had been reported to the Inquisition for asserting that Christ was not the true Messiah, that his miracles had all been accomplished with the aid of the Kabbalah, that all who believed in Christ were lost and damned, that the Gospels were not true, and that the Virgin and the saints were incapable of interceding for humanity. He had also told a notary that the law of the Jews was better than that of the Christians, because it had been given to the Jews by God himself, while that of the Christians had only been given by the apostles, and attributed most of his wild statements to conversations with the Jews. When the Inquisition claimed that all persons believed in their soul the things that they expressed in words since the mouth was the organ of the heart, he responded that his remarks proceeded from the looseness of his speech and that he did not believe what he had said.[84]

Even more seriously from the perspective of the Venetian government, employment of Christians by Jews could actually lead the Christians to convert to Judaism. For example, Francisco Carraton, a Venetian who had been employed by a Christian bookseller, left around 1655 to work for two Jewish booksellers for two-and-a-half years. Later, he related to the Venetian Inquisition that his employers, along with some other Jews, sometimes together and sometimes separately, had spoken to him two or three times a week about Judaism and Catholicism, claiming that their religion was better, and persuaded him to convert to Judaism. They then paid his expenses to go to Amsterdam for that purpose, and promised him an additional sum of money after he got there. However, after he arrived in Amsterdam, he was told that he would only be paid after he let himself be circumcised, and so out of necessity he had worked for two months in a Jewish bookstore, conducting himself as a Jew and attending synagogue. But since he really wanted to remain a Catholic, he left for Rome where, persuaded by the convert Giulio Morosini and his confessor, he went to the Inquisition, confessed, and sought a pardon and absolution. The Venetian Inquisition was informed of the course of events, but after investigating, could not confirm his story, yet ordered his brother, who was still working for those Jewish booksellers, to find other employment as soon as possible and to inform it after he had done so.[85]

In 1660 Prudenza Pasquali, after serving for eight months in the dwelling of Abram Papo, came on her own to the Inquisition and confessed that she had fallen into apostasy. She related that she had received permission from the Cattaveri to work in the dwelling of Papo by falsely declaring her age as forty, instead of only twenty-three or twenty-four. After her Jewish employer and his mother convinced her of the superiority of Judaism, telling her that she should not believe in a piece of wood and that Mary was a prostitute who claimed to be a virgin, and promised her 300 ducats to enable her to go to the Ottoman Empire, she stopped believing in Jesus, Mary, and the saints and no longer went to church but instead attended synagogue and observed the Jewish dietary laws and fasts, while eating meat on Fridays and Saturdays and during Lent. The Inquisition absolved her after imposing on her abjuration, some spiritual penalties, and the promise never again to work for Jews, but did not start an investigation of her Jewish employer.[86]

Contact between Jews and Christians could also occur in the context of Jews providing for Christians services in the grey area of exorcism and divination, often to locate stolen or lost objects. For example, in 1584 two Jews performed rites of exorcism on a Christian child allegedly possessed by spirits, commanding them 'by the God of the Christians and by the God of the Jews, and by the saints of the Christians and by the saints of the Jews, to come out of this body.'[87] Also interesting due to the personality of the defendant as well as the nature of the activity are the charges against Isacco Levi, presumably identical with Isaac min Ha-Leviim, the grandson of Leon Modena.[88] In 1658, Isacco was accused by a Christian of having found a stolen silver belt by means of a procedure involving a 'king figure' seated on a throne and dressed in black who had revealed the identity of the thief and the circumstances of the theft. However, the Christian related, despite the success of the necromancy, neither he nor the other Christian present had believed in the undertaking nor had either collaborated in the magic ritual, and finally Isacco had received a smaller sum than he had requested. Another Christian claimed that he had used Isacco to locate some stolen pawnshop tickets, while still another Christian had been persuaded by him to learn the art of distillation. In a somewhat different vein, in 1620 Ricca and Regina, the daughters of Reggio, the beadle of the Levantine Jews, were accused of sexual relations with Christians and of witchcraft, with which they had ruined some poor young men, while Ricca had even dared to be outside the ghetto at night to engage in witchcraft.[89]

Sexual relations between Jews and Christians were certainly not unknown in Venice. When in 1635 the Jewish merchants were negotiating the renewal of their expiring charter of 1625, they complained that often the Cattaveri would initiate proceedings against a merchant for minor reasons and suddenly arrest him, possibly causing not only confusion but also such a fear of loss among his creditors that it could lead to significant trouble. Therefore, the merchants requested that in all matters in which the Cattaveri could impose punishment, they only be allowed to arrest merchants in connection with charges of relations with Christian women. The government accepted this request, and the new charter provided that the Cattaveri could only actually arrest Jewish merchants for confirmed cases involving relations with Christian women.[90] Then, in 1641, it was provided in the new charter of the Tedeschi Jews that cases involving relations between Jewish men and Christian women were to be punished by the Cattaveri, while those involving Christian men and Jewish women were to be punished by the Essecutori contro la Bestemmia; however, it was stated that these provisions were only to go into effect after they had been approved by the Maggior Conseglio, and, to date, no such approval has yet been found.[91] Given these measures, it would appear that the already noted constant reiteration of the need for the Jews to wear their distinguishing head-covering and to observe the ghetto curfew in order to minimize sexual contacts between Jews and Christians reflected not only general religious teachings but also an attempt to eliminate actual occurrences. To give some specific examples, in 1576, the Jewish merchants complained that the Ghetto Vecchio had become a den of thieves and prostitutes.[92] Then in 1615, Allegra, a Jewish prostitute, became a major protagonist in an important case involving the forced baptism of her daughter Savia, whom she boarded out to a Christian in the neighbouring parish of San Marcuola, during the course of which the distinguished Venetian *consultore in iure* Paolo Sarpi issued a *consulto* on the issue of the forced baptism of Jewish minors against the will of their parents.[93]

Let us return to the ghetto. Three basic issues must be clarified. First, on the basis of the special characteristics of the Venetian ghetto, the first Jewish quarter to be referred to as a ghetto, and those that followed it on the Italian peninsula, the pre-emancipation ghetto should be defined as a compulsory, segregated, and enclosed Jewish quarter. It was only in the nineteenth century that the word ghetto came to be used in a wider and looser sense.[94] Second, not every Jewish quarter was a ghetto.[95] Indeed, the ghetto was characteristic only of the Counter-Reformation Italian peninsula.[96] Third, many of the alleged influences of the ghetto upon the Jews and their communal, cultural, intellectual, and religious life require systematic reappraisal far beyond the scope of this essay. Here, it can only be stressed that the purpose of the ghetto was never to end all contact between Christians and Jews. The clearest indication of that basic reality is that the ghetto gates were open for a very extensive portion of the twenty-four-hour day, generally from sunrise to slightly after sunset. This gave the Jews ample time to leave the ghetto at their pleasure, while Christians were allowed to enter it. Indeed, the pawnshops, for whose operation the Jews had initially been allowed to settle in Venice, had to be located in the ghetto according to the terms of their charter. Accordingly, all Christians who wished to borrow money were compelled to enter the ghetto, where they had to interact with those Jews who were providing them with the desired loans, and once they had entered the ghetto, they could have further contact of all kinds with Jews. Yet on the other hand, the institution of the ghetto did eliminate much everyday casual contact that would have taken place at all times between Jews and Christians had the Jews not resided in a separate quarter,[97] and it did greatly curtail the presence of the Jews outside the ghetto during the dark and mysterious night, when many undesirable things could occur. Certainly of great significance was the symbolic function of the compulsory, segregated, and enclosed ghetto in serving as an always visible institutional embodiment and reinforcement of the long-standing view that the Jew constituted the Other from whom the faithful were to stay away as much as possible. However, the ghetto did not represent the beginning of the policy of marginalizing the Jews in Christian society, but rather constituted yet another manifestation – perhaps the ultimate – of their already existing marginalization. Yet at the same time, paradoxically, the ghetto was a constantly encountered indication of the basic acceptance of the Jews within Christian society, for they were assigned their own specific space integrated into the larger urban context. When any premodern Christian society came to consider the Jews as being so Other that it did not wish to tolerate their presence, it would then expel them – as England did in 1290; as France did in 1394; as Spain did in 1492 after the failure of the program to isolate them in compulsory, segregated, and enclosed Jewish quarters so that they could not influence New Christians to return to Judaism;[98] as Spanish Naples did in 1541; as the Papal Bull *Hebraorum Gens* of 1569 did from all locations in the Papal States except for Rome and Ancona; and as Lombardy did in 1597.

To conclude this brief discussion of the ghetto, we should note the assertion of Richard Sennett that 'the ghetto represented something like an urban condom.'[99] It is a striking – and perhaps even appealing –

image, but to fully understand the actual situation of the Jews in the ghetto of Venice and in other places in which ghettos existed, it must be noted that the so-called urban condom was never intended or designed to provide complete protection for the Christian inhabitants, for its creators constructed it with holes, or more accurately gates, that were open to constant two-way traffic during daytime hours. Indeed, the authorities acknowledged the ineffectiveness of their 'urban condom' and provided reinforcement, what one may term a spermicide, to make it more effective. Often, especially from the later seventeenth century on, the authorities associated in legislation and in administrative rulings frequently printed on broadsides that were posted in the ghetto, the requirement for the Jews to observe the ghetto curfew with that to wear the special Jewish head-covering at all times. The specific justification for this was to prevent Jews who supposedly otherwise would not be recognized as such from being outside the ghetto after hours and committing many evils, especially having relations with unsuspecting Christian women.[100]

Consequently, while certainly the ghetto hindered intercourse, in all senses of the word, between Jews and Christians, it never served as a complete and effective barrier and indeed was never intended to. Therefore, any attempt to characterize the nature and extent of the relationship between the Jews and their Christian neighbours cannot merely assert that a ghetto existed and assume that constitutes an adequate explanation. Rather, one must take into consideration both the permeability of the ghetto walls in law and especially in practice, and also the attitude of the native Christian population towards the Jews. Although indeed usually associated with a varying wide range of restrictions, it must always be kept in mind that ultimately the word *ghetto* only referred to the basic housing arrangements for the Jews.

Notwithstanding Simone Luzzatto's clear and immediate apologetic intention in writing his *Discorso*, not everything that he wrote should be rejected out of hand. His claim that in Venice 'the common people are more peaceful and docile toward the Jewish nation than in other parts of the world'[101] is at least partially supported by the fact that there were no major incidents against the Jews in Venice, as the Venetian government represented a restraining force which protected the Jews and strove to maintain law and order, albeit within the framework of the highly restrictive provisions on the books. To give one example, according to the mid-eighteenth century report issued by Cardinal Ganganelli (later Clement XIV) investigating the charge of alleged ritual murder, when in 1705 a large painting depicting 'Jews killing a child with other figures and inscriptions' was displayed on the Rialto bridge, an 'order was made for the said picture to be wholly and entirely effaced and deleted.'[102]

Indeed, Luzzatto's assertion that 'there is no doubt that among all the states and places in the world, the Jewish nation is pleased by the very gentle government of the Most Serene Republic, because its government is stable and not variable on account of the mutability of the thoughts of one sole ruler and the instigation of counsellors'[103] may have been based on his own experiences as a leader of the Jewish community.[104] Luzzatto was well aware that although the everyday life of the Jews was restricted in numerous ways and they resided in Venice on sufferance and not as of right, nevertheless the Venetian government did not act towards them in an arbitrary manner, but on the contrary, manifested a serious concern that the due process of law be applied in all matters involving the Jews. His very favourable assessment of the Venetian government is corroborated by other Jewish authors of the period, and their perception that Venice constituted an attractive place to reside was shared by some Christians, although of course such positive evaluations must always be placed in the context of the condition of the Jews elsewhere at that point in time.[105]

Yet there were limits to what the Jews could expect. Well aware of the situation, Luzzatto stressed that the Jew is 'occupied only in overcoming his urgent needs and necessities, and does not aspire to improve in any way his general condition.'[106] Significantly, Luzzatto did not seek any innovation in, or amelioration of, the condition of the Jews of Venice – as did Menasseh ben Israel and John Toland, who were both profoundly influenced by him,[107] on behalf of the Jews of England – but rather only the maintenance of the Venetian status quo. And that status was always governed by the policy articulated by Pope Gregory I and subsequently reiterated by medieval popes, which asserted that while the Jews ought not to claim more than was permitted to them by law, on the other hand, those rights which had been granted to them were to be observed.

To conclude, although the Jews were always considered to constitute a people of a different religion who were to inhabit their own separate space, to be readily distinguishable from the Christian population of the city, and to be subject to various discriminatory laws, and clearly their status was not – and could never be – the same as that of the native Christian inhabitants of the city, nevertheless they constituted an integral and integrated part of the Venetian system and scene. Certainly, their Otherness did not lead to their demonization, despite occasional harsh language in government legislation and decrees. Indeed, as noted, it was better in many respects to be an infidel Jew in early modern Catholic Venice than to be an Orthodox Greek, a heretical Protestant, or an infidel Moslem. Clearly, in Venice itself, different individuals manifested different attitudes towards the Jews and reflecting those differences of opinion, on occasion, the individuals, legislative assemblies, and administrative committees that comprised the Venetian government were very divided on the question of what policy to adopt towards the Jews, and one cannot assume that legislation and administrative rulings which were not favourable to the Jews represented the unanimous attitude of all members of the Venetian government and of the population of the city at large.[108] Accordingly, one must resist the temptation to assume that the mere assertion that the Jews always constituted the 'Other' represents a meaningful description of the actual state of affairs in Venice and throughout the premodern European Diaspora. Rather than generalizing on the basis of the official policy of the Catholic Church and of some major legislation of the secular authorities, one must always take into consideration the realities of the complex and varied dynamics existing in each location in order to arrive at a balanced and nuanced understanding of the actual position of the Jews.

Notes

1 See Robert Bonfil, 'A Cultural Profile,' *The Jews of Early Modern Venice*, ed. Robert C. Davis and Benjamin Ravid (Baltimore 2001), 169. For a brief overview of the history of the Jews of Venice, see Benjamin Ravid, 'The Venetian Government and the Jews,' in ibid., 3–30.

2 For a recent reinterpretation which sees the Serrata as a gradual process that took place in the late thirteenth and early fourteenth centuries rather than the result of specific legislation of 1297, see Gerhard Rosch, 'The *Serrata* of the Great Council and Venetian Society, 1286–1323,' in *Venice Reconsidered: The History and Civilization of an Italian City-State, 1297–1797*, ed. John Martin and Dennis Romano (Baltimore and London 2000), 67–88.

3 See Brian Pullan, 'Poverty, Charity and *Raison d'état*,' *Bollettino dell'istituto di storia della società e dello stato veneziano* 2 (1960), 28, and Frederic C. Lane, *Venice: A Maritime Republic* (Baltimore 1973), 113–14, 151–2, 196, 430. For a recent discussion of the *cittadini*, see James S. Grubb, 'Elite Citizens,' in Martin and Romano, *Venice Reconsidered*, 339–64; also Matteo Casini, 'La cittadinanza originaria a Venezia tra i secoli XV e XVI: Una linea interpretiva,' *Studi Veneti Offerti a Gaetano Cozzi* (Venice 1992), 133–50; Andrea Zannini, *Burocra-*

zia e burocrati a Venezia in età moderna: I cittadini originari (sec. xvi–xvii) (Venice 1993); Luca Mola and Reinhold C. Mueller, 'Essere straniero a Venezia nel tardo Medioevo,' *Le migrazioni in Europa, Secc. XIII–XVIII*, ed. Simonetta Cavaciocchi (Florence 1994), 839–51; and Reinhold C. Mueller, '"Veneti facti privilegio": Stranieri naturalizzati a Venezia tra XIV e XVI secolo,' *La città italiana e i luoghi degli stranieri, XIV–XVIII secolo*, ed. Donatella Calabi and Paola Lanaro (Rome 1998), 41–51.

4 See Benjamin Ravid, 'An Introduction to the Charters of the Jewish Merchants of Venice,' *The Mediterranean and the Jews II: Society, Culture and Economy in Early Modern Times*, ed. Elliott Horowitz and Moises Orfali (Ramat Gan 2002), 204–6, photo-reproduced in Benjamin Ravid, *Studies on the Jews of Venice, 1382–1797* (Aldershot Hants 2003; hereafter *Studies*).

5 See David Chambers and Brian Pullan, *Venice: A Documentary History, 1450–1630* (Oxford 1992), 276–8.

6 See Daniele Beltrami, *Storia della popolazione di Venezia dalla fine del secolo XVI alla caduta della repubblica* (Padua 1954), 72. The number of *cittadini* given there should be reduced for our purposes, since some were only *cittadini de intus*, who could not engage in the Levant trade as could native citizens by birth and *cittadini de intus et de extra*.

7 On the Jewish moneylenders of Venice, see Brian Pullan, *Rich and Poor in Renaissance Venice* (Cambridge 1971), 476–578, and Benjamin Ravid, 'On Sufferance and Not as of Right: The Status of the Jewish Communities in Early-Modern Venice,' *The Lion Shall Roar: Leon Modena and his World*, Italia: Conference Supplement Series, vol. 1, ed. David Malkiel (Jerusalem 2003), 18–43.

8 See Ravid, 'Introduction to the Charters,' 207–38.

9 See Benjamin Ravid, 'Venice, Rome, and the Reversion of Conversos to Judaism: A Study in *Ragione di Stato*,' in *L'identità dissimulata: giudaizzanti iberici nell'Europa cristiana dell'età moderna*, ed. Pier C. Ioly Zorattini (Florence 2000), 162–93, photo-reproduced in Ravid, *Studies*.

10 'Che gli Ebrei di Venezia e dello stato e qualunque altro Ebreo non possa pretender ne goder mai diritto qualunque di sudditanza, e non dovendo goder in qualunque tempo e luogo di qualsisia privilegio riservato a soli sudditi veneti, non dovranno mai in conseguenza in qualunque tempo e luogo esser considerati per tali'; Archivio di Stato di Venezia (henceforth: ASV), Senato, Terra, filza 2660, 27 Sept. 1777. The charter was printed under the title of *Capitoli della ricondotta degli Ebrei di Venezia e dello stato veneziano* (Venice 1777).

11 For details, see Benjamin Ravid, 'Curfew Time in the Ghetti of Venice,' *Medieval and Renaissance Venice*, ed. Ellen Kittell and Thomas Madden (Urbana 1999), 237–75, photo-reproduced in Ravid, *Studies*.

12 On the special Jewish head-covering, see Benjamin Ravid, 'From Yellow to

Red: On the Distinguishing Head-covering of the Jews of Venice,' *Jewish History* 6 (1992), 179–210, also published in book form under the title *The Frank Talmage Memorial Volume II*, ed. Barry Walfish (Hanover NH 1992), photo-reproduced in Ravid, *Studies*.

13 See Ravid, 'Curfew Time,' 248–51. Legislation of 1424, apparently never repealed, provided that Jewish men having relations with prostitutes of the Rialto were to pay a fine of 500 lire and spend six months in jail, while for relations with any other Christian women, they were to pay the same monetary fine but be jailed for the longer period of one year, indicating that financial considerations were secondary to socio-religious ones; see Benjamin Ravid 'The Legal Status of the Jews in Venice to 1509,' *Proceedings of the American Academy for Jewish Research* 54 (1987), 185–6. I have not yet found even an echo of the demonization professed by one eighteenth-century Venetian author who alleged that sixteenth-century Venice considered such relations with Jews to be on a level with relations with animals and corpses; see Guido Ruggiero, *Boundaries of Eros: Sex Crimes and Sexuality in Renaissance Venice* (New York and Oxford 1985), 70-88.

14 See David Malkiel, *A Separate Republic: The Mechanics and Dynamics of Venetian Jewish Self-Government, 1607–1624* (Jerusalem 1991), 130–2.

15 Christian printers did however publish Hebrew, Latin, and Italian books written by Jews, and Jews served as proofreaders and also typesetters; see Benjamin Ravid, 'The Prohibition against Jewish Printing and Publishing in Venice and the Difficulties of Leone Modena,' *Studies in Medieval Jewish History and Literature*, vol. 1, ed. Isadore Twersky (Cambridge 1979), 135–53.

16 On Jewish doctors ministering to Christian patients despite periodic objections, see Benjamin Ravid, 'In Defense of the Jewish Doctors of Venice, ca. 1670,' in *Man tov be-Mantova: Studi giudaici in onore di Vittore Colorni per il suo 90 compleanno*, ed. Mauro Perani (Florence 2004), 479–506.

17 See ASV, Senato, Terra, reg. 19, cc. 95r–96r, 29 March 1516, published in Benjamin Ravid, 'The Religious, Economic and Social Background and Context of the Establishment of the Ghetti of Venice,' *Gli Ebrei e Venezia*, ed. G. Cozzi (Venice 1987) 248–50.

18 ASV, Conseglio dei Dieci, Comune, reg. 4, cc. 26v–27v, 5 Sept. 1528; Senato, Secreta, reg. 66, cc. 74v–77v, 18 Dec. 1548.

19 For details on the establishment of the synagogues of Venice and their numbers, see Benjamin Ravid, 'Christian Travelers in the Ghetto of Venice: Some Preliminary Observations,' *Between History and Literature: Studies in Honor of Isaac Barzilay*, ed. Stanley Nash (Bnai Brak 1997), 115-16, photo-reproduced in Ravid, *Studies*. On synagogues previously in fifteenth-century Venice, see Ravid, 'Legal Status of the Jews,' 185, 189.

20 For the text of the charter of the Tedeschi Jews of 1634, see Benjamin Ravid, *Economics and Toleration in Seventeenth Century Venice: The Background and Context of the* Discorso *of Simone Luzzatto* (Jerusalem 1978), 105–26; for the text of the charter of the Levantine and Ponentine Jewish merchants of 1589, see Benjamin Ravid 'The First Charter of the Jewish Merchants of Venice,' *Association for Jewish Studies Review* 1 (1976), 219–22, and for that of 1636, Ravid, *Economics and Toleration*, 100–5.

21 See the pamphlet entitled *Leggi circa il sabbato e feste*, printed after 1738, containing appropriate verses from the biblical books of Genesis, Exodus, Leviticus, Numbers, Deuteronomy, and Jeremiah, as well as a memorandum of the Avogadori to the Senate of 7 May 1727 and the Senate legislation of 22 May 1727, preserved in ASV, Inquisitorato agli Ebrei, b. 19, cc. 39r–46v.

22 See Benjamin Ravid, 'The Forced Baptism of Jewish Minors in Early Modern Venice,' *Italia* 13–15 (2001), 259–301, photo-reproduced in Ravid, *Studies*.

23 See ibid., 277–80, 282–3.

24 Ibid., 273–4n32.

25 See ASV, Senato, Terra, filza 1083, 26 June 1687.

26 See Ravid, 'Forced Baptism of Jewish Minors,' 280–1.

27 For details, see Benjamin Ravid, 'The "Translator of the Hebrew Language" of the Venetian Republic and the Venetian Government as Preserver of Documents of the Venetian Jewish Community,' to appear in a Festschrift for Robert Bonfil.

28 For a general introduction to foreign groups in Venice, see Giorgio Fedalto, 'Le minoranze straniere a Venezia tra politica e legislazione,' *Venezia: Centro di mediazione tra oriente e occidente, secoli XV–XVI: aspetti e problemi*, 2 vols., ed. Hans-Georg Beck, Manoussos Manoussacas, and Agostino Pertusi (Florence 1977), 1: 143–63; Giorgio Fedalto, 'Stranieri a Venezia e a Padova,' *Storia della cultura veneta*, 6 vols. in 10, ed. Girolamo Arnaldi and Manlio P. Stocchi (Vicenza 1976–1986), 3:1, 499–535; Giorgio Fedalto, 'Stranieri a Venezia e a Padova; 1550–1700,' *Storia della cultura veneta*, 4:2, 251–79; Paolo Preto, *Venezia e i Turchi* (Florence 1975); Paolo Preto, 'I Turchi e la cultura veneziana del Seicento,' *Storia della cultura veneta*, 4:2, 313–41; and Donatella Calaba, 'Gli stranieri e la città,' *Storia di Venezia dalle origini alla caduta della Serenissima*, ed. Gino Benzoni, 12 vols. (Rome 1991–7), vol. 5. Alberto Tenenti and Ugo Tucci, eds., *Il Rinascimento: società e economia* (Rome 1996), 913–46.

29 See Brian Pullan, *The Jews of Europe and the Inquisition of Venice, 1550–1670* (Oxford 1983), 154.

30 For further details, see below, and also Ravid, 'Christian Travelers in the Ghetto.'

31 See Chambers and Pullan, *Venice*, 335.

32 For details, see Ravid, 'Religious, Social and Economic Background,' 243–4. On the attitude of Querini, see Deno J. Geanakoplos, *Greek Scholars in Venice* (Cambridge 1962), 67.
33 See Fedalto, 'Stranieri a Venezia e a Padova,' 265.
34 See Lane, *Venice*, 395.
35 See Ravid, 'Religious, Social and Economic Background,' 234.
36 See ibid., 238. A remarkably similar assessment of the status of the Jews is to be found in the *Discorso* of Simone Luzzatto (see below, n48) 22r, Hebrew translation, 92: 'ma la Natione Hebrea dispersa e disseminata per il mondo, priva d'alcun capo di protetione'; see Ravid, *Economics and Toleration*, 70–1.
37 For details, see Ravid, 'Religious, Economic and Social Background,' 234–43, and Pullan, *Jews of Europe*, 154; also Chambers and Pullan, *Venice*, 350–2.
38 See Maximilien Misson, *A New Voyage to Italy*, 5th enlarged ed., 2 vols. in 4 (London 1739) 1: i, 256, reprinted in Ravid, 'Christian Travelers,' 132–3.
39 See Lane, *Venice*, 395.
40 See Marino Berengo, *La società veneta alla fine del Settecento: ricerche storiche* (Florence 1956), 172–3.
41 Leon Modena, *The Life of Judah of Judah Arye of Modena*, ed. Daniel Carpi (Tel Aviv 1985); English translation, on the basis of the original manuscripts: *The Autobiography of a Seventeenth-Century Venetian Rabbi: Leon Modena's Life of Judah*, ed. and trans. Mark R. Cohen (Princeton 1988), 131, with introductory essays by Theodore K. Rabb, Mark R. Cohen, Howard. E. Adelman and Natalie Z. Davis, and historical notes by Howard. E. Adelman and Benjamin Ravid; Italian translation: *Vita di Jehudà: autobiografia di Leon Modena, rabbino veneziano del XVII*, ed. Elena Rossi Artom, Umberto Fortis, and Ariel Viterbo, trans. by Emanuele Menachem Artom, introduction by Umberto Fortis, and notes by Daniel Carpi (Turin 2000).
42 See Howard Adelman, 'Jewish Women and Family Life,' in Davis and Ravid, *Jews of Early Modern Venice*, 146–9; Robert Bonfil, 'Cultural Profile,' 188; and Don Harrán, 'Jewish Music Culture,' in Davis and Ravid, *Jews of Early Modern Venice*, 214. Also Carla Boccato, 'Sara Copio Sullam: la poetessa del ghetto di Venezia: episodi della sua vita in un manoscritto del secolo XVII,' *Italia* 6 (1987), 104–218; Don Harrán, 'Doubly Tainted, Doubly Talented: The Jewish Poet Sara Copio (d. 1641) as a Heroic Singer,' *Musica franca: Essays in Honor of Frank A. D'Accone*, ed. Irene Alm et al. (Stuyvesant NY 1996), 367–422; and Marina Arbib, 'The Queen Esther Triangle: Leon Modena, Ansaldo Cebà, and Sara Copio Sullam,' in Malkiel, *Lion Shall Roar*, 103–35.
43 See Giulio Morosini, *Via della fede* (Rome 1683), 1413. On Morosini, see Benjamin Ravid, 'Contra Judaeos in Seventeenth Century Italy,' *Association for Jewish Studies Review* 7–8 (1982-83), 328–51, photo-reproduced in Ravid, *Studies*,

and Pier C. Ioly Zorattini, *Processi del S. Uffizio di Venezia contro ebrei e giudaizzanti* (14 vols.), vol. 11 (Florence 1980–99), 14–15.
44 See John Clenche, *A Tour in France and Italy in 1675*, quoted in Abraham Cohen, *An Anglo-Jewish Scrapbook, 1600–1840* (London 1943), 155, and reprinted in Ravid, 'Christian Travelers,' 130.
45 See Alexandre-Toussaint Limojon de Saint Didier, *The City and Republic of Venice* (London 1699), 2: 60–1, reprinted in Ravid, 'Christian Travelers,' 131–2.
46 See Misson, *A New Voyage to Italy*, 1: i, 311, reprinted in Ravid, 'Christian Travelers,' 132–3.
47 Quoted in Jean Georgelin, *Venise au siècle des lumières* (Paris and The Hague 1978), 676, reprinted in Ravid, 'Christian Travelers,' 142n85.
48 The *Discorso* is also available in a Hebrew translation by Dante Lattes, ed. Aaron Z. Aescoly (Jerusalem 1950). An annotated English translation is in preparation. On the *Discorso*, see Ravid, *Economics and Toleration*, and Ravid, 'Contra Judaeos in Seventeenth Century Italy'; also Abraham Melamed, 'The Myth of Venice in Italian Renaissance Jewish Thought,' *Proceedings of the First International Italia-Judaica Conference, Bari, 1981* (Rome 1983), 401–13; Abraham Melamed, 'Simone Luzzatto on Tacitus: Apologetica and Ragione di Stato,' in Twersky, *Studies in Medieval Jewish History and Literature, II* (Cambridge 1984),143–70; and Bernard Septimus, 'Biblical Religion and Political Rationality in Simone Luzzatto, Maimonides and Spinoza,' *Jewish Thought in the Seventeenth Century*, ed. Isadore Twersky and Bernard Septimus (Cambridge MA 1987), 399–433.
49 See Gaetano Cozzi, *Giustizia 'contaminata': vicende giudiziarie di nobili ed ebrei nella Venezia del Seicento* (Venice 1996), esp. 77–85.
50 See Ravid, 'Christian Travelers,' 116–17, and the extended accounts of Thomas Coryat, in ibid., 120–3, Philip Skippon, in ibid., 128–30, and Richard Lassels, in ibid., 130, and the passage from the biography of William Bedell, in ibid., 125.
51 Modena, *Autobiography*, 131; see also Ravid, 'Christian Travelers,' 95–6, 117, 128. Modena was also referred to favourably by Christian preachers in their sermons; see ibid., 109 and 151.
52 See Morosini, *Via della fede*, 790, with the prayer for the government, in Hebrew and in Italian, 575–6. For further details, see Benjamin Ravid, 'Between the Myth of Venice and the Lachrymose Conception of Jewish History: The Case of the Jews of Venice,' *The Jews of Italy: Memory and Identity*, ed. Bernard Cooperman and Barbara Garvin (Bethesda MD 2000), 179–80n18, photo-reproduced in Ravid, *Studies*.
53 See Georgelin, *Venise au siècle des lumières*, 676, 944n56.

54 See Edwin Seroussi, 'In Search of Jewish Musical Antiquity in the 18th-Century Venetian Ghetto; Reconsidering the Hebrew Melodies in Benedetto Marcello's "Estro poetico-armonico,"' *Jewish Quarterly Review* 93 (2002), 149–99.
55 See Benjamin Ravid, '*Cum Nimis Absurdum* and the Venetian Republic: Precedents, Parallels, Differences and Cardinal Priuli.' Paper presented at the Seventh Italia Judaica Conference, Reggio Emilia, June, 1998.
56 See Marino Sanuto, *I Diarii* (56 vols.), vol. 54 (Venice 1879–1903), 146.
57 For examples, see Pullan, *Rich and Poor*, 553; also Ravid, 'Curfew Time,' 243–6, and Ravid, 'From Yellow to Red,' 196.
58 ASV, CL, Ebrei, 16 Nov. 1609 and 1 Jan. 1609 (*more veneto* [henceforth m.v., i.e., according to the Venetian calendar which began on 1 March]), from the *capitolare* of the Cattaveri; see also Giacomo Carletto, *Il ghetto veneziano nel settecento attraverso i catastici* (Rome 1981), 38n77.
59 ASV, Cattaveri, b. 247, reg. 8, c. 77v, 21 Jan. 1609 (*m.v.*).
60 ASV, Cattaveri, b. 246, reg. 7, c. 45v, 26 June 1613.
61 See Zorattini, *Processi*, 7: 18, 69, and Zorattini, 'Jews, Crypto-Jews and the Inquisition,' in Davis and Ravid, *Jews of Early Modern Venice*, 104.
62 See Ravid, 'Legal Status of the Jews,' 186. See also Ruggiero, *Boundaries of Eros*, 88, for the association of this legislation with measures adopted against homosexuality.
63 'Far cosa grata al nostro Signore Doge ... facendoli qualche cosa di gusto, come per esempio balletti et cose simili, nel giorno della sua allegrezza;' see Malkiel, *Separate Republic*, 160, 231, text of the Libro Grande, c. 77r, 377–8.
64 See Zorattini, 'Jews, Crypto-Jews, and the Inquisition,' 98–9.
65 See Pullan, *Jews of Europe*, 104, 172, and Zorattini, *Processi*, 6: 24.
66 See Pullan, *Jews of Europe*, esp. 231–3, 237–40; Zorattini, *Processi*, vol. 5 (all); and Zorattini, 'Jews, Crypto-Jews and the Inquisition,' 100–1.
67 Although reliable figures regarding the number of Jews in Venice are limited, it would appear that starting with perhaps around 700 Jews when the ghetto was established in 1516, their numbers gradually reached close to 3,000 by the earlier part of the seventeenth century, and then gradually declined to 1,626 at the time of the abolition of the ghetto in 1797. For the latest discussion of the population of the Jews in Venice, see Giovanni Favero and Francesca Trivellato, 'Gli abitanti del ghetto di Venezia in età moderna: dati e ipotesi,' *Zakhor* 7 (2004), 9–50. Compare the graph on p. 41 with the figures in Beltrami, *Storia della popolazione di Venezia*, 72.
68 Simone Luzzatto claimed in his *Discorso*, 28v–9r, that because of the various restrictions imposed on the Jews, they required a large number of people to provide them with food and services. Although he conceded that he did not

know how many individuals were included in this category, he assumed that their number amounted to around 4,000; see Ravid, *Economics and Toleration*, 78–9. Luzzatto had his apologetic reasons for proceeding in this manner, but it would seem preferable to conceive of the 'Jewish contribution' more in terms of potential additional earnings for Christians already otherwise engaged in their activities rather than in the creation of new full-time jobs.

69 ASV, Senato, terra, reg. 46, 31r–37r, 2 April 1566.
70 ASV, Cinque Savii alla Mercanzia, second series, reg. 141, 32v, 20 Feb. 1602.
71 For cases of Jewish children being taken care of by Christians outside the ghetto, see Ravid, 'Forced Baptism of Jewish Minors,' 264–5, 268.
72 ASV, Cattaveri, busta 2, 27r–v, 20 Feb. 1615 (m.v.). In 1638, the Cattaveri ruled that the notary was not to issue mandates or licences of any sort unless approved by all three of them, subject to deprivation of office and whatever other punishment was to be considered appropriate; ASV, Cattaveri, busta 2, 95r–6v, 21 Aug. 1638.
73 See Ravid, 'Prohibition against Jewish Printing and Publishing,' 142–3 and 151n35.
74 Broadside of 22 March 1703, preserved in ASV, Compilazione delle Leggi, Ebrei.
75 Broadside of 29 Nov. 1716, preserved in ASV, Compilazione delle Leggi, Ebrei.
76 Broadside of 26 Jan. 1738 (m.v.), preserved in ASV, Inquisitorato sopra gl'Ebrei, busta 24, 98r.
77 ASV, Senato, Terra, filza 2106, 7 Aug. 1760.
78 ASV, Cattaveri, busta 3, 195r.
79 See Pullan, *Jews of Europe*, 160. On Saruc, see Benjamin Arbel, *Trading Nations: Jews and Venetians in the Early Modern Eastern Mediterranean* (Leiden 1995), 95–168.
80 See Pullan, *Jews of Europe*, 160–1, who observed that the same story, originally related by Boccaccio, was again related to the Inquisition in 1599, and Zorattini, *Processi*, 4: 39, 129–30. The parable is also invoked in the play *Nathan the Wise* (1779), by the German Enlightenment figure Gotthold Ephraim Lessing.
81 See Pullan, *Jews of Europe*, 161; M. Milani, 'Indovini ebrei e streghe cristiane nella Venezia dell'ultimo '500,' *Lares* 52 (1987), 207–13; Zorattini, *Processi*, 8: 23–4, 177–99; and Zorattini, 'Jews, Crypto-Jews and the Inquisition,' 114.
82 See Pullan, *Jews of Europe*, 165–6; Zorattini, *Processi*, 8: 16–17, 81–97; and Zorattini, 'Jews, Crypto-Jews and the Inquisition,' 101–2.
83 On the role of the Jews in providing Christians with relief from Lenten restrictions, see Pullan, *Jews of Europe*, 163–7.

84 See ibid., 61–2; also 47–8, 65, 66, 77, 96, 110, 113, 114, 124, 134, 137–8, 153.
85 See ibid., 162, and Zorattini, *Processi*, 11: 17–19, 125–36.
86 See Pullan, *Jews of Europe*, 162; Zorattini, *Processi*, 11: 19–20; and Zorattini, 'Jews, Crypto-Jews and the Inquisition,' 111.
87 See Pullan, *Jews of Europe*, 77, and Zorattini, *Processi*, 6: 25–6.
88 See Pullan, *Jews of Europe*, 90–1; Zorattini, *Processi*, 11: 9–12, 107–23; Zorattini, 'Jews, Crypto-Jews and the Inquisition,' 114–15; and Modena, *Autobiography*, 40–1.
89 See Zorattini, *Processi*, 9: 33, 49, 55
90 See Ravid, 'Introduction to the Charters,' 221–2, 228–9.
91 ASV, Senato, Terra, reg. 123, cc. 159r–161r, 5 June 1641; see also Pullan, *Jews of Europe*, 79–80.
92 See Pullan, *Jews of Europe*, 157, and Benjamin Ravid, 'New Light on the Ghetti of Venice,' *Shlomo Simonsohn Jubilee Volume: Studies on the History of the Jews in the Middle Ages and Renaissance Period* (Tel Aviv 1993), 157n21.
93 See Pullan, *Jews of Europe*, 277–8, and Ravid, 'Forced Baptism of Jewish Minors,' 264–6.
94 I plan to trace this development further in a forthcoming study. In the interim, see Benjamin Ravid, 'From Geographical Realia to Historiographical Symbol: The Odyssey of the Word Ghetto,' *Essential Papers on Jewish Culture in Renaissance and Baroque Italy*, ed. David Ruderman (New York 1992), 373-85.
95 Benjamin Ravid, 'Alle Ghettos waren jüdische Viertel, aber nicht alle jüdischen Viertel waren Ghettos,' *Die Frankfurter Judengasse: Jüdisches Leben in der Fruehen Neuzeit*, ed. Fritz Backhaus, Gisela Engel, Robert Liberles, and Margarete Schlüter (Frankurt 2006), 13–30, to appear in an English version in *Jewish Culture and History*.
96 See Ravid, 'From Geographical Realia.'
97 See Ravid, 'Curfew Time,' 254–6, for an interesting case that arose in 1699–1700.
98 For details, see Ravid, 'Alle Ghettos waren jüdische Viertel,' 18–21.
99 Richard Sennett, *Flesh and Stone: The Body and the City in Western Civilization* (New York 1994), 237.
100 See Ravid, 'From Yellow to Red,' 187–8, and Ravid, 'Curfew Time,' 248.
101 See Luzzatto, *Discorso*, 32r-34r; Hebrew translation, 101–2.
102 See Cecil Roth, *The Ritual Murder Libel and the Jews: The Report by Cardinal Lorenzo Ganganelli (Pope Clement XIV)* (London 1935), 44, 48–9, 50, English translation, 72, 77–8, 79. For further examples of the protective attitude of the Venetian government towards the Jews, see Ravid, 'Between the Myth,' 159–64.

103 See Luzzatto, *Discorso*, 15v–16r; Hebrew translation, 87.
104 See Ravid, 'On Sufferance,' 58–9.
105 For details, see Ravid, 'Between the Myth,' 154–69.
106 See Luzzatto, *Discorso*, 41v; Hebrew translation, 109.
107 See Ravid, 'How Profitable the Nation of the Jewes Are,' and Isaac Barzilay, 'John Toland's Borrowings from Simone Luzzatto,' *Jewish Social Studies* 31 (1969): 75–81.
108 For a detailed discussion of this very important point, see Ravid, 'Between the Myth,' 165–9, and Ravid, 'On Sufferance,' 51–4.

chapter two

Emotion and Acculturation: Masquerading Emotion in the Roman Ghetto

KENNETH STOW

Every man has his mask. So said Erwin Schenkelbach, noted Jerusalem portrait photographer. For mask, the kind one wears on the face, we might also substitute masque (with a q), the drama. And as dramaturges like the noted Emile Pin might observe, for masques to be believable, they must never distort reality beyond recognition. Otherwise, both they and the theatre where they are props become absurd. They cease to address the audience or to have meaning even for the players themselves.[1]

This theatrical vision epitomizes the 'state' (the reason for the quotation marks will soon be apparent) of Roman Jewry in 1555. To parry, emotionally and practically, the blow they received when the Roman ghetto's establishment shattered their previously stable existence, Rome's Jews metaphorically donned masks and staged theatrical shows: masks, therefore, to play out masques. These mask/ques (I mean both costume and drama), which were often intentionally crafted, did not fail. Through them, Rome's Jews moulded, yet never lost sight of, their real selves – or the reality of their ghetto lives – and, in doing so they achieved considerable control over their lives and their community. This was vital for ghetto survival. No less importantly, through the masques, Rome's Jews were able to persuade themselves that although 'divorced,' as they put it, from their former civic partner – they called the ghetto *nostro ghet*, our bill of divorce (in Hebrew) – they were still Romans, as they had always been, neither immigrants nor outsiders, as Jews were nearly everywhere else.

When the ghetto was decreed, Rome's Jews did not simply turn in on themselves and accept being cut off. Nor did they exploit their enclosure to adopt, now without fear of contamination, Italian ways; this adoption had taken place centuries earlier, whether through speech, food, or dress.[2] In the period shortly before and during the early decades of the ghetto itself, Rome's Jews demonstrated an especially sophisticated 'Romanity' through their recourse to notarial acts that deliberately replicate the forms and procedures used by Christian practitioners of the notarial art, the *ars dictaminis*. The sole difference was that the bulk of these acts, drawn between about 1538 and 1605 by the father and son, Rabbis Judah and Isaac Piattelli, were written in Hebrew.[3] At the same time, paralleling the Piattellis' Hebrew texts are Samuel Castiglione's volumes of Jewish notarial records written in Italian in the mid-sixteenth century; Rome's Jews were using Italian formally, and in writing, from well before the ghetto's time. These acts, taken together (no pun intended), were the scripts of the dramas, the masques, that Rome's Jews acted out.[4]

These scripts represent, and are a window onto, the doings and 'misdoings' – and, I would argue, the consciousness – of a large swathe of Rome's Jews, especially as they dealt with each other. This, simply, was because acts drawn by medieval and early modern notaries embody not only the mundane: rentals, contracts, apprenticeships, and the like (they are never the simple validation of identity and signature that is the burden of the contemporary American 'notary public'). They also record, and officially so, what, today, would be testimony in court. The contents of the notarial act are thus not so much the words of the notary himself, but those of the persons who entered his 'office' to make a deposition, the words of defendants, plaintiffs, and the like, which have been cast into formal, and sometimes not so formal, judicial parlance. When we interpret these acts, therefore, we are interpreting the thoughts, the will, and the desires of a great many people. The acts convey far more than what notaries themselves were thinking.

We may also say that the notarial act permitted Rome's Jews to exploit their pre-existing high level of acculturation and carry it a major step forward, which was to 'imitate' the state-building that was then going on throughout Europe, and the Italian peninsula, in particular. The goal, although unspoken and perhaps not fully articulated, was to create a *virtual* (Roman) Jewish state.

The word state must be used with care. Rome's Jews never adopted the word itself, nor can they have imagined themselves exercising unsupervised coercive powers such as those of taxation or of policing their neighbourhoods by force of arms. But as I deduce from the (notarial) acts about to be reviewed, the notaries who drew them – and with some degree of awareness those who accepted their lead through their large-scale willingness to depose before them – were determined to create quasi-formal regulatory procedures that would serve as vehicles for resolving intra-Jewish disputes and managing internal Jewish affairs, procedures that would be much like those (statutory ones) that Rome's Jews saw coalescing about them in the Papal State as it matured in the sixteenth century. Accordingly, these procedures had to be endowed with greater credence than that normally accorded the institutions and ways of civil society, to wit, the bodies that operate in the undefined region between state and individual. They also had to be widely acknowledged, for only in this way would Rome's Jews be able to control their *universitas* (as both they and Roman authorities called their community) like a true corporation, which is to say, like a true State; and this was despite these Jews' certain awareness that *ius commune*, Roman law as then used in Italy, forbade Jews from enjoying full corporate status or rights.[5] Put otherwise, the Jews had to find a way to secure and exercise powers they did not truly possess, powers, which, needless to add, had to be as informal, as they were formidable, and, perforce, derived from popular, not legislative, consent – and consensus – for the latter was impossible.

Yet how was this to be accomplished in an ultimately metaphoric Jewish state, whose attributes were so very limited? Besides lacking powers of taxation and the right of resort to arms, this 'state' possessed no geographical borders (although I believe that the Jews saw the ghetto as their private sacred space).[6] Neither was it animated by perfecting pre-existing or nascent governing councils or offices, the so-called *Congrega* of sixty and the three rotating *Fattori;* these were always weak. Nor was it coterminous with Rome's synagogues or confraternities, whose role was ancillary.[7] What created Jewish 'statehood' was the coalescence of a Jewish public sphere or, more precisely, a realm of Jewish 'publicity.' Following Nancy Struever, I am using publicity to refer to a (public) sphere where decisions are openly, and commonly, arrived at, but, even more, a sphere where self- or auto-regulation prevails and, within which, a modest – and, of course, highly limited – form of '(Jewish) sovereignty' could be exercised.[8]

That which created Jewish 'publicity' in Rome, as the reader may well have imagined, was the notarial act. One vehicle of acculturation was simultaneously catalyzing a second. Yet the key to success, as observed above, was selectivity, the careful choice of what to absorb, so that the essentially Jewish nature of the Jewish notarial act and its contents would not be obscured. This basic principle guided the Jewish notaries in their work. Hence, although the Jewish notarial act was not necessarily unique to Rome,[9] the acts drawn in Rome were unique in that the Jewish notaries of the sixteenth century who drew them, whether in Hebrew or Latin letters, tellingly concluded each of their texts by adding that the act was valid as though drawn by a *notaio publico autentico in forma camerae*. This borrowing from outside legal terminology, to close what could have otherwise been a wholly internal document framed within strictly Jewish legal language, meant that beyond satisfying truly Jewish needs, the act would also be recognized, even registered, by Roman authorities as one that was judicially correct; *ius commune* had accepted over the years that Jews could resort to internal arbitration in civil disputes, and it was only consequential that when Jews starting drawing (what were effectively) juridical acts, these acts be considered valid.

Nonetheless, arbitration among Christians had been on the wane since the fifteenth century, replaced by governmental tribunals. Had Jews, too, abandoned internal arbitration, it would have spelled the end to judicial self-control; indeed, it was likely toward this end that the papal vicar closed down the Jewish notaries, with their arbitration-facilitating acts, in 1640. The existence of (officially) recognized notarial acts drawn by Jewish notaries thus forwarded arbitration – as well as Jewish 'publicity.' Yet how did both manage to gain the required consensus to make them work? They did so by going a step beyond the 'publicity' of the authentic public record that notarial acts normally constitute – that public record which Laurie Nussdorfer has called a repository of public truth, in the sense of a publicly credible version of what litigants and witnesses said, not only that of veracity.[10] Such a repository is crucial in founding reliable public bodies; and such a repository is what the Piattelli documents provide. But to compensate for their lack of true authority, the legal obligation, not only the option, to turn to (Jewish) arbitration – for this, even the registration of a notarial document did not provide – Rome's Jews needed something more. And this, as we said above, they acquired by perfecting structured theatrical illusion, including costume and stage. They developed what I have called elsewhere a 'social theatre,' a system of carefully elaborated public behaviour[11] whose repeated observance – its theatrical performance – created, as well as it reflected, public consensus. The setting, if not the vehicle, of this illusion, this theatre's script, as said, was the notarial act. The performance itself was Jewish 'publicity.'

The emphasis, moreover, falls on the broad consensus of Rome's Jews to resort to the notaries (and their acts). The stage of the Roman Jewish 'social theatre' was far wider than the breadth of the literary imagination of two or three notaries drawing standardized, if well-wrought, acts. The persons standing before the notary – who numbered perhaps in the hundreds, all intent on initiating or resolving litigations – were surely themselves aware of how their statements, containing, as we are about to see, often turbulent emotions, were being put down on paper. Indeed, in the present context, 'scripted' might be a more precise term, for those making depositions had to have sensed that they were participating in a well-prepared performance, to which they had first given their assent through their very participation. The Roman Jewish notarial theatre was one in which Roman Jews chose to participate out of free will. Roman Jewish 'publicity', therefore, was the property of the many, not the few. If one would like to call this a 'self-fashioning,' although I hesitate to use the term, it was a communal one, not the pose of a restricted, if inventive, elite.

As just indicated, the existence of Roman Jewry's social theatre may be most obvious in the matter of emotion. It was on emotion and its modes of articulation that the consensus necessary to stage performances was dependent; and the emotion we see in the notarial acts is staged. It is 'masqued' (here, the pun is intended) in order to cover over true emotion, although not so entirely as to obscure, for both performers and the audience, the reality of what was truly being felt and why arbitration was needed. Operated on the basis of orchestrated emotional expression, Roman Jewish arbitration worked; without it, the Jewish notarial *ars dictaminis* was insufficient. Standardized formulae can go only so far to guarantee orderly public life, and for this reason, the Piattellis innovated to invent (what I am convinced is) a coded 'public emotional scale.'[12]

Of itself, linking emotion and publicity was no Jewish novelty. Like the Jewish notarial act, the idea of public emotion, too, was a product of acculturation. Guido Ruggiero points out that a woman going to confession was also restoring her *fama*, her (deeply felt) reputation and honour, publicly, in a public event.[13] Jews, first, individually and, then, collectively and standing before the notary (not, of course, before the priest in the confessional) did precisely that. Jews frequently supported arguments made before the notaries by emphasizing that a contract, for example, had been made public or, more concernedly, that an insult, by husband, wife, or business colleague, had been made in front of all. They were retaining their self-respect, their reputations, but making these reputations a part of the *fama* of the whole.

Linking emotion and publicity also turned aspects of Jewish private lives into public ones. Legal adoption, as we know it, is a product of about the last 150 years. The Jews of Rome were very close to realizing this institution fully during the sixteenth century. Christians, in order to adopt, would give the child (or adult) they had taken into their homes an irrevocable gift, a *donatio inter vivos*, to cement the relationship. The Jews, using the same concept of *donatio* – it parallels perfectly the talmudic *matanah gemurah* – said that the gift was the child itself, affecting, as adoption does today, the child's legal status. But to seal the public act as a truly Jewish one – even beyond the changes worked by the revision of terms – Jews renamed the adopted child, calling it after the father or mother of the adopting parents. This was precisely as all Roman Jewish children were named. Renaming thus created lineage of both descent and affection. As created here, this lineage was also strictly Jewish. It was also 'publicly' affirmed.[14]

It was the linkage of publicity and emotion in the notarial act that overcame the Jewish community's lack of true legal and judicial empowerment. However, openly to assert this fact would have raised eyebrows, to begin with, Jewish ones. It would have also been dangerous. The authorities could close one eye to a quasi-public Jewish sector, but not two. Jewish self-regulation, even where grudgingly sanctioned, competed with that imposed from above. It was the papal vicar's privilege to interfere in Jewish litigation, and, intermittently, he did. Complementarily, Jews themselves sometimes turned to the vicar, especially when emotionally provoked. For example, Haim Anav's unbridled expression of anger not only stimulated outside attention, it also moved Anav himself to disregard the norms of Jewish publicity and turn to civic authorities instead of to Jewish arbiters. The result was Raffaele di Sezze's being tortured by the *Conservatore*. This was succeeded by interference on the part of both the *Auditore* and the vicar. Unfettered emotional publicity had brought all three competing Roman Christian jurisdictions: the municipality, the papal governor, and the papal vicar, respectively, into play.[15]

There was also a second internal issue. As Barbara Rosenwein has pointed out, people live in more than one 'emotional community,' civic, social, professional, and familial, and the emotions generated in these communities overlap.[16] Among Roman Jews, the overlap came from emotion generated in ghetto neighbourhoods (*vicinati, shekhunot*, as the texts call them), the holy space of the ghetto as a whole, the synagogues, the *havurot*, even the formal communal organization, the *Congrega*, and, of course, the family. Each one of these spheres produced a burden of emotion and, perhaps more importantly in the immediate context, potentially unchecked emotional expression that might – no doubt would – work its way to the vicar's ever-attentive ear.

'Unmasqued' emotion thus risked upsetting delicate structural balances. Its expression had to be tempered, and it is here that the invented notarial emotional scale enters. In the approximately 6,000 notarial acts the Piattellis drew, which, let it be remembered, constitute the body of acts drawn for the entire community, encompassing the lives of both its rich and its far less well-off, not a segment of it alone, emotional expression is minimized. When emotion was expressed, its terms were carefully chosen. They are, in fact, encoded. The anthropologist Rom Harré has said that 'the analysis of ... interrelated systems of [religious, moral and political beliefs ... and values] should be prior to our analysis of the emotions which feature in, and support such systems.' Here, it is the opposite, the other way around: emotion sheds light on the 'system,'[17] albeit prudence dictates calling the process reciprocal. To understand Roman Jewish emotion and its manipulation in the notarial acts, we would do well to observe bi-directionally, moving simultaneously from emotion to system (and context) and from context (and system) to emotion.

As said, constant resort by petitioners to the Piattellis' coded emotional scale demonstrates its effectiveness and common acceptance. Petitioners themselves were no doubt aware of how notarial acts containing their depositions represented, however formally and in judiciously judicial terms, their current emotional state. By purposefully containing emotional expression, these acts 'managed,' channelled, and even controlled potentially explosive 'feelings.' They also created a 'public emotional standard.' (There is no way to gauge how often this framework was rejected, but the frequency with which Roman Jews resorted to it – 860 litigations during about eighty years in a community averaging 3,500 total residents – indicates a high level of acceptance).[18]

Free emotion in the texts (as opposed to emotion voiced on the street or within family walls) is rare. It appears only when extraneous to the core of the act. A man, now dead, is said to have been *inamorato* of a woman, for whom he left his wife – but the suit was over the paternity of his now mature son, who was seeking to inherit property. There was also a father's compassion for his daughter beaten by her husband – surely derived from the fact that his own mother had been beaten – yet expressed to strengthen the argument in favour of returning her dowry. All in all, *inamorato* appears but once, 'compassion,' twice. The desire that the poor or old not be made to 'suffer,' appears three times.

In the 860 acts whose subject is litigation, strong emotions like anger or insult appear fewer than 40 times. Overall, there are about 250 traces of emotion in the entire body of 6,000 Piattelli acts. Petitioners and notaries observed emotional 'conventions.' To be 'content' meant invariably to accept stipulations and avoid conflict; to 'honour,' to give a person his or her due; to 'make peace,' formally to end a quarrel; to 'take an oath,' to put one's honour at stake and allay anxieties; and to be 'faithful,' as well as to be credited with 'love,' to be loyal – although the Italian *amorevole* seems to convey a measure of true affect. These terms' appearance is also skimpy: content (willing, accepting), 43 times: honour, 20; make peace, 26; oaths, 98 (including 24 over taxes and a large number simply to repay a loan or to stop gambling); faithfulness and love, together, 29 times.

At the same time, I again recall what I began by saying: that the emotional coding and masking, the emotional masque itself, could never so greatly pervert authenticity that for either players or audience, the dramas and the illusion of 'publicity' Rome's Jews created through their social theatre embodied the preposterous.[19] Emotion was to be imaginatively covered over, masked, masqueraded, and even inverted, yet not so distorted that it betrayed reality, depriving the dramas being played out on its stage of their powers satisfactorily to resolve actual tension and dispute.

To illustrate the point, I turn to the coded emotion expressed in documents of conflict. It is the costuming of illusion at its best. What we see is not what really was. Yet what we see is still sufficiently anchored in actual event to reveal how Jewish publicity and the social theatre that served it were needful of emotional codification in order to survive. Code, theatre, and publicity joined hands to be at once acculturational products and producers, without which Rome's Jews would have lost their sense of living alongside Rome's Christians – in what I have called elsewhere a 'tense intimacy' – as both Romans and Jews. In fact, they never did. Even after three hundred years in the ghetto, Rome's Jews remained essentially Roman. Theatre and drama had worked well.

The workings of Roman Jewish dramatic emotion are clearest in conflicts involving engagements, betrothals, and marital failure. Here coded emotion and notarial scripting become a true art.[20] In these seemingly private disputes, we should expect emotion to have free reign – but it did not. Almost without exception, broken engagements at Rome are simply recorded as having been annulled. No reason is provided, except for the one or two times when we hear that 'the match was not made in heaven,' or 'the pair did not like each other or get along.'[21] One match was said to have ended 'amicably.' Should we believe this? We are never wholly privy to the details; the conventions of displaying only coded emotion were in effect. They were observed even by advocates like Rabbi Abramo ben Aron Scazzocchio (whose inventiveness is the subject of a study unto itself), aware as he was of the need to prevent 'excessive publicity.' As one text says, 'the Vicar, to some extent, is always involved.'[22] How then was vicarial involvement to be minimized, limiting debate – as this same text also says – to 'the Jewish Tribunal?'

In cases of marital strife, moreover, where emotions so easily explode and issues get out of hand, people might turn to the vicar more freely. Sometimes, they had no choice. Before approaching the Jewish notary to begin proceedings to issue a *get*, the banker Mrs Rosetta appeared before the vicar with her husband Angelo (= Mordecai) di San Giusto to say she would accept a *get* after a year, should he leave Rome during that time. There it came out that Rosetta's son Angelo had once threatened to kill Rosetta's husband Angelo (eventually she had three husbands), to which husband Angelo had responded and 'shouted curses and lewdness [at Rosetta] on account of his enormous anger.'[23] Criminal threat was more than the Jewish notary could (allow himself to) handle. Open anger had brought even the halachic issue of a *get* under the vicar's purview.

Instead of such endangerment – of both the parties and also Jewish communal self-regulation – seasoned advocates like Abramo Scazzocchio preferred the kind of situation where he, as an arbiter, along with Joshua Corcos, convinced the wife to accept the *get* as one who had *hit-payyesah* and was *meruzet*: 'made her peace and was pacified' – and the husband felt that the payments asked of him were justified;[24] or a broken engagement, where the erstwhile groom took an oath – a sign, often, of emotions on the brink of explosion, yet which had been brought under control – 'not to put out a *dibah*, to speak wickedly,' but to announce to all that his previously promised was *kevodah*, *zenua*, and *kesherah*.[25] Thanks to notarial prodding, and irrespective of what they really felt, the parties had publicly and legally agreed to part in a spirit of (public) – 'amity.' Samuele (Musetto) and Caricciola, it was said, were 'fighting and there was no way to pacify them.' Yet, almost idyllically, an apparently quiet divorce was arranged.[26] The report has the air of make-believe.

Other instances of domestic violence, whether verbal or physical abuse, required a full-blown script. The plot itself was reasonably banal: charge, counter-charge, resolution. The nature of the resolution is financial satisfaction, sometimes satisfaction of honour, but most often, the satisfaction of halachic need, to prove why a dowry should be returned, nor the less, why it may be returned even though the wife has left her husband's 'bed and board.'

Thus Bella Fiore accuses Gabriele of impotence: 'she has [also] had enough of him.' Gabriele threatens to bring witnesses that he is potent; what precisely he intended we may only guess. But only three weeks later, Gabriele reappears before the notary to say he wants to divorce Fiore; she, in accordance with the centuries-old halachic ordinance of Rabbenu Jacob Tam (d. 1171), is asked whether she consents. Gabriele says he will accept the arbitrators' decision about a financial settlement.[27] The actors are disturbingly acquiescent. They are playing roles, ones likely drafted by the arbitrators themselves – or, more likely, the notary.

Roles are also being played in the case of Marchigiana. She had either committed adultery or cursed her husband, Beniamino, in public, or likely both. He had struck her. She had taken his money and given it to her parents. She also refused to go to the ritual bath – leaving her sexually unavailable. Beniamino was admonished not to remind Marchigiana of her past (and to maintain her). He was also to stay away from inns, bad company, and not to gamble, and the pair should unite as one flesh.[28] This was a tall order, in fact, an impossible one, and its issuance seems to have been directed at creating conditions facilitating a parting of the ways, not for restoring *shelom babyit* (family peace). The real picture was probably less misogynous than it appears.[29]

The smoke screen parts somewhat in the story of Laura and Sabato. Both sides had come to blows, Laura inciting her brothers to strike Sabato. Or had they been the initiators? Both sides, therefore, swear not to repeat the action, nor is Sabato to 'call Laura a whore or lewd, *mufkeret*,' charges that would justify (her seeking a) divorce – although he may strike her *be-moser kal*, with a light strap, or what the Italian in the margin says: *Salvo d'una legere gastigatione come la legie prometta*, 'except for some light castigation, as the law allows' (these people were not Ashkenazim, with their absolute prohibition against hitting a wife, but neither did corporal punishment make them content). All of these conditions, Sabato either accepts, or he divorces Laura 'within five days' – the exact words of the text.[30] The point of the drama was to force a resolution, the emotion staged.[31]

In all of these tales, there are really two actors, two protagonists – actually, two antagonists. The only way to make peace was through the final separation of divorce, much as one woman was told simply to take the *get*: 'You cannot' [as the Talmud puts it] live together in a basket with a snake.' But who of this pair was the snake?

One asks the same question with respect to Gratia, the wife of Agnilo; this was as late as the 1620s, which shows how resilient was the structure erected in the 1540s and 1550s. Agnilo was penniless, but Gratia 'was still content to return to Agnilo,' a real attempt at *shalom bayyit*, a household truce; the truce lasted for about six years. Then, we find Agnilo (had he become solvent in the meanwhile?) agreeing to pay support for six months. And Gratia 'is [again] content – but this time that Agnilo eats, drinks, and sleeps wherever he wishes during this time.' In short, she had thrown Agnilo out of the house, and she was also getting away with it.[32]

The will of Fiore, too, was respected (a second Fiore, not Bella Fiore of above). But it was she who had left 'bed and board' and would not return.

> Berechiah's wife, di Città Ducato ... has left her husband and has left his house against his will, without his permission, and against law and right ... And since she has enjoyed from him his wealth and his love, he orders her to go back to his house and not to be wandering homeless here and there in the markets and squares. His honour will not allow that. To this she responded that she does not want to go back to his house. And on this very day Isach Piattelli went again and tried to convince Fiore to go back to her husband's house, but she refused to listen and said that she does not want to go back to her husband and to his house.[33]

This, too, was drama, intended to make Fiore confront the seriousness of her predicament. But it was also a predicament that Jewish authorities both accepted and understood. As the notary wrote with respect to Stella and Giuseppe, 'the arbiters had tried to restore *ahva* and *re'ut*, warmth and loving companionship, in the way of honest and pure people. But both of them were stubborn, and they would not listen ... Both had a passion, *ta'avah*, to separate. They had no intention, *da'atam*, to unite as one flesh as they had done in times gone by.'[34]

The problem, therefore, was to facilitate separations like these, to script halachic dramas that would allow coping with emotion, to keep it from running amuck, yet not pretending it was non-existent. This accounts for the case-by-case variation on the basic single plot. And to judge from the many times when the drama is nearly invisible, the arbiters succeeded in their tasks. The masks were apt. Interpersonal and communal peace was preserved. The vicar's role was limited to what it 'preferably' was – no role at all.

Even the individual as individual might profit. For how, in the absence of dramas that controlled society by regulating public emotional expression, could one ever – in the supposedly patriarchal sixteenth century – imagine the following: 'Samuele di Isach and his bride Sara, daughter of Isach Frascati, agree to annul their engagement agreement and not to ask anything of each other. They interrupt the negotiations and Isach gives back to Sara 10 sc. of gold. For Sara had vowed to go to "*Erets Yisrael.*"' She would join a group of Jews now set to depart.[35]

Coded emotion, harnessed dramatically to a notariably sophisticated version of traditional Jewish arbitration, had led to this almost incredible tale.[36] By finding ways to be so thoroughly and intrinsically Roman, yet alongside the capacity 'to erect' a virtual Jewish 'state' (defined by its consistently maintained and consensual Jewish 'publicity' and self-regulation) – acculturation, therefore, at its maximum – this most Jewish of ends, a voyage to the Land of Israel, was forwarded. That Sara was a woman did not affect the result.

An Afterthought

Richard Hofstadter (writing in Fritz Stern's *The Varieties of History*), trying to discern the role of social sciences in historical writing, but realizing full well that such a role meant anything but trotting out theories and hanging events on them like clothing on a tree, ultimately spoke out in favour of historical imagination. Maybe, he wrote, history is literature, by which he meant fiction: that history as it is written is all imagined, that none of us today do any better than the sixth-century Gregory of Tours, who openly admitted he was expressing his bias, ending his stories the way he wanted them to end, regardless of 'what really happened.'

Hofstadter was tweaking our historiographical nose. He knew that about some things, we can be reasonably sure; and he, of all people, understood historiographical sophistication. However, he also knew there were areas where claiming certainty was perilous. We may achieve reasonable certainty about public emotion and public mechanisms of acculturation and self-regulation – we may also know, as Natalie Davis has shown us, that the scripted legal document, replete with staged emotion, was not a Jewish monopoly; for Jews, it was indeed the fruit of acculturational dialogue. But what did acculturation mean for the individual, the private Roman Jew? What did it mean to survive in the ghetto under conditions of 'tense intimacy?' This question presses enormously against the confines of historical certainty. To assay a firm response in cases like those of Sara, Fiore, and Gratia pushes us, against our will, to the limits –

or over them – of writing not history, but fiction, certainly of working violence on the normal historiographical canon.

These people are not Menocchio; we know them more through lacunae than a full set of texts. To tell what they thought, and felt, we must go far beyond the written text. Hermeneutical principles, no matter how skilled the exegete, will allow going only so far. By opening the question of illusion and emotion as a way to understanding Roman Jewry, how it coped and acculturated with, and to, the wider Roman world, especially the coping of the individual Roman Jew, we perforce place ourselves on a historical precipice, challenging ourselves not to fall off the scholarly edge. Yet, to complete the enquiry we have begun, we are, I believe, left with precious little choice. Dipping into the barrel of emotion forces us to ask that ultimate of historiographical questions, to enquire just how far we as historians may legitimately go.

Notes

1 Emile J. Pin and Jamie Turndorf, 'Staging One's Ideal Self,' *Life as Theater: A Dramaturgical Source Book*, ed. Dennis Brissett and Charles Edgley (New York 1990), 163–81, esp. 177.
2 Jews were clearly so indistinguishable from Christians that this transparency was no doubt a factor in 1215, when Innocent III ordered Jews to wear special garb, to avoid social – read, sexual – mixing; for this order, at the Fourth Lateran Council, see Solomon Grayzel, *The Church and the Jews in the Thirteenth Century* (New York 1964), 308–9.
3 The father and son drew acts between about 1536 and 1605; Isaac was active for nearly sixty years, and Jewish notaries kept drawing acts until the vicar closed them down about 1640.
4 On these acts and in general on the subjects discussed here, see Kenneth Stow, *The Jews in Rome*, 2 vols. (Leiden 1995–97), and Stow, *Theater of Acculturation: The Roman Ghetto in the Sixteenth Century* (Seattle 2001).
5 On this issue, see Kenneth Stow, 'Corporate Double Talk: *Kehillat Kodesh* and *Universitas* in the Roman Jewish Sixteenth Century Environment,' *Journal of Jewish Thought and Philosophy* 8 (1999), 283–301, and Stow, 'Holy Body, Holy Society: Conflicting Medieval Structural Perceptions,' *Sacred Space: Shrine, City, Land*, ed. J. Prawer, R.J.Z. Werblowsky, and Benjamin Z. Kedar (New York 1998, 151–71).
6 See Kenneth Stow, 'Sanctity and the Construction of Space: the Roman Ghetto,' *Luoghi sacri e spazi della santità*, ed. S. Boesch and L. Scaraffia (Turin 1990), revised in *Jewish Assimilation, Acculturation and Accommodation*, ed. M. Mor (Lanham, MD 1992).

7 See esp., Attilio Milano, 'I Capitoli di Daniele da Pisa e la Comunità di Roma,' *La Rassegna Mensile di Israel* 10 (1935), 324–38 and 409–26; and see also Milano, *Il Ghetto di Roma* (Rome 1964), *passim.*
8 See Nancy Struever, *The Language of History in the Renaissance* (Princeton 1970), 140.
9 See Robert I. Burns, *Jews in the Notarial Culture: Latinate Wills in Medieval Spain, 1250–1350* (Berkeley 1996), 41, and Benjamin Gampel, *The Last Jews on Iberian Soil: Navarrese Jewry 1479 to 1498* (Berkeley 1989).
10 See Laurie Nussdorfer, 'The Politics of Space in Early Modern Rome,' *Memoirs of the American Academy in Rome* 42 (1999), 161–86.
11 I am using theatrical metaphor purposefully. My theatrical framework is also broader than Victor Turner's, who spoke of 'social dramas.' I prefer to speak of a 'social theatre.' Social dramas, as Turner viewed them, offer a means for resolving individual conflicts through acting out standardized scripts. See Victor Turner, *Dramas, Fields, and Metaphors: Symbolic Action in Human Society* (Ithaca 1974), 121, also Turner, *From Ritual to Theatre: The Human Seriousness of Play* (New York 1982).
12 An orderly system of notarial acts and voluntary arbitration, as Thomas Kuehn has explained, especially with regard to the latter, was the key to urban peace. The more formal court system with its authoritarian sense of finality had the potential for dissent more than for reconciliation. Kuehn, *Law, Family, and Women: Toward a Legal Anthropology of Renaissance Italy* (Chicago 1991), 19–26.
13 Guido Ruggiero, *Binding Passions: Tales of Magic, Marriage, and Power at the End of the Renaissance* (Oxford 1993), 142–3.
14 On Jewish adoption, see Stow, *Theater of Acculturation*, and *Jews in Rome*, doc. No. 1271, but esp., Archivio Storico Capitolino, Rome, Section III (hereafter ASC, Sec. III), Fascicle 2, bk. 3, f. 9r–v; and Kristin Gager, *Blood Ties and Fictive Ties* (Princeton 1996), on adoption in general in this period.
15 Discussed in Stow, *Jews in Rome*, nos. 1654 and 1656.
16 See now, too, Barbara H. Rosenwein, 'Controlling Paradigms,' *Anger's Past: The Social Uses of an Emotion in the Middle Ages*, ed. Barbara Rosenwein (Ithaca 1998), on anger as a social instrument; and Rosenwein, 'Worrying about Emotions in History,' *American Historical Review* 107 (2002), 821–45.
17 Much work has been done on the question of understanding emotions by understanding the cultural setting in which emotion is expressed. See J. Coulter, 'Affect and Social Context: Emotion Definition as a Social Task,' *The Social Construction of Emotions*, ed. Rom Harré (Oxford 1986), 127: 'Types of situation are paradigmatically linked to the emotions they afford *by convention*. The link is neither deterministic, nor biological, but sociocultural'; or Harré himself, 'An Outline of the Social Constructionist Viewpoint,' ibid., 81:

'to the extent that emotions reflect and sustain the religious, moral, and political beliefs, interests and values of a community, then ... the analysis of these interrelated systems should be prior to our analysis of the emotions which feature in, and support such systems.' Emotion thus is viewed as a relative expression, measuring among other things degrees of reaction to various stimuli, reaction that is controlled or unbound, considered legitimate or illegitimate, depending on circumstance and (specific cultural) setting. And see the fundamental anthropological studies of Catherine A. Lutz, *Unnatural Emotion: Everyday Sentiments on a Micronesian Atoll and Their Challenge to Western Theory* (Chicago 1988); and Catherine Lutz and Lila Abu-Lughod, eds., *Language and the Politics of Emotion* (Cambridge 1990).

18 It is well to note, for our purposes, that in making the system of notarial-based arbitration work, Rome had an advantage over other Italian Jewish communities. The Piattellis were ancient Roman Jewish aristocrats, which perhaps obviated the competition normal elsewhere between rabbis and lay leaders or even between rabbis themselves; there is no need for researchers to search out subtexts of power conflict in the texts.
19 Pin, *Life as Theater*, 177.
20 The examples to follow are individual social dramas, but taken together as reflecting a wider social system whose 'rhythmic rituality' may be demonstrated in all aspects of Roman Jewish life, the term *theatre* is more apt.
21 Archivio Storico Capitolino, Rome, Section III, Fasc. 12, book 1, f. 83v.
22 ASC, Sec. III, Fasc. 12, bk. 1, f. 40v, 41r, and 42v–43r; and on the issues involved here, in which Jews varied from Christians in allowing women the right to refuse a proposed match, see Kenneth Stow, 'Marriages Are Made in Heaven: Marriage and the Individual in the Roman Jewish Ghetto,' *Renaissance Quarterly* 48 (1995), 452–91.
23 Stow, *Jews in Rome*, nos. 449, 451, 452, 454.
24 ASC, Sec. III, Fasc. 7, bk. 1, f. 167v.
25 ASC, Sec. III, Fasc. 2, bk. 3, f. 20r.
26 ASC, Sec. III, Fasc, 11, bk. 4, f. 3r
27 ASC, Sec. III, Fasc. 11, bk. 1, f. 53r–54r; see also Fasc. 11, bk. 3, f. 53r on the custody battle between Marchigiana and Moise.
28 Stow, *Jews in Rome*, no. 291.
29 The idea was really to spread the blame, not condemn just one of the pair. See the similar case of Buonuomo and Ricca (another Ricca), who had left her husband's dwelling of her own accord, which was theoretically most prejudicial to her; Stow, *Jews in Rome*, no. 1094.
30 Ibid., no. 394.
31 See, for comparison, the case of another Ricca and Gabriele, where the arbiters order a 'trial separation,' ASC, Sec. III, Fasc. 12, bk. 1, f. 96r.

32 ASC, Sec. III, Fasc. 5, bk. 3, f. 155v: 'Contenta tornar con suo marito Agnilo [q.m Graziadio] ovve oggi lui habita con suo figliolo Moise; et si compiace m.a Gratia di riportarse con lei tutte le robbe che si havea portato con lei quando sera partita da suo marito' (the language has switched to Italian) 'quali sono per li alimenti fine a pasqua nostra ... de' quale detta Grazia li da ampla autolita e se contenta che lui Agnielo vada a magniare e bevere dormire dove pare a lui per le dette sei mesi' (original orthography).
33 ASC, Sec. III, Fasc. 9, bk. 1, f. 124r.
34 Stow, *Jews in Rome*, no. 21.
35 Ibid., no. 52.
36 It is important in closing to note that none of the above is to negate the existence of real emotion, certainly on the part of couples divorcing, women harried, and the like. What has concerned me here exclusively is what I perceive to be the intentionally erected formal emotional structure intended to foster some measure of true communal (self)control.

chapter three

Between Exclusion and Inclusion: Jews as Portrayed in Italian Music from the Late Fifteenth to the Early Seventeenth Centuries

DON HARRÁN

To Joseph Kerman, a birthday offering

Oh earthly orb, here's the whole Jewish mob ... You've got to take heart. But if they speak to me in Hebrew, I'm lost. I'll pretend to be dumb. Ba, be, bi, bo, bu?[1]

For Christians, in early and more recent times, the Jews offer a salient, if not quintessential example of alterity, which led more often than not to their exclusion from one or another kind of participation in a Christian-dominated society.[2] In this essay I shall treat their alterity from a novel perspective: the Jews as portrayed in Italian vocal works of the outgoing fifteenth to the first years of the seventeenth century.[3] I shall define them not only as liable to exclusion however, but also more supplely as poised in their attitudes and activities between exclusion and inclusion. The Jews in early modern Italy operated within the perimeters of their rejection or acceptance by the ruling majority. As in life, so, I premise, and propose to demonstrate, in music.

Before proceeding any further, let me introduce the repertory of works on which the investigation is based, or at least as many of them as to my knowledge have been preserved in their poetry and music. Ten, perhaps eleven or even more, are relevant: they date from the last decades of the fifteenth century until 1605 and, for the basic ten, are ascribed to eight different composers, some of them major figures in Renaissance music.[4] Though written variously for three or more voices as carnival songs, *canzone villanesche, mascherate,* and so forth, the works are best characterized as illustrating a single species, the *ebraica*, or song about Jews.[5] It ranges, in its subject matter, from Jews at prayer to Jews as converts, moneylenders, (female) prostitutes, tradeswomen, *mohalim* (circumcisers), and butchers. For practical reasons (space, consistency), I shall concentrate on a selected, yet representative number of works, leaving the rest to future studies (among the 'excluded' few are those about Jewish women, which, in moving in their own conceptual orbit, are best treated separately).[6]

The examples are as piquant in their verses as they are unique at times in their music. Yet it should be mentioned that the *ebraica* is but one of several ethnic types, from the *veneziana* or *napolitana* to the *todesca, spagnola*, and so on. The Jews, in short, were on the map of Renaissance poetry and music as a representative part of Italian demography.

When compared with the thousands of Italian secular compositions from the later fifteenth to seventeenth centuries, the *ebraiche* are almost negligible. Others may have been improvised, as was the practice in the *commedia dell'arte* (about which more below); still others may have been written, though are no longer extant.[7] Whatever the case, the repertory is precious for its singularity. Nor is its limitation to the time frame of what is traditionally labelled the Renaissance a true indicator of its importance. The ten or so works actually constitute the only existing compositions of their kind in the Italian repertory at large, which invests them, obviously, with interest for the history of music and, more generally, for Italian culture. Yet the roots of the *ebraica* go back to an earlier period, to satirical pieces about Jews in liturgical dramas, Passion plays, and *sacre rappresentazioni*, only to be perpetuated in the *giudíate*, or Jew-bating scenes, in later theatrical productions. Crescimbeni said of these *giudíate* that 'the whole point was to ape and mock the Jews in the strangest ways, now hanging them by the throat, now strangling or torturing them, and now making them the butt of every other obnoxious entertainment ...' They comprise 'all sorts of languages corrupted and maimed and blended together, nor do they have any order beyond proceeding with the long-drawn-out tunes of many foolish persons who revel in the joke one plays on the supposed Jew.'[8]

In the following sections, I will establish, as a frame of discussion, the dialectic of setting and removing boundaries. Its operations will be observed in examples where the Jews are portrayed as either outsiders or insiders. But these operations are complicated, in real life, by the vacillation of their practitioners: Christians who see Jews as alien, yet integrate them into their activities by utilizing their services; or, contrarily, Jews who see Christians as alien, yet imitate their arts or adopt their customs.

To instantiate the vacillation, I shall, to conclude, raise the question whether, in the examples discussed, the portrayal of the Jews according to the perhaps overly rigid dialectic of exclusion and inclusion can in fact be pragmatically sustained. The last section would appear to nullify the previous ones, but in effect it underlines the semantic polyvalence of the examples as perceived in different frames of reference: behavioural, literary, and musical. Clearly, the subject is too variable in its components to spawn a set of homogeneous conclusions; nor can the exclusionist and inclusionist propositions for its investigation be easily confirmed or confuted. Though existent on maps, boundaries collapse under the weight of human interaction: in the concourse of daily events they are often removed or displaced or circumvented. The examples show Jews and Christians in variant situations of confrontation, some of them authentic, others imaginary. Where reality ends and fantasy begins is itself a liminal question, to be raised towards the close.

Setting Boundaries, Removing Them

Under this rubric, I will, as said, expand on the antithetic thematics to which the works are related in the continuation. The tone is general, and the content synthetic, as befits a set of prolegomena.

Exclusion and inclusion are forces that work separately, yet also in oppositional co-dependency. Jewish identity is usually defined by exclusion, as is, vicariously, the identity of those who, by excluding the Jews, define themselves.[9] Boundaries separate persons into rationally perceptible entities, by nations, peoples, languages, religions, and so on; they signal majorities and minorities, centres and peripheries, in an unending process of triage, for sorting persons by their sameness or diversity. On every level there are insiders and outsiders, and the Jews were normally considered the latter, hence excluded.

Boundaries may be set, but in the thoughts and actions of those who are confined by them, they are often removed. The lines of demarcation thus blur and there is a running over, or what Jacques Derrida calls *débordement*, of elements from one to another area.[10] Christians and Jews defined their own cultures and customs as separate, but Christianity and Judaism, by the very nature of their relationship within a larger Judeo-Christian tradition or of their coexistence within Italian society, were mutually influential. With each bordering on the other, it was only inevitable that the lines of division be traversed in both directions.

The Christians worked to narrow the distance between Christians and

Jews by a concerted effort to convert infidels to the true faith. Theirs was a double-edged sword: mendicant friars aroused antagonism to the Jews, the populace often responded with physical violence upon them, the authorities exerted social and economic pressures to constrain the Jews, yet, as a countermeasure, the Church wooed them with promises of clemency and deliverance. Embittering their lives and reducing them to poverty, and at the same time preaching the benefits of the new faith, the Christians hoped that by force or persuasion the Jews would in fact apostatize for their own safety and salvation. Many of them did, crossing the lines to pass over into the Christian camp and thereby eradicate the traces of their erstwhile estrangement. But many more resisted, indeed we read, in a report of John Evelyn, who visited Rome in 1645, that 'a Sermon was preach'd to the Jewes at Ponte Sisto, who are constrain'd to sit, till the houre is don [= dawn]; but it is with so much malice in their countenances, spitting, humming, coughing & motion, that it is almost impossible they should heare a word, nor are there any converted except it be very rarely.'[11]

But the Christians had other ways of blurring the divisions. They turned Jewish Kabbalah to their benefit by treating it typologically as foreshadowing the mysteries of the Church. The aim was to obliterate the distinctiveness of the Jewish mystic tradition by incorporating it into the larger body of Christian theology. Christians learned their Kabbalah from the Jews, but the teachers were soon supplanted by the students who so adapted the Jewish mystical tenets to their own ends as to proclaim the inevitability and inviolability of Christian truth. In latching on to Kabbalah and directing it to their own ends, Christians succeeded in confounding the boundaries: where does Jewish Kabbalah end? Where does Christian Kabbalah begin?

Nor could or would the Christians peremptorily forbid concourse with the Jews, for their services proved essential to their own maintenance and well-being. Jews were drawn into Christian affairs as moneylenders, providers of merchandise, and middlemen; their talents were sought as physicians; their acting, dancing, and musical skills were exploited for theatrical and private diversions. They sold clothes and cosmetics to Christian women; they taught Christian children how to dance, sing, and play instruments.

The Christians invaded Jewish space, visiting the synagogues and attending their prayer services out of curiosity or for their own amusement. Travellers from abroad scheduled visits to the ghetto as part of their itinerary.[12] They were present at circumcisions, describing their execution with surprise or repugnance, yet always with a relish for particulars (blood, knives, cutting, sucking, spitting, crying). By entering the dwellings of the Jews, and observing their customs, the Christians expanded their own intellectual frontiers, absorbing the Jewish component into the larger space defined by their own knowledge and experience. Thus Gregorio Leti observed that by travel 'we become acquainted with an endless number of relatives who have never been seen by us, yet by all being humans born of the same Father and the same Mother are consequently all relatives of each other.'[13]

The Jews, for their part, lived on the borderline between their own and Italian culture. They crossed over into the Christian camp to serve its rulers by will or command; they spoke Italian as a lingua franca, often adapting it, among themselves, to their own dialects, yet plying normative Italian ably enough to converse and correspond with Christians to their joint advantage; they adopted Italian habits of dress or modes of behaviour; and they learned and practised Italian arts (music, poetry, theatre). Jewish musicians and actors consorted with notables in the court or theatre or private homes; moneylenders, physicians, and merchants catered to their needs or wants. Jewish composers embraced the styles of writing practised by the Christians in their art music, shaping pieces to their models (madrigals, *canzonette*, and motets). The lines between Christian and Jewish were so blurred that Leon Modena wrote about Salamone Rossi's Hebrew songs, or as it were motets, that their composer 'worked and laboured to add from his secular to his sacred works,' 'secular' betokening the influence of Gentile customs (*ḥukat ha-goy*), as they pertained to music, on the formation of specifically Hebrew artefacts.[14]

The Jews, in short, were constantly crossing the borderline. Usually they returned to the fold. Yet there were some who, for a variety of reasons, decided not to. Once they left the faith of their fathers, be it voluntarily or compulsorily, there was no return, or usually none: the backsliders were subject to the strictures of the Inquisition. Here the authorities were inexorable in their application; and for the community the converts were often as good as dead and buried.

How do the operations of setting and removing boundaries reflect in the works themselves?

The Portrayal of Jews as Outsiders

Lines are carefully drawn between Jews and Christians in their mutual description and evaluation. Aron (English, Aaron), in one poem, identifies the Christian who came to exchange a pawn on the Sabbath as a *goy*

Figure 3.1. Christian knocking on the door of a Jewish pawnbroker; woodcut, in Orazio Vecchi's *Amfiparnaso* (1597), p. 33, to illustrate the *argomento* of Act 3, Scene 3 (beginning 'Tich tach toch').

(see figure 3.1).[15] He and other members of the household appear agitated, less so perhaps for having to deal with the *goy* than for being disturbed on the Sabbath. So, rather breathlessly, Aron summons his brother or father Samuel to handle the matter. The *goy* is already upset at having to wait so long for the door to open, saying that by habit he expects to be properly received, yet will doubtless be even more upset when he is sent away with the announcement that no business is done on the Sabbath:[16]

> ARGUMENT: Francatrippa goes to the Jews to deposit a pawn;
> He bangs loudly on the door ...

FRANCATRIPPA:	Hurry up, open, hurry up,
	I'm used to being treated like a gentleman ...
JEWS:	Goodness gracious!
	What does he want?
	What is he saying? ...
[ARON]:	Oh Samuel, Samuel,
	Come on down, come on down!
	Oh my god! there's the *goy*
	Who came with the pawn
	And wants the credit slip.
JEWS:	But it's the Sabbath, we can't [help him].

In another poem, the Jews visit Florence, in the later fifteenth century, to sell their wares.[17] By law, they say, their stay was limited to three days ('[By the lure of] the beautiful city / ... / We have been induced to stay with you / For three days, as the law guarantees us').[18] Being aliens, they feared for their safety, uncertain of how they would be received ('We've come here today, / Though in staying we're wary and worried').[19]

In a third poem, another Aron is in consternation over the theft, by the *goyim*, of his goose and gander.[20] He rushes back and forth, to the delight of the 'robbers,' who shout 'run! run!'[21] One is reminded of the nasty races in sixteenth- and seventeenth-century Rome where, during Carnival, Jews, stripped naked, were made to run for their lives.[22] Aron protests: how could you? The goose and gander are 'ours':[23]

[GOYIM]:	Run, run, Mr Aron!
[ARON]:	Oh the *goyim*, the *goyim*,
	Have killed the gander and our goose:
	It's *our* gander, it's *our* goose!

But the best part was still to come – after stealing the feathered creatures, the *goyim* flayed and ate them:[24]

[ARON]:	Oh my god! they've stabbed them,
	They've strangled them,
	They've skinned them!
	Oh shit [*merdochai*]!
	They've, they've gobbled them up!

The portrayal may have been directed at Jewish butchers. When Aron implies that the *goyim* are cruel to his animals, the poet seems to be saying the reverse, namely, that for the *goyim* it is the Jews who are cruel in their methods of slaughtering them.

As outsiders, the Jews have their own language: to the Christian ear, Hebrew must have sounded like gibberish. When the same *goy* who came to leave a pawn stands at the door, what he hears is 'a hubbub of voices and horrifying utterances.'[25] The Jews are busy at prayer and their words are as far removed from Italian as, say, night from day: 'Ahi Baruchai / Badanai Merdochai / An Biluchan / Ghet milotran / La Baruchabà.'[26]

Is this Hebrew? Yes and no: some of the words are, others could be. Thus *baruchabà* derives from 'Barukh ha-ba' (Psalm 118, the opening of verse 26);[27] *baruchai*, from a possible conflation of *barukh* and *adonai*; and *ghet* not only from the Italian *ghetto*, but perhaps from the Hebrew *get*, 'divorce,' or *ḥet*, 'sin.' Many locutions can be overlooked as merely 'exotic' (*nai, balachot, mallacott*,[28] etc.). Yet some are crucial to the understanding of the poetry, such as *bezza*, from the Hebrew *betsaʿ*, for 'greed' or 'unjust gain' (usury),[29] or *moscogn*, from the Hebrew *mashkon*, for a 'pawn.'[30] In all this commotion, the Christian's knock on the door was inaudible. So he knocked again, only to hear more prattle ('Oth zorochot, / Aslach muflach, / Iochut zorochot, / Calamala balachot').[31] If ever one were to define the *ebraica* for its earmarks, one might cite its inclusion of Hebrew or Hebrew-sounding vocables.[32]

Hebrew also has its own intonation: nasal, whining, guttural, or so it was perceived. In the poems one finds strings of words, in fact, with *ai* or *nai* ('*Ahi* Baruch*ai* Bada*nai* Merdoch*ai*') or with *ch* ('Mordo*chi* mordo*chai*'; 'As*sach* mus*tach*').[33] Because the speech is unintelligible to the *goi*, the Jews seem to be blabbering much the same thing. So if it is not *latrai nai nai nai nai*, etc., it is *sinagoga*, to which the singers add 'go go go go ga,' or *baruccabà* (thus spelled), to which they add 'bà bà bà bà,'[34] which, in English, would be equivalent to saying *blah blah blah blah*. Reporting on a prayer service in a Venetian synagogue (1611), the English traveller Thomas Coryate wrote that the rabbi spoke 'before the congregation not by a sober, distinct, and orderly reading, but by an exceeding loud yaling [= yelling], undecent roaring, and as it were a beastly bellowing of it forth. And that after such a confused and hudling [= huddling][35] manner, that I thinke the hearers can very hardly understand him.'[36]

But where the Jews stand apart most notably is in their customs. From the poems it is clear that, as prescribed by Jewish rite, they have their formularies and ordinances. They 'make synagogue' (*fanno sinagoga*),[37] that is, pray, at dawn or midday or sunset; they have their rules of ritual slaughter; they circumcise their male offspring. All of these, to the observer, made the Jews extremely, if not enticingly interesting as a subject for both the poetry of the *ebraica* and its music.

And what about the music? In the early examples, one has to admit, there is nothing particularly 'Hebrew' about it. Yet from the 1590s a distinct attempt was made to simulate, in composition, the same kinds of idiosyncrasy heard in speech: disorder, agitation, babbling, whining, aimlessness, redundancy, the Jews as it were aping Christian 'song' but getting it wrong. In describing Jewish singing at a circumcision in Rome, 1581, Michel de Montaigne remarked on the 'extreme *desaccord* [= discordance] from the confusion of so many voices of every variety of ages,' namely, adults down to the tiniest children, singing together.[38]

The *desaccord* might, in technical terms, be described as 'heterophony,' or voices not sounding simultaneously, but entering on different beats or pitches. To illustrate it, see the excerpt from a piece describing the prayers of two Jews on their way to Padua (figure 3.2).

The voices wander aimlessly, without a clear melodic or rhythmic profile; they repeat themselves; they lack cadences for their syntactic articulation; the top voice straggles, by a beat, behind the bottom one, or vice versa (measures 21, 23, 25–6); the middle voice, with nothing better to do, sometimes reiterates a single note (measures 25–6, 27–8); tonally, the lines are at odds, with conflict between F sharp and F natural, or C sharp and C natural, or B flat and B natural; expectancies are aroused, then frustrated, as when the top line moves (in measure 25) towards what would seem to be an approaching melodic cadence on g, then at the last minute shifts away to d' (beat 4 of same measure); and all this, here and there, to the accompaniment of stuttering speech, as in 'go-go-go-ga,' or 'hò-hò-hò-hò,' or 'bà-bà-bà-bà.'

Were one to describe the example, one might say that it exhibits confusion and disorder. Somehow they became synonymous with synagogue chant. Orazio Scaletta remarked that 'if all [singers] should want to perform a trill at the same time (try it and you'll hear it), you'd think you were actually in a Jewish synagogue.'[39]

While the Christian pawner cools his heels, waiting for a response to his knock, the Jews earnestly pray: they execute a lavish cantorial recitative on 'oth zorochot,' then proceed with staggered syncopations on 'Aslach muflach,' etc. With the inconsistencies between the parts, the presentation (from measure 29 on) is typically muddled (see figure 3.3).

The Christian joins in, mimicking the Jews in their moans ('U, uhi! o, ohi!') and helter-skelter rhythms (see figure 3.4).

Figure 3.2. Adriano Banchieri, 'Latrai nai' (*Barca di Venetia per Padova*, 1605, measures 21–30).

It is no wonder that the famed music historiographer Charles Burney, two hundred years later, described synagogue song, with tongue in cheek, as 'very unlike what we Christians are used to in divine service.'[40]

The Portrayal of Jews as Insiders

The Jews could not be insiders; and if they were, it was rather because they tried or hoped to be or because, in crossing the lines, they thought, in a moment of self-deception, they could be. They yearned for integration within the larger complex, so much so that, for example, in returning to Florence, from which they had been expelled, they remarked on 'The beautiful city, which, by nature, / Is shared today by you and us.'[41]

Figure 3.3. Orazio Vecchi, 'Tich tach toch' (*L'Amfiparnaso*, 1597), measures 26–32.

Its charms are no less apparent to the Jews than to the Christians; thus *by nature* one would expect, reading the poetry between the lines, that persons who serve, and honour, a city should not be denied rights of residence in it. The Jews elaborate on the point, saying that after having instructed Christians in the art of glassblowing, they trusted their own works would be recognized for their superior craftsmanship:[42]

> We brought along some of our goblets
> Which we taught you how to make

Figure 3.4. Ibid., measures 36–8.

And are much better and more beautiful than some of yours;
And you'll see for yourself in trying them out.

Though displaced by their pupils, they hoped nevertheless that, as teachers and artisans, they could be of further service to their neighbours.

The same displacement occurred in moneylending. Here too the Jews taught their neighbours the tricks of the trade, if not by formal instruction at least by example:[43]

A thousand times did you already borrow money
From us with a pawn in your hand;
Ever since you acquired from me the skills of ours,
We've become poor.

Wishing to be useful, though, the Jews advised the Christians on how to increase their profits ('Don't lend to anyone on faith, / As if it makes no difference,' but rather on interest).[44] Nor should the Christians, they say, have misgivings about earning money, for 'if you gain some, it is fair and honest.'[45]

The Jews chafed at being squeezed for their knowledge and talents, then discarded. When they say that 'our goblets ... are much better and more beautiful than some of yours; and you'll see for yourself in trying them out,' they are saying: allow us to work again at our old professions; when they say that ever since the Florentine moneylenders usurped their services, they've 'become poor,' they're saying: is that reasonable? It hurts them to see a Christian, who doesn't have to wear an identifying sign, and is unrestricted in his place of habitation, exercise the same profession in the very city from which they were excluded:[46]

> But it seems strange to us
> That he [the Christian] who lends for a pawn
> Doesn't wear our sign
> And stays within your walls as much as he wishes.

The Jews were aware that the Christians had replaced their pawnlending shops by the *monti di pietà*.[47] But they pleaded their case for lending on interest, as if they were defending themselves in the law courts. They assert, to start with, that the Christian form of moneylending has certain advantages:[48]

> We well know that not only for gain
> Do you lend with surety,
> But also to help a poor fellow,
> By which you do much good.

Then they proceed to describe its liabilities. One of their arguments is that there is nothing wrong with exacting interest, for it's not the lender who makes a bad name for monetary gain, but the borrower who calls it extortion ('For he who lends does no harm, / But he who borrows does harm to usury').[49] Another argument is that by lending on good faith, the lender is likely to be deceived:[50]

> Only he is cheated who believes too much,
> For he will be sorry for having dispensed with collateral.

It follows then, and here is where the Jews hope to offer sound advice, that to retain one's wealth one should be careful in its distribution:[51]

> May he who has wealth and repute from it [= lending money]
> Now be wise and cautious,
> For whatever good comes of a poor acquisition
> Evaporates quickly and is of short duration.

The conclusion: the Jewish method of lending money provides the best guarantee against financial debit. With the deposit of a pawn the lender neither has to resort to brokers or lawyers to recuperate his losses, nor will he ever be accused of inexperience or ineptitude:[52]

> By receiving a pawn, a person is secure and without any need
> Of brokers, illicit gains, and papers to be signed
> To recover a loan; nor will there be reason for him to be ashamed,
> For he well knows how to practise his trade.

The arguments seem to have won some support. One year later, the Jews returned to Florence, encouraged by what they thought was a change of attitude. 'You recognized,' they declare, 'the excessive injury we suffered from your lending [money in our stead] and our being expelled.'[53] Yet they paid a heavy price for the change: they converted to Christianity. In a new burst of confidence the Jews exclaim: 'How happy is he who on earth is born / Of a good Christian, especially so in Florence!'[54] They seem to have achieved their goal of being 'insiders,' but reality proved otherwise. As the Christian loan bankers who, the Jews had warned, would be victims of their own benevolence, so the Jews were victims of their own faith in the Christians. In the end, they had to admit that their Christianity was acquired, not inherited. 'We have left the Jewish faith / And been baptized, as everyone can see,'[55] which is the reason perhaps why they went to great lengths to prove their sincerity. Thus the words 'How happy is he who on earth is born / Of a good Christian, especially so in Florence!' assume a new meaning. *Born* into Christianity reads as against converting to it, being *in* Florence reads as against being out of it. Try as he may, the convert retained the taint of his Judaism and felt uncertain in his new surroundings. 'The beautiful city' may have been 'shared today by you and us' (see above), but it rightly belonged to Christians born of Christians.

Can the Dialectic of Exclusion and Inclusion be Sustained?

So far the Jews as portrayed on both sides of the fence: outside, inside. But one wonders whether the exclusionist or inclusionist tendencies discerned in the works themselves necessarily betoken negative or positive attitudes towards the Jews at large. At least four qualifying points bear mention, to assure a more balanced interpretation of *ebraiche* than might seem possible from a literal reading of their outwardly discriminatory or non-discriminatory contents:

One, the various *ebraiche* constitute examples of 'lighter' or 'popular' music, in contrast to *musica erudita*. They were meant to be humorous and entertaining. Thomas Morley said of '*villanelle*, or country songs' that their composers 'make a clownish music to a clownish matter.'[56] Orazio Vecchi commented on his popular compositions: 'What better way could the musician ... delight [his audience] than with the comical?'[57] In Vecchi's *Veglie di Siena* the participants react to one or another piece, gushing: 'Oh it's charming, oh it's gracious and delightful, full of jokes and entertaining!'; 'Oh what fun! oh what pleasure we experience!'; or 'Oh what a silly story! oh it's enchanting! oh it's lovely!'[58] The singers who imitate the Jews in the *Veglie* do so for amusement, though no less so than those who, in the same work, imitate, among others, 'a Sicilian madly in love,' 'a country girl who thinks that of all others she's the most beautiful,' and 'a Spaniard who speaks to his Lady in great grief.'[59] It fell to Lady Giulia, as 'the highest honour,' to 'imitate the Jews,' whereby she was instructed to depict them 'from life.'[60] The spectators can't wait: 'Oh what fun! oh what fun!'[61]

Two, as lighter music the *ebraiche* convey mixed messages: what appears to be antagonistic in their verses is often neutralized by their ludic function. When Francatrippa comes to deposit a pawn, then addresses the Jews in faulty Latin ('O Hebraeorum gentibus'), do we identify with Francatrippa who, as a Christian, is entitled to demand services of the Jews at any time and in any place? Or do we with the Jews who are alarmed by an intruder on the Sabbath? One wonders who is being laughed at: the Jews, as they mumble their prayers? Or Francatrippa, whose name 'Greedyguts' reveals his contemptible character and whose boorish Latin reveals his stupidity?[62]

Three, Italian portrayals of Jews are only part of the story. To fill in the missing details, one needs to know how the Jews would have portrayed Christians if they were able to (which they were not) or, at least, how they would have portrayed themselves. Hannah Arendt wrote that 'in a society on the whole hostile to the Jews ... it is possible to assimilate only by assimilating to anti-Semitism also.'[63] Did the Jews, in short, ever assimilate, musically, to the 'anti-Semitism' of their neighbours?

One example might suggest they did. To celebrate the nuptials of Duke Ferdinando Gonzaga and Caterina de' Medici in 1617, the Mantuan court staged the (Christian) sacred drama *La Maddalena*, about Mary Magdalene's penitence and conversion, for which five composers, among them Claudio Monteverdi and the one Jew Salamone Rossi, were requested to write music to some of its poetry.[64] But how could Rossi *ebreo*

Figure 3.5. Salamone Rossi, 'Spazziam pronte' for three voices from Giovanni Battista Andreini's sacred play *La Maddalena* (1617), first two of four stanzas (top voice only).

participate in a Christian play? While Monteverdi and the others devised 'serious' works to verses of genuinely Christian content, Rossi was assigned the text of a light-hearted, rather witless *balletto*, to be danced by the Magdalene's three lady's maids and her two dwarf servants, who, to judge from their names (Stella, Rosa, Aurora, Aron, Leone), were all Jews. The first two stanzas read:[65]

Stanza 1 Come on, old women, let's sweep
This floor;
Our only wish
Is to make birds our fairest prey.

Stanza 2 Hurry, let's have a race to move our arms,
For the rooftop
Is the grove
Where snares and traps are laid.

In the stage directions to this *balletto* we are informed that the lady's maids are 'old women of little worth' and that 'they move, bent over, holding little sticks.'[66] While the women sweep the floor, the servants are charged with watering the plants (elsewhere in the play 'water' signifies baptism). The *balletto* is delightful in its sprightly rhythms and catchy tunes (see figure 3.5), but in portraying the antics of old crones and dwarfs, cavorting about the stage with brooms and watering-cans, it preserves the conventional image of the Jews as servants and fools.

Rossi was clearly engaging in an act of self-satire. His picture of the Jews was drawn after the Christian stereotype.[67] But all this is good slapstick humour, in the *commedia dell'arte* tradition. Self-satire, yes, but also entertaining, as one would expect of a *balletto*. Rossi cannot have taken himself seriously, for if the *balletto* were performed before Jews, they, too, would probably have laughed at themselves.[68]

The fourth, and last, point concerns the late Renaissance notion of the world as a theatre. The Jews are one of many ethnic groups within the complex of Italian society. Each of them is recognizable for its separate traits, as schematized not only in comedies, but also in literary treatises. We learn from Giovan Giorgio Trissino, for one, that

> nations subdivide into countries, just as foreigners do into Turkish, French, German, English, and such similar. The Turk strikes one as arrogant, homicidal, illiterate, and hostile to virtues, intellects, and the nobility; the Frenchman as impetuous, inconsiderate, fickle, and thankless; and the English ... as sitting at the table, from morning to evening. Throughout the world the proverbs of countries and cities denote some inclinations or deficiencies commonly known among their denizens. Thus one says of the Spaniard: 'beautiful on the outside and tainted on the inside'; of the Lombard: 'faithful and fawning'; of the Florentine: 'set on farthings, in his body and soul'; of the Roman: 'with weapons in hand, day and night'; of the Sienese: 'crazy at his own expense'; of the Genoese: 'a white Moor'; of the Neapolitan: 'golden on the outside and vain on the inside'; and so forth with many others.[69]

Here's how the German, Mr Tutesch, for *Deutsch*, tells the audience, in Banchieri's *Barca di Venetia per Padova*, that in performing a 'concerto' with four others (a Neapolitan, a Florentine, a Venetian, and a Bolognese), he will be singing the bass:[70]

> Mi star Tutesch, mi canter un bassott;
> Mò prima foller far un trinc e sgott.

Or to translate the macaronic speech:

> Me am German, me sing bass;
> But want first have drink,[71] *Grüss Gott* [God bless you].

In Renaissance theatre and *musica popolaresca*, not only are different ethnic types delineated, but so are different character types, from doctors and soldiers to gypsies, beggars, and clowns. Represented were the rich and mighty along with the poor and miserable, to form a colourful picture of society in all its shapes and shades. It was drawn in the later fifteenth century in the Florentine *canti carnascialeschi* and, more fully, in the sixteenth century after the example of the *commedia dell'arte* with its stock figures and situations. Garzoni's idea of Venice as a 'universal square with all the world's professions, both noble and ignoble,'[72] is a case in point. It might be coordinated with the explanations of the literary theorists who expected comedy to mirror real life. Thus Nicolò Barbieri defined comedy, in 1634, as a 'popular chronicle ... with incidents so depicted as to be lifelike: and how could one write or depict chronicles without telling the truth?' It revolves, for its content, around 'the ruthlessness of princes, good and bad governance, magnanimity, stinginess, losses and victories, in short, evil and good.'[73]

A musical illustration can be found in Vecchi's *Amfiparnaso*, which, according to the composer, 'depicts through diverse characters almost all the actions of private individuals, thus showing a mirror to human life.'[74] Venice, 'the city where this work is performed,' becomes, in his words, 'the great theatre of the world.'[75] In this 'great theatre' there are, we know, Jews and Christians, Germans, Turks, Greeks, Spaniards, and so forth. They form part of that great *comédie humaine* that, long before Balzac, played itself out, in a series of colourful tableaux, on the stage of early modern Italy.

Although often treated shabbily, the Jews were regarded as no less an integral part of the whole. In the *ebraiche*, true, they have their troubles and voice their grievances. But from the nature of the *ebraiche* as wholesome entertainment, all this is good theatre, in which the spectator was expected to sit back, enjoy himself, and laugh. Everyday life may have been different, but 'on the stage' its darker shades were removed by make-believe. So let's pretend, for one brief moment, that the Jews were considered as delightful in reality as they were in their droll musical representation. Although we know this was not so, the thought at least, for whatever compensation it is worth, is entertaining.

Notes

1 'O corpo del mondo, è qui tutta la turba israelittica ... Bisogna far buon cuore. Ma se mi parlano in ebraico sono spedito. Farò il muto. Ba, be, bi, bo, bu?': Giovanni Battista Andreini, *Lo schiavetto*, Act 2, Scene 10 (Milan 1612). For more on this comedy, see below.

2 The theme of 'the Other' infiltrates into the main body of literature on Jews

in the Renaissance, let alone other periods, in the sense that Jews are ineluctably treated for their individuality, hence as different from or in conflict with Christians. Rather than refer to relevant passages in key works (by, among others, Robert Bonfil, Daniel Carpi, Josef Kaplan, Benjamin Ravid, Cecil Roth, David Ruderman, Shlomo Simonsohn, Kenneth Stow, and Ariel Toaff), I will mention a few general studies on outsiders versus insiders: Hans Mayer, *Outsiders: A Study of Life and Letters* (Cambridge MA 1982), translated from *Aussenseiter* (Frankfurt am Main 1975); David Novak, *The Image of the Non-Jew in Judaism: An Historical and Constructive Study of the Noahide Laws* (New York 1983); Laurence J. Silberstein and Robert L. Cohn, eds., *The Other in Jewish Thought and History: Constructions of Jewish Culture and Identity* (New York 1994); Jacob J. Schacter, ed., *Judaism's Encounter with Other Cultures: Rejection or Integration?* (Northvale NJ 1997); Jacob Neusner and Ernest S. Frerichs, eds., *'To See Ourselves as Others See Us': Christians, Jews, 'Others' in Late Antiquity* (Chico CA 1985); Bernhard Blumenkranz, *Le juif médiéval au miroir du chrétien* (Paris 1966); Kenneth Stow, *Alienated Minority: The Jews of Medieval Latin Europe* (Cambridge MA 1992); and Robert Bonfil, 'Aliens Within: The Jews and Antijudaism,' in *Handbook of European History 1400–1600: Late Middle Ages, Renaissance, and Reformation*, 2 vols., ed. Thomas A. Brady Jr, Heiko A. Oberman, and James D. Tracy (Leiden 1994–5), 1: 263–302. The dichotomy outsiders/insiders expands, in its ramifications, to encompass the literature, from various angles, on early Christian-Jewish debates, the Inquisition, and, more broadly, anti-Semitism.
3 See next note for details.
4 Alessandro Coppini, 'La città bella,' entitled 'Canzona de' giudei' (late fifteenth century); Giovanni Serragli, 'Per non trovar,' entitled 'Canzona de' giudei battezzati' (late fifteenth century); Giovanni Domenico da Nola, 'Ecco la nimpha ebraica chiamata' (1545); Lodovico Novello, 'Quatro hebbree madonne siamo' (1546); Ghirardo da Panico, 'Adonai con voi lieta brigada' (1569); Orlando di Lasso, 'Ecco la nimph'Ebrayca chiamata' (1581; same lyric as in Nola's work); Andrea Banchieri, 'Samuel, Samuel, vu che havite' (1597), and 'Latrai nai nai' (1605); Orazio Vecchi, 'Tich tach toch' (1597), and 'Corrit! corrit! Messer Aron' (1604). For details of sources and editions, see variously below. As a possible eleventh work, one might mention 'Barachim e za chai' from a German publication (*Musikalischer Zeitvertreiber*, 1609, extant in only one of its six voices), where it is entitled 'Judenschul,' or synagogue; its composer is unnamed, although one suspects he was Italian.
5 No literature proper is available, although *ebraiche* are fleetingly mentioned in any number of monographs, from Alfred Einstein's by-now classic study on *The Italian Madrigal*, 3 vols. (Princeton 1949; repr. 1971), to, most recently,

Judith Cohen, 'The Bergamasca: Some Jewish Links,' in *Studies in Honour of Israel Adler*, ed. Eliyahu Schleifer and Edwin Seroussi (Jerusalem 2002), 396–420. Two of the *ebraiche* properly classify as carnival songs (Coppini's 'La città bella' and Serragli's 'Per non trovar'), two as *mascherate* (Novello's 'Quatro hebbree' and Banchieri's 'Samuel, Samuel,' the latter published in a collection of the composer's *canzonette*), three as pieces in madrigal comedies (Vecchi's 'Tich tach toch' and his 'Corrit! corrit!,' Banchieri's 'Latrai nai nai'), two as *canzone villanesche* (Nola's and, later, Lasso's 'Ecco la nimpha'), and one as a *villotta* (Ghirardo da Panico's 'Adonai con voi'). The classification follows the titles or contents of their publications. Yet the differences between the generic types are inconsequential for present purposes: all the works exemplify 'popular songs' of one particular variety, namely, as said above, the *ebraica*, and it is with Jewish character portrayal in the *ebraica*, not its typology, that this study is concerned.

6 They include Nola's and Lasso's settings of 'Ecco la ninfa ebraica chiamata,' both of which can be consulted in *Orlando di Lasso et al.: Canzoni villanesche and Villanelle*, Donna G. Cardamone (Madison 1991), 78–81 (Nola), 39–41 (Lasso).

7 Banchieri, e.g., prepared a three-voice arrangement of Vecchi's *ebraica* 'Tich tach toch,' originally for five voices, along with other portions from the source, viz., Vecchi's *Amfiparnaso*, publishing them as a collection entitled *Il studio dilettevole a 3 voci nuovamente con vaghi argomenti e spassevoli intermedii fioriti dal Amfiparnasso* (Milan 1600). Of the three voices, only the *canto* remains (in a unique copy in Bologna, Civico Museo Bibliografico Musicale), and precisely those pages with the *ebraica* (29–32) are missing: one suspects they were expurgated.

8 After Giovanni Mario de' Crescimbeni, *Istoria della volgar poesia*, 6 vols. (Rome 1702–11), 1: 198–9: 'in esse non si tratta d'altro che di contraffare e schernire gli Ebrei in stranissime guise, ora impiccandone per la gola, ora strangolandone ed ora scempiandone ed ora facendone ogn'altro più miserabile gioco ... sono composte ... d'ogni sorta di linguaggi corrotti e storpiati e mescolati insieme: né hanno altro ordine che di condursi con lunghissime cantilene di molti sciocchi personaggi allo spettacolo della burla che si fa al supposto Ebreo.' Expanding on Crescimbeni, Pietro Toschi discusses the *giudíata* in *Le origini del teatro italiano* (Turin 1982; 1st ed., 1955), 333–40.

9 On exclusion as self-definition, see, e.g., Jacques Derrida, 'Deconstruction and the Other,' in *Dialogues with Contemporary Continental Thinkers: The Phenomenological Heritage*, ed. Richard Kearney (Manchester 1984), 107–26, esp. 116–17.

10 Derrida, 'Living On: Border Lines,' in *Deconstruction and Criticism* (a collec-

tion of various authors' essays, prefaced by Geoffrey Hartman) (New York 1979), 75–176, esp. 83–4.

11 *The Diary of John Evelyn*, 6 vols., ed. Edmond Samuel De Beer (Oxford 1955; originally 1645–6), 2: 291–2. Ponte Sisto refers to the Oratory of the Compagnia della Santissima Trinità.

12 See Benjamin Ravid, 'Christian Travelers in the Ghetto of Venice: Some Preliminary Observations,' *Between History and Literature: Studies in Honour of Isaac Barzilay*, ed. Stanley Nash (Benei Berak 1997), 111–50; reprinted in idem, *Studies on the Jews of Venice, 1382–1797* (Aldershot, Hants 2003), same pagination).

13 '... con questo mezzo impariamo à conoscere un'infinità di Parenti, che mai da noi erano stati visti, perché essendo tutti gli Huomini nati d'un medesimo Padre, e d'un'istessa Madre, sono per conseguenza gli uni, agli altri tutti Parenti': Gregorio Leti, *L'Italia regnante, ò vero Nova descritione dello stato presente di tutti prencipati, e republiche d'Italia*, 2 vols. (Geneva 1675–6), 1: 3–4.

14 From Modena's foreword to Rossi's collection of *Ha-shirim asher li-shelomo* [Songs of Solomon] ('pa'al ve-'asa le-hosif mi-ḥol 'al ha-kodesh'), after Lev. 10:10, Ezek. 22:26, 42:20, etc. See, for original and translation, Salamone Rossi, *Complete Works* (Corpus Mensurabilis Musicae, 100), 13 vols., ed. Don Harrán (Neuhausen-Stuttgart, Middleton WI 1995–2003), 13a:175–86, esp. 179.

15 Orazio Vecchi, 'Tich tach toch' (*L'Amfiparnaso*, 1597; Act 3, Scene 3). For a recent edition, see *L'Amfiparnaso*, ed. Cecil Adkins (Chapel Hill 1977), 74–9.

16 '*Argomento*: Va à gli Hebrei Francatrippa à porr'un pegno; / La porta forte scuote' (lines 1–2). '*Fran.[catrippa]*: Sù prest, avrì, sù prest; / Da hom da be cha tragh zo l'us' (7–8). '*Heb.[rei]*: Badanai, Badanai, / Che cheusa volit? / Che cheusa dicit?' (27–9). '[*Aron*]: O Samuel, Samuel, / Venit à bess, venit à bess! / Adanai, che l'è lo Goi / Ch'è venut con lo moscogn, / Che vuol lo parachem. / [*Hebrei*]: L'è Sabbà, cha no podem' (31–6).

17 'Canzona de' giudei,' by the poet Giovambattista dell'Ottonaio: for its musical setting by Alessandro Coppini (after Florence, Biblioteca Nazionale Centrale, MS Banco Rari 230, fols. 42v–3r; late fifteenth century), see Frank A. D'Accone, ed. *Music of the Florentine Renaissance* (Corpus Mensurabilis Musicae, 32), 12 vols. (Rome, Neuhausen-Stuttgart 1966–96), 2: 11–13. On moneylending practices in Florence, see variously in Umberto Cassuto, *Gli ebrei a Firenze nell'età del Rinascimento* (Florence 1918), and B. Di Porto, ed., *Gli ebrei in Toscana dal Medioevo al Risorgimento: fatti e momenti* (Florence 1980).

18 'La città bella ... / Ci à mossi a star con voi / Tre dì, come la legge ci sicura' (lines 1, 3–4).

19 'Sian oggi qui venuti, / Benché no' stian con sospetto et paura' (11–12).

20 Orazio Vecchi, *Le veglie di Siena* (Venice 1604), end of 'first *veglia*'; see *Le veglie di Siena* (Capolavori polifonici del secolo XVI, 2), ed. Bonaventura Somma (Rome [1944]), 37–41.
21 The imperative 'run' can be traced to any number of precedents in the madrigal literature, for example: 'Correte, amanti, a veder questa fiamma' (N.V. [Il Nuovo Vogel]: Emil Vogel, Alfred Einstein, François Lesure, and Claudio Sartori, eds., *Bibliografia della musica italiana vocale profana pubblicata dal 1500 al 1700*, 3 vols. [Pomezia 1977], nos. 955–8, 2853, 3015–18), 'Correte, fiumi, a le vostre alte fonti' (N.V., nos. 787–90), 'Correte, ninfe leggiadrette' (N.V., nos. 777, 2322), 'Correte tutti quanti, o sventurat'amanti' (N.V., nos. 731, 961–3, 2607); or 'Corri, corri, ben mio' (N.V., no. 1960), 'Corri, corri, infelice' (N.V., nos. 2702–3), 'Corri, Filli, corri al prato' (N.V., nos. 238, 1306).
22 See, e.g., Richard Lassels, *The Voyage of Italy: or, A Compleat Journey through Italy* (London 1686; 1st ed., 1670), pt. 2: 119: 'Crossing from hence [the square before the church of SS Apostoli] into the *Corso*, I took an exact observation of this Street, which is the fairest in *Rome*. Its [*sic*] called the *Corso*, because here it is that they make Horses run aginst [*sic*] Horses, Jews against Jews, Boys against Boys, and the like, in *Carneval* time.' Similar passages can be found in the travel reports of Fynes Moryson, viz., the unpublished chapters in his *Itinerary* (1617), 2nd ed., ed. Charles Hughes (New York 1967), 458, 487–97, and Francis Mortoft, *His Book; Being His Travels through France and Italy, 1658–1659*, ed. Malcolm Letts (London 1925), 136. On the mortification of Jews during Carnival in Rome, see Attilio Milano, *Il ghetto di Roma: illustrazioni storiche* (Rome 1964), 307–28; and Elio Toaff, 'Il carnevale di Roma e gli ebrei,' *Scritti in memoria di Sally Mayer (1875–1953): saggi sull'ebraismo italiano*, ed. Umberto Nahon (Jerusalem and Milan 1956), 325–43.
23 '[*Goyim*]: Corrit! corrit! Messer Aron! / [*Aron*]: Che gli Goi, che gli Goi / Hanno ucciso lo Peper e 'l nostro Ochon, / È 'l nostro Pepere, è 'l nostro Ochon!' (lines 10–13).
24 '[*Aron*]: Badanai, se l'han traffughet, / Affagatet, / Se l'hanno pelet! / Merdochai, / Se l'han, se l'han papet!' (14–18).
25 Vecchi, 'Tich tach toch': ' ... e una Babelle / S'ode di voci, e horribili favelle' (2–3).
26 Ibid., 9–13.
27 'Barukh ha-ba [be-shem adonai]' ('Blessed is he who comes [in the name of the Lord]').
28 Or perhaps *ballachot* is a distortion of *berakhot*, 'blessings,' and *mallacott* of *makkot*, 'blows.'
29 Or possibly *petsaʻ*, 'wound,' which, in the same poem ('Adonai con voi lieta brigada'), can be sustained as a second reading.

30 The word *mashkon* seems to have been borrowed into Venetian as 'moscogn' (Vecchi's 'Tich tach toch'). See Giuseppe Boerio, *Dizionario del dialetto veneziano*, 2nd rev. and enl. edn. (Venice 1856; repr. Turin 1964), 429: 'far un moscón,' an expression of local jargon ('locuzione di gergo fam.'), meaning to pledge goods ('far un pegno [= impegnar della roba]').

31 'Tich tach toch,' lines 19–22.

32 The same could be said of the *giudíata*. Laura Falavolti, for one, placed G.B. Andreini's *Lo schiavetto* (from which an excerpt was drawn for the epigraph to this essay) 'in the context of a recrudescent anti-Jewish satire,' yet noted its 'interest for us,' moreover, 'as a demonstration of the author's acquaintance with both Hebrew and *giudeo-italiano*': see the introduction to her edition of *Commedie dei comici dell'arte* (Turin 1982), esp. 32–3.

33 Respectively, Vecchi, 'Tich tach toch', lines 9–10; Banchieri, 'Samuel, Samuel, vu che havite' (from his *Canzonette* for three voices [Venice 1597], 20, where it is entitled 'Mascherata di Hebrei'), lines 4, 8, 12; Banchieri, 'Latrai nai nai' (from his *Barca di Venetia per Padova* [Venice 1605]; see modern edition by Elio Piattelli [Capolavori polifonici del secolo XVI, 9; Rome 1969], 60–3), line 8.

34 Both from Banchieri, 'Latrai nai nai.'

35 That is, jumbled.

36 Thomas Coryate, *Coryats Crudities: Hastily Gobled Up in Five Moneths Travells in France, Savoy, Italy* [etc.] (London 1611), 231.

37 From both Vecchi, 'Tich tach toch' (as 'fa sinagoga'), and Banchieri, 'Latrai nai nai' (as 'fan sinagoga'). For 'fare sinagoga' in the added, figurative sense of making noise or a commotion, which, too, fits in with the same texts, see under 'sinagoga' in *Grande dizionario della lingua italiana*, ed. Salvatore Battaglia and Giorgio Barberi Squarotti, eds., 21 vols. (Turin 1960–2000), 19: 42–3 (meaning 4).

38 Michel de Montaigne, *Journal de voyage*, ed. François Rigolot (Paris 1992), 102: 'Ils ont ... un desaccord estreme, pour la confusion de tant de voix de toute sorte d'aages: car les enfans jusques au plus petit aage, sont de la partie.'

39 'Ma se tutti vorranno in un'istesso tempo far gorga, (provalo & lo sentirai) ti parerà d'esser proprio in una Sinagoga d'Hebrei' (the last words could also be translated as 'right in the middle of a Jewish prayer service'): Orazio Scaletta, *Scala di musica molto necessaria per principianti* (Venice 1626; repr. Bologna 1976), 23.

40 Charles Burney, *An Eighteenth-Century Musical Tour in Central Europe and the Netherlands* (first published in 1773 under the title: *The Present State of Music in Germany, the Netherlands, and United Provinces*), in the series of the author's *Musical Tours in Europe*, 2 vols., ed. Percy A. Scholes (London 1959), 2: 230.

41 'La città bella et conforme natura / Ch'oggi è fra voi et noi' (lines 1–2): Alessandro Coppini, 'Canzona de' giudei' (see above).
42 'Portato abbian de' nostri calicioni / Che v'insegnamo fare, / Ei [*sic*] son de' vostri assai più begli et buoni / E 'l vedrete al ghustare' (ibid., 5–8).
43 'Già mille volte da noi achattas[t]i / Danar col pegnio in mano; / Hor poiché l'arte me' di noi imparasti, / Pover venuti siano' (13–16). The *di noi* of 'l'arte me' di noi imparasti' could be construed as 'from us' or 'of ours' ('my skills' which are 'ours,' i.e., of the Jews at large); both readings are awkward (and have been levelled by the translation above).
44 'Non prestate a nessuno in sulla fede / Ché non ce n'è niente' (29–30).
45 'Et se voi guadagniate, / È giusto et cosa honesta' (25–6).
46 'Ma parci un caso strano, / Che chi presta col pegnio / Non porti el nostro segnio / Et stia quanto e' vuol drento a vostre mura' (17–20).
47 In governing Florence, the Medici protected, and encouraged, the Jewish moneylenders. With the death of Lorenzo de' Medici in 1492, however, a new period of religious stringency was inaugurated by the dour friar Girolamo Savonarola, who rescinded the earlier privileges. On the *monti di pietà*, see Marino Ciardini, *I banchieri ebrei in Firenze nel secolo XV e il monte di pietà fondato da Girolamo Savonarola: appunti di storia economica con appendice di documenti* (Borgo S. Lorenzo 1907), and, most recently, Daniele Montanari, ed., *Monti di pietà e presenza ebraica in Italia: secoli XV–XVIII* (Rome 1999).
48 'Noi sappian ben che non sol per guadagnio / Con sicurtà prestate, / Ma l'aiutare un povero compagnio: / Il che molto ben fate' ('La città bella,' lines 21–4).
49 'Ché non fa mal chi presta; / Ma chi achatta, fa mal dell'usura' (ibid., 27–8); read 'does harm to usury' as 'makes a bad name for usury.'
50 'Et sol ghabbato è quel che troppo crede, / Po' che danno [= dannò] si pente' (31–2).
51 'Hor sia saggio et prudente / Chi n'a richeza et stato, / Ch'un ben, male acquistato, / Se ne va in fummo [*sic*] presto et pocho dura' (33–6).
52 'Col pegnio è l'huom sicuro et non bisognia / Sensal, trabalzi et carte / Per ricoprir; ché non s'à aver vergognia / Di far ben la suo [*sic*] arte' (37–40).
53 'Dove intendesti el troppo nostro danno / Per prestar voi et esser noi chacciati': from 'Per non trovar,' or 'Canzona de' giudei battezzati' (lines 7–8), by the poet Giovambattista dell'Ottonaio; for its musical setting by Giovanni Serragli (after Florence, Biblioteca Nazionale Centrale, MS Banco Rari 230, fols. 97v–9r, anon., though ascribed to Serragli in ibid., MS Banco Rari 337, fol. 79v, there as 'So'; late fifteenth century), see D'Accone, ed., *Music of the Florentine Renaissance*, 2:11–13.
54 'Quanto è felice in terra un che sia nato / Di buon cristiano et maxime in Fiorenza!' (ibid., lines 29–30).

55 'L'ebrea [fede] lasciata abbiano / Et battezati sian, com'ogniun vede' (3–4).
56 Morley, *A Plaine and Easie Introduction to Practicall Musicke* (London 1597), ed. R. Alec Harman (London 1952), 295.
57 'Come meglio potrà il musico ... dilettare che col ridicolo?': *Le veglie di Siena*, preface 'Ai lettori' (fol. A 1v).
58 Ibid.: 'Oh l'è galante, oh l'è gentile e dilettevole, pien di ridicoli, e solazzevole'; 'O che solazzo! oh che piacer si sente!'; 'Oh che sciolta favella! oh l'è vaga! oh l'è bella!' (the first two exclamations from the *Prima veglia*, 'proposta prima,' and the third from same, 'proposta seconda').
59 Ibid.: 'un siciliano, d'amor insano' (from *Prima veglia*, 'proposta prima'); 'una contadinella, che si creda fra l'altre la più bella' (same, 'seconda proposta'); 'uno spagnolo, che parli alla sua dama con gran duolo' (same, 'quarta proposta').
60 Ibid.: 'Nell'imitar gli ebrei ha 'l primo onore Giulia ... Imitate gli ebrei del naturale' (from *Prima veglia*, 'chiusa del giuoco').
61 'Oh che riso! oh che riso!' (ibid.).
62 On Francatrippa as a *commedia dell'arte* figure, first created in 1577, see Pierre Louis Duchartre, *The Italian Comedy: The Improvisation, Scenarios, Lives, Attributes, Portraits, and Masks of the Illustrious Characters of the Commedia dell'Arte*, translated from the French by Randolph T. Weaver (London 1929), 20, 87, 177.
63 *Rahel Varnhagen: The Life of a Jewess*, ed. Liliane Weissberg and translated from the German by Richard and Clara Winston (Baltimore and London 1997), 256. The portion omitted (under the ellipsis points) reads: 'and that situation obtained in all countries in which Jews lived, down to the twentieth century.'
64 G.B. Andreini, *La Maddalena, sacra rappresentatione* (Mantua 1617). For all five works, see Salamone Rossi, *Complete Works*, ed. Harrán, 8:xlvii–lix (texts), 48–67 (music).
65 *Stanza 1*: 'Spazziam pronte, o vecchiarelle, / Questo suolo, / Vaghe solo / Far d'augei prede più belle.' *Stanza 2*: 'Su affrettiamo a gara i bracci, / Già che 'l tetto / È 'l boschetto / Ove stan le panie, i lacci.' Two stanzas follow; see ibid., 8, esp. lvi–lviii (poetry), 64–7 (music).
66 'Vecchie di bassa stima serve di Maddalena' (1617), 'anderan curve, con bastoncelli' (later ed., 1652); for details on editions, see ibid., 8:lxvii.
67 On the way the Jews, in forming their own identity, appropriated the stereotyped images of their alterity as defined by Christians, see Sander L. Gilman, *Jewish Self-Hatred: Anti-Semitism and the Hidden Language of the Jews* (Baltimore and London 1986). In Andreini's *Lo schiavetto*, already mentioned for the author's clever simulation of Hebrew speech, the Jews are especially harsh on themselves, inveighing against their rabbis as 'irate, full of grievances, de-

ceits, and stupidities' and against their brethren as belonging to an 'excommunicated, condemned, and diabolic race' ('Rabini arrabbiati, pieni di mormorazzione, di falsità, e d'ignoranze ... razza scomunicata, dannata, indiavolata,' ibid., Act 2, Scene 7; Laura Falavolti, ed., in *Commedie dei comici dell'arte*, 110, 112).

68 On this *balletto* in the context of Rossi's theatre music, see Don Harrán, 'Salamone Rossi as a Composer of Theatre Music,' *Studi musicali* 16 (1987): 95–131; also idem, *Salamone Rossi, Jewish Musician in Late Renaissance Mantua* (Oxford 1999; repr. in paperback, 2003), 174–200. For laughter and mockery in sixteenth-century Italian literature, see Anna Fontes Baratto, ed., *De qui, de quoi se moque-t'on? Rire et dérision à la Renaissance* (Paris 2004).

69 'Le nazioni poi si subdividono in paesi come il barbaro si subdivide in Turco, in Francese, in Tedesco, in Inglese, e simili. Onde il Turco se introdurrà arrogante, omicidiario, ignorante, inimico delle virtù e dell'ingegni e della nobiltà; il Francese veemente, inconsiderato, mutabile, et ingrato; Inghilterra, come dice il Giovio, alla tavola dalla mattina alla sera. Et universalmente i proverbi dei paesi e delle città dinotano qualche disposizione o vizio che comunemente hanno quelli di quei luochi. Come è Spagna: "di fuori bello e dentro la magagna"; Lombardo: "fedele e leccardo"; Fiorentino: "il corpo e l'anima al quattrino"; Romano: "giorno e notte con l'arme in mano"; Senese: "pazzo a sue spese"; Genovese: "moro bianco"; Napolitano: "fuori d'oro e dentro vano", e così di molti altri': Trissino, *La quinta e la sesta divisione della poetica* (Venice 1562, originally c. 1549), *Trattati di poetica e retorica*, 2 vols., ed. Bernard Weinberg (Bari 1970), 2: 64.

70 'Cinque cantori in diversi lenguaggi, concerto di cinque cantori ... *Argomento*: Ecco un Napoletano, e un Fiorentino, / Venetian, Bolognese & un Thedesco / Che in Barca voglion far un concertino': Banchieri, *Barca di Venetia per Padova*, no. 7. The German appears to have carried the day, for his partners finish with the couplet 'O buono, o buono, hor cinque siamo, / Prima si bevi, doppo cantiamo' ('Oh great! oh great! now we're five, / But first let's drink, then after we'll sing').

71 Or possibly 'make a toast.'

72 *La piazza universale di tutte le professioni del mondo, e nobili e ignobili* (Venice 1585).

73 'La comedia è una cronica popolare ... un caso rappresentato al vivo; e come si può scrivere o rappresentare croniche senza dire la verità? ... Si raccontano nelle croniche le tirannie de' Prencipi, i buoni e tristi governi, le magnanimità, le avarizie, le perdite e le vittorie, ed in somma il male ed il bene': Nicolò Barbieri, *La supplica, discorso famigliare a quelli che trattano de' comici* (Venice 1634), ed. Ferdinando Taviani (Milan 1971), 34–5.

74 '... rappresenta sotto diverse persone, quasi tutte le attioni dell'huomo privato, la onde come specchio dell'humana vita': *L'Amfiparnaso*, from preface 'Ai lettori,' fol. [vi]v.
75 'E la città dove si rappresenta quest'opra è 'l gran Theatro del mondo': ibid., from 'Prologo' to Act 1.

chapter four

Can Fundamentalism Be Modern? The Case of Avraham Portaleone (1542–1612)

ALESSANDRO GUETTA

One of the protagonists of the great scientific renaissance in sixteenth-century Europe was an Italian Jew. Avraham Portaleone (1542–1612) practised medicine, one of the traditional professions of the Jewish intellectual elite, in Mantua. Under the rule of the Gonzaga dynasty, the city was one of the main cultural centres during the Renaissance and the Baroque period. Situated on the plain of the river Po to the southeast of Milan, Mantua became a kind of laboratory for the arts, the sciences, and music, while its Jewish community, fairly well-established since the fifteenth century, flourished to such an extent that in many fields Mantuan Jews paved the way for what could be termed 'Jewish modernity.'[1]

Avraham Portaleone was heir to a long tradition of prestigious physicians and enjoyed a privileged status among his colleagues in North Italy. Close to the court of the Gonzagas, he was called upon to give lessons to the doctors of Lombardy and to make written pronouncements on controversial medical subjects. In parallel, he treated the Jewish community free of charge. Portaleone was a man of considerable culture, since he had been educated to an advanced level in traditional Jewish studies and in medicine, a discipline which then required a vast knowledge not only of science but also of literature and classical philosophy.

His written oeuvre consists of two printed books (and a medical manuscript which will not be examined here), the first written in Latin, the second in Hebrew. His Hebrew-Latin bilingualism, extremely rare for the period, is noteworthy from a historian's point of view, but it is the nature, content, and style of the two texts which demand comparison – one conducive to the understanding of a mentality typical of a period of European history that experienced both a huge growth in scientific knowledge and a renaissance of religious piety.[2]

The Latin book, *De Auro dialogi tres* (Venice 1584),[3] is a discussion of the properties of gold, and seeks to address a question debated by scientists at that time (and one that would continue to be debated for over a hundred years after the book's publication): can gold cure certain illnesses? The prestige gold had enjoyed since Antiquity had given it a special status among metals, to the extent that ancient and modern scientists shared the conviction that gold, if used in the right way, could be a panacea capable of treating all illnesses. Medical literature prescribed grinding it into a very fine powder and its ingestion, mixed with water, or slicing it into thin strips to be heated in the fire and then cooled with wine to produce the *vinum aureum*, the golden wine, believed to have great powers.

Contemporary medical authorities were divided into two camps on this – those who denied its powers and those convinced of them. Portaleone's position lay midway between. In his view, although the hypothesis that gold had powerful medicinal properties was true, in light of the knowledge at that time it remained a mere hypothesis since such properties do not reside within gold as we know it (*aurum vulgare*) but in its quintessence (*succum aurum*), a substance perfectly pure and balanced in composition.[4] But, in truth, nobody had yet succeeded in extracting this essence, on which the *Ars chimica* had focused its efforts; consequently, the long list of healings that ancient and modern doctors had attributed to the ingestion of 'common gold' mixed with water or wine was the fruit of ignorance and charlatanism.[5] As for gold's capacity to cauterize wounds, it has this in common with many other metals with the same characteristics.

As was often the case with scientific works of the period, the subject provided an opportunity to discuss other, sometimes unrelated subjects. In *De Auro*, alongside the strictly medical argument, there are incursions into Greek, Latin, and Italian literature, mythology, and a host of other disciplines. But two themes stand out for their importance and de facto constitute a sort of epistemological framework that organizes the empirical observations and gives them coherence: (1) the relationship between the ancients and moderns and (2) the closely related theme of the place of experience in scientific argumentation or, in a more general sense, the roles of reason and experience in human knowledge.

The beginning of the third dialogue effectively presents the first theme, the relationship between the scientific authorities of the past and the 'moderns.' The two characters are the author's alter ego, Dynachrisus, a doctor very erudite in the Greek, Latin, and Arab medical tradition but who never tires of experimenting, and Achryvasmus, whose role is to ask the questions and who is sceptical of this tradition and of scientific opinions devoid of common sense.

Dynachrisus is shut up at the back of the library. The candle burning at his side is to invoke the help of the dead, as 'magicians, diviners and enchanters used to do,' but the dead don't reply. Achryvasmus, concerned, fearing his friend has gone mad, asks him where the dead he is talking about are. Dynachrisus, indicating the books around him, concludes dryly, 'May they stay away from here! There is no kinship between them and me!'[6]

The library-cum-cemetery, dimly lit by a candle, corresponds in every way to the image formulated by other scientists of Portaleone's generation and the next. The Jesuit astronomer Giovan Battista Riccioli (1598–1671) criticized those who exercised their minds purely theoretically, 'intra sua cubicula meditando' (in meditating in their little rooms).[7] To represent this science of the past, Galileo, Francis Bacon, and Descartes proposed the same metaphor of an enclosed space where light never reaches, full of books that seem to offer protection from new things outside rather than constitute a source of knowledge.[8]

The second theme, the central role of experience, runs through the whole of Portaleone's book and is its fundamental epistemological notion. Portaleone constantly repeats that experience is the only legitimate source of knowledge and formulates this in a manner reminiscent of Martin Luther's *sola scriptura*: even where reason is incapable of inferring the cause of a natural phenomenon, we can have a certain knowledge of it through experience, without other aids, *experientia sola*.[9] The two interlocutors agree on this: 'Experience [says Achryvasmus] is celebrated as a source of knowledge for all natural things. If you were to deny this, you would deserve not only to be reproached but also punished.'[10]

Reason can refer back to general laws based on the regularity of phenomena, affirms Dynachrisus, alias Portaleone, but the real causes will always elude man because it would take infinite science to know the infinite properties of the innumerable things of the world. Nevertheless, one should not be deterred by the complexity and obscurity of phenomena but experiment relentlessly: the enemies of the good scientist are negligence, specious reasoning, and defective analysis, which cause him to lose sight of the truth.[11] Knowledge, Achryvasmus reminds us, is a duty, and stupor in the face of natural phenomena is the son of ignorance.[12]

This exaltation of experience goes hand in hand with an overt closeness to the alchemists, not to the details of their ideology, which the author openly mocks ('God protect me, I do not suffer from that form of stupidity'),[13] but to their empiricist readiness to soil their hands using ovens and alembics. The love of truth pushes Portaleone to seek it where it can be found, to, if need be, unashamedly resort to the techniques of the artisans (*mechanici*).[14] In his view, alchemic medicine was a viable alternative to traditional medicine, and it is the good doctor's duty to master both. But certain questions can be resolved solely by practical means (i.e., of the alchemists), hence Dynachrisus' peremptory exhortation: 'Work and you will find!'[15]

The epistemology of *De Auro* is therefore based entirely on experience. One could object that the importance attributed to the unproven notion of quintessence, on which he has part of the properties of bodies depend, is contrary to his empiricist *credo*. Quintessence does, however, represent the hypothetical solution to which the human intellect resorts when it is incapable of finding something out by merely observing phenomena. If my interpretation is correct, quintessence is a notion destined to remain void: 'Dynachrisus: When human reason endeavors to find the causes of certain phenomena, it is incapable of affirming anything at all, and so falls back on specific form, in other words, on the totality of the substance or force of the medicine, on a magical property, as though clinging to a sacred anchor.'[16] The true causes, including the magical quintessence, remain mysterious in the end. Radical empiricism results in a religious attitude: 'Achryvasmus: It leads the ship into the most feeble of ports, into the shakiest of shelters, since only God, Creator of the entire universe, knows perfectly the substances capable of producing wonderful effects.'[17]

It is an attitude that returns twenty-five years later in Portaleone's second book, in an entirely different existential context with its own very different rhetoric. A quotation from this second book immediately conveys the intervening change of tone. The author is still reserved concerning the authorities of the past but gives them a religious and national tone:

> Understand and see that, just as one has to accept that precious stones and some animals possess – by God's decree – many virtues for avoiding man's illnesses and for preserving their health, for us it would be a fault, an impediment, an obstacle, a great sin to believe in everything these philosophers [i.e., non-Jewish scientists] have to say on the subject; theirs are vain, false and untrue words in which one must not have faith. One must attribute these effects to God alone, to Him alone belong the riches, the glory, the kingdom ... in heaven and on earth, only He has the power to make all grow

and give it strength. We praise His Name always since he is God above all blessings ... He created the sky ... and all its armies, the Earth and everything on it, the oceans and all they contain. He gave life to us all ... and we are His people and the flock He leads ... and we prostrate ourselves before Him in fear.[18]

The difference is dramatic. The declared reason was that, in 1605, a sudden attack of apoplexy forced Portaleone to change course; the confident scientist was supplanted by a religious figure tormented by guilt for having neglected the Torah. Therefore, he decided to embark on a work the function of which is atonement for his sins, *Shilte ha-Giborim* (Shields of the Mighty),[19] an extraordinary book that is both a comprehensive survey of empirical knowledge in the most varied domains and a manual of devotion. The well-known beginning of *Shilte ha-Giborim* introduces us to an intellectual world very distant to that of Dynachrisus, the intrepid harbinger of modern science:

> When God wanted to chasten me I fell ill. Two years ago the whole left side of my body became as if dead and I could no longer touch my hand to my breast nor walk in the street, even leaning on a cane, because of the loss of feeling and the ability to move my limbs.
>
> I searched my behavior and saw (after Him who sees all) that in addition to my sins, which were more numerous than the hairs on my head, the clamor of my neglecting the Torah rose before the face of God. For I had dealings with the children of Greek wisdom, I sought to reach the heights through philosophy and medicine, which lured me with their honeyed words to seek salvation in the ways of darkness, and thus prevented me from devoting myself to the heritage of the community of Jacob, as I should have done.
>
> This is why God was angered against me, dire maladies have darkened my days and defeated me; my nerves are ruined, my sighs do not cease, so that with the bitterness of my soul, sleep has left me and I cannot recover my strength. Happiness has fled and pain increased. So I raised my eyes upward and made repentance (*teshuvah*) in my heart. I told myself that sin might be forgiven if, after repairing what he had damaged, the father were to teach his children that they would be victorious with God if they would put His Law in their hearts, meditate on it day and night and observe prudence and good counsel; by so doing they would be blessed.[20]

The partisan of scientific method makes way for the pious Jew intent on atoning for the wrongs of his youth. Galileo becomes Pascal; one could even say that through a kind of self-censorship, Portaleone exercises the same violent control and censorship that the Church had applied to both Galileo's theories and Galileo the man.

His *teshuva*, repentance, consists in providing his children and readers in general with an anthology of sacred texts that they can browse through daily, thereby observing the duties of the good Jew without too much difficulty. To render this reading more effective, he precedes it with a description of the Temple in Jerusalem, so that the reader can identify with the Jews of the past who offered sacrifices, according to the well-known principle of prayer and the study that replaced sacrifices. I have noted – as Avraham Melamed has done before me in another context[21] – the parallel between Portaleone's reasoning and that of Ignatius Loyola, who in his *Spiritual Exercises* exhorts the faithful to imagine scenes in the life of Christ to heighten their concentration (and *kavanah* is a recurrent word in Portaleone's writing) and to mentally transfer themselves into the past.[22]

Avraham Portaleone's description of the architecture of the Temple in Jerusalem and its ceremonies in ninety chapters is a preparation for the reading of the sacred texts which, conducted with the right *kavanah*, will act on God and consequently on the children of Israel.

Despite a certain mysticism in the introduction – the author also declares his admiration for the kabbalists by acknowledging that he has not had the privilege of penetrating their secret garden – this description is absolutely realist, with one highly significant exception that I will discuss further on. Portaleone the scientist never wavers in this pious work, despite the affirmations in the introduction mentioned above; he is extremely clear and precise and concerned with verifying the coherence of his sources. When these seem in conflict with one another he embarks on lengthy discussions that do not always achieve a satisfactory outcome, in which case he frankly acknowledges this. One should add that, despite expressing regret for his profane studies at the beginning of *Shilte ha-Giborim*, Portaleone does not seem to be denying the experiments he carried out in his youth. He even refers the reader of the Hebrew book to *De Auro* for fuller information on his scientific opinions. One can therefore conclude that they have not changed; what has changed is the overall conception within which they are set.[23]

In this book, the Jewish Sages have replaced the Greek, Latin, and Arab philosophers and scientists, and, quite naturally, here the scathing criticism of the authorities of the past is absent. On the contrary, Portaleone, the repentant, sees the sages of the Mishna and the Talmud as absolute, infallible authorities, and when perceptible experience contradicts their affirmations (we are in the thick of Galileo's problematic here), he resorts to strange balancing acts to justify two truths – one addressing the man of religion, the other the scientist. Nevertheless, instead of looking forward with the optimism of the explorer, here Portaleone looks back, following the typical schema of the traditionalist Jew for whom all has already been said and generations to come have only to organize the knowledge that is progressively forgotten in time.

But we have said that there is one exception to the author's realism; it concerns his perception of historical time. Because one should add that *Shilte ha-Giborim* is not a straightforward description of the Temple in the manner of the traditional Jewish texts (essentially the Mishna with Bertinoro's commentary and the relevant chapters of Maimonides' *Mishneh Torah*): whenever the opportunity arises the author adds little essays in various disciplines. These essays reveal his vast knowledge of contemporary learning of non-Jewish origin and, even more striking, they are resolutely 'modern' in conception. Together, the essays comprise a kind of encyclopedia, for which the description of the Temple, like a *Theatrum memoriae*, acts as a supporting structure, and which Portaleone systematically justifies by anachronisms (see Miletto, *Glauben und Wissen*, 108–75).

Let us give an example. Discussing the music and songs of the Levites, Portaleone resolutely denies that this is simple, primitive music and describes in minute detail the *shir mahshavti* (which could be translated as 'artistic song') of his time with evident admiration – remember that he lived in Mantua, then one of Europe's musical capitals. Contemporary music, which was highly elaborate, was for him *the* music of the Temple, and he makes this explicit by using the expression 'like today'; 'they played and sang the psalms of David son of Ishai in many kinds of instrumental and vocal music, basing this on books, like today.'[24]

This collapsing of present and past, which reflects the well-known tendency of the Jews to appropriate contemporary knowledge elaborated by others over which they then claim paternity, must be seen alongside the spiritual displacement into the past recommended for the pious Jew. These anachronisms – there are many in the work – indicate an acute perception of historical time rather than great naivety. It is as if the man who twenty-five years earlier had taken a clear stance in a scientific quarrel between ancients and moderns, now found himself in the uncomfortable position of wanting to glorify the Jewish past while recognizing the greatness of contemporary culture, non-Jewish in origin. He beholds two privileged eras, that of the Judaism of the first and second Temple and the contemporary age, out of which he fashions an imperfect synthesis bespeaking a tension that is difficult to resolve.

We have evoked Portaleone's methodological probity in this work full of religious piety. One would have expected at least a selective choice of sources excluding everything non-Jewish, in conformity with his admission of having sinned by allowing himself to be fascinated by 'foreign' sciences. Nothing of the sort. True, he proposes the above-mentioned model of 'Israel mother of all sciences' (including the art of war, which suggests a frustration vis-à-vis the affairs of the real world and alludes to the still-embryonic notion of Israel as a 'normal' nation among others), and he attributes infallibility to the rabbis of the Talmud, which has led me to define him as a 'fundamentalist.' But elsewhere, he cites a great many non-Jewish sources, past and present, and openly declares this; better, at the end of his introduction, when he gives a list of 196 Jewish and non-Jewish authors and books, he assigns to this ensemble, as a mnemonic verse: 'As for me, I will behold thy face *in righteousness* ('be-tzedek,' equivalent to the number 196): I shall be satisfied, when I awake, with thy likeness (Psalms 17, 15).'[25] In other words, by subtle allusion, Portaleone links the contemplation of the face of God or, from his perspective, the obtaining of truth, to the use of all sources, Jewish and non-Jewish, that, together, form righteousness, a human and religious value. He makes a point of indicating that none of these authors of the Nations took up a position against the Torah; and one should add that they were scientists not theologians, which suggests the idea of the establishment of a neutral ground, that of science, on which the pious Jew can move freely and without danger.

Not only does Portaleone not renounce non-Jewish scientific contributions, he does not abstain from using numerous languages, indispensable for the mastery of his rich bibliography. Above all, he manifests his appreciation, I would say his love even, for the Greek language. He justifies its constant use in the book by the use the sages of the Talmud made of it, which imposes that one establishes its correct spelling, given the mistakes made by typographers – the rabbis, remember, never made mistakes. I think that this justification smacks of dissimulation, and the following passage bears this out.

In Chapter 35, Portaleone describes the three chests in the Temple, in which worshippers left money for sacrifices. In the Mishna, to which he refers (*Shekalim*, chapter 3), it is written that the letters *alef*, *bet*, and *gimel* were inscribed on the chests or, according to another authority, the

Greek letters *alpha, beta,* and *gamma.* Portaleone unhesitatingly accepts the second hypothesis and cites Bertinoro: 'It is written that (Genesis 9, 27): *God shall enlarge Japheth, and he shall dwell in the tents of Shem,* [implying that] the beauty of Japheth may dwell in the tents of Shem. But, for Japeth, nothing is more beautiful than the Greek language.' (In Bertinoro's text: 'For Japheth, there is no more beautiful language than Greek.') By citing the Jewish authorities (*Shilte ha-Giborim,* 31b), Portaleone is surreptitiously expressing an opinion on the Greek language – evidently the famous and controversial Azariah de' Rossi, although never mentioned, had not written in vain. It is, moreover, almost certainly to de Rossi's *Me'or 'enayim* (Part 3, chapter 4) that Portaleone is referring in the rest of the passage, in which, by developing Bertinoro's commentary, he explains that the Jews during the Second Temple period were better versed in Greek than in Hebrew. The development consists in taking Philo, the Jewish philosopher from Alexandria, as an example of poor knowledge of Hebrew. He calls him Yedidia, the Hebrew version of Philo by de Rossi, and some of the lines he writes about him are identical to those in the *Me'or 'enayim.* This work, considered as one of the first examples of modern Jewish erudition, which Italian rabbis were far from unanimously agreeing with, has, in certain respects, an unexpected continuation in the *Shilte ha-Giborim.*[26]

Let us now examine another striking example of Avraham Portaleone's oscillation between modernity and tradition, his discourse on the properties of precious stones in *De Auro* and *Shilte ha-Giborim.* In both works, the author discusses the subject at length. In *De Auro,* he does so by inserting it into a broader examination of the classification of beings as animal or mineral. His conclusions are categorical: metals and stones are inanimate beings, since their growth process does not depend on any kind of nutrition or process one could call 'organic' (and which he calls 'intrinsic') but on a juxtaposition of parts: 'Dynachrisus: Note, Achryvasmus, that when one says that stones feed and grow one uses an inappropriate expression (*æquivoce nutriuntur, & æquivoce augmentatur*). Indeed, they do not increase in volume for an internal but for an external reason, and grow through the juxtaposition of parts, which should not be considered as true nutrition or autonomous growth (*propria auctio*) but rather as an addition. This is why we affirm that these mixed bodies are totally lacking in soul.'[27]

In *Shilte ha-Giborim,* the discourse on precious stones is introduced via the description of the breastplate of the High Priest, which was adorned with twelve precious stones. As usual in this work, the description of a ritual garment is transformed into a veritable little treatise in which Portaleone displays his scientific knowledge. The phenomenon of the growth of stones is discussed here by bringing to the fore its quasi-miraculous aspect, without bothering to give general definitions. When he writes about the diamond, Portaleone cites the mineralogist Francesco Roheo's account of the phenomenon of diamonds occasionally giving birth to other, identical diamonds,[28] an observation that he does not doubt but explains by natural laws: 'If one wanted to understand this using natural laws, one could say that the celestial energy that God gave them and which enables them to produce similar diamonds is first transformed by the pure air around it into water, which solidifies and becomes ice. Then, thanks to the energy inherent in precious stones, the water changes into diamonds.' He continues, citing Theophrastus and Pliny, who respectively talk of precious stones 'giving birth' using the divine energy animating them within, and of the 'pregnancy' of another stone lasting three months.[29]

This acritical acceptance of quasi-miraculous phenomena related by others clashes with the empirical attitude to which Portaleone has accustomed us, especially as it contrasts completely with the very clear position set out in *De Auro*. But in the cases already examined, the difference between the two works lies in their general frames of reference, scientific in one, religious in the other, not in the recourse to experience and observation as the true source of truth.

To understand this discrepancy, one has to return to the general examination of the virtues of precious stones in *De Auro*. Having discussed the curative properties of certain fossils and several animals – about which his interlocutor is sceptical – Dynachrisus enumerates the qualities of precious stones. The almandine garnet protects from or heals all poisons, renders its wearer invincible in battle, and enables one to interpret dreams; beryl wards off arguments and danger from enemies and makes one calm and sincere; jasper stops the menstrual cycle, wards off lust and heals fever and dropsy, and so on. True, Dynachrisus does take pains to attribute these opinions to other authors (*dixit ... fertur ... asseverant ... affirmant*), but at the same time he readily sings the praises of these stones, whose transparency and luminosity enables them to receive their particular properties, which he likens to various parts of the heavens.[30]

In the Hebrew work, the lengthy description of the qualities of precious stones follows a philological and scientific analysis of the identification of the stones on the breastplate of the High Priest, attempting to put some order into the multiplicity of denominations attributed – often wrongly – by traditional Jewish exegetes. Here, the Hebrew book is more 'scientific' than the Latin one. But, immediately after, Portaleone inserts a rather strange passage:

> Some of my masters, having read these pages, were dissatisfied when they noticed I had not discussed the essences of precious stones on the mantelet and breastplate [of the High Priest]. Numerous authorities vigorously requested, ordered me to do everything in my power to seek these essences so as to consign them to my book, in which case they would have been satisfied. But, for me, this is very difficult, particularly because the great [non-Jewish] scientists of the past never agree.
>
> But I did my utmost, I hastened to find pertinent answers through the light of my reason ... by trying to attain good results through well conducted reasoning, and I wrote them in conformity with the orders of many great Sages.
>
> If I have said true things, I thank God for His bounty in opening my eyes to the way: from His mouth comes knowledge and intelligence. I may not have attained complete knowledge of their essence and qualities, in which case, those who have confidence in me should not blame me, as I must write only what my eyes have seen, in a just, correct and true way (*be-tzedek*).[31]

It seems clear from these lines that Portaleone had come under pressure from rabbis to include edifying notions in a religious subject such as the High Priest's clothing, and not limit himself to the work of the scientist or philologist – which the Mantuan doctor duly did, imbuing the precious stones adorning the sacerdotal vestments with manifold properties, finding correspondences between the twelve stones and the twelve tribes of Israel,[32] and identifying fanciful etymological links between Hebrew and Italian words. In one instance, he even creates an interpretation from a *gematria*, that is, a correspondence between the equal numerical value of two different Hebrew words – a method which has nothing to do with science.

In short, in the many pages Portaleone devotes to precious stones, the scientist is eclipsed by the preacher. But he does from time to time recall the 'sin' of those who deny perceptible experience,[33] and concludes his peculiar mineralogical treatise by insisting on the primacy of 'plain experience' (*nisayon pashut*) over theoretical study, adding, 'Without experience, the doctor had no superiority over other men,'[34] which seems to be a warning to the reader about the profound convictions from which rabbinic pressure has forced him to depart.

Complex, strange, and fascinating, the *Shilte ha-Giborim* can be read as an attempt to give Jews a concise handbook of general culture, written in Hebrew, and keeping talmudic knowledge as its basis of reference.[35] But one should not forget that this text is above all a description of the Temple, even if the modern researcher is understandably attracted by its divergences, discrepancies, disparities, deviations, and originality, above all in its reference to non-Jewish knowledge. To evaluate its own characteristics, a systematic examination of this description in comparison to the sources must be undertaken. An initial analysis yields the following results:

1. *Shilte ha-Giborim* is more synthetic than its sources, to which the reader is sometimes referred. It is also more systematic (or follows another system), since it brings together the subjects that in the sources are scattered in different parts.
2. It is interested in *halakhah* only when it gives details of the Temple's *realia*. The book aims to be an historical reconstruction not a book of laws.
3. In places, we are dealing with a veritable exegesis in the traditional sense. In particular, one finds explanations of the Mishna, in which Portaleone develops hypotheses rendered necessary by the impossibility of consulting the Talmud, forbidden at the time. Or he adopts a position among ancient and modern commentators whose opinions differ.
4. The author sometimes enlarges on his sources when he thinks that his scientific experience and readings can help a better understanding of the subject. In so doing he produces a kind of 'scientific midrash.' This *amplificatio* can develop into a full-blown fictional account in which the author imagines scenes that could have taken place in the Temple, complete with dialogues and oratories. This is the case in chapters 18–21, in which he stages a conflict between priests, Levites and Israelites, or in chapters 41–2, with the speech of the priest in charge of war.

In the works of Avraham Portaleone, one recognizes the intellectual tensions of his time: the great broadening of the horizons of knowledge, the manifestation of both a scientific vision of reality and great religious devotion, a change in the perception of space and, for the Italian Jews in particular, an oscillation between openness and closure to the non-Jewish world together with a shift towards an increased use of Latin and then Italian as a written language (*Shilte ha-Giborim* contains many Italian terms, which are used to better explain the subject to the reader). This work, with its reversals and difficulties, is part of what one could call the movement of Italian Jewish culture towards modernity, or the Jewish declension of a movement throughout European culture.

Notes

1 The most important representative of Jewish culture either born or living in Mantua were: Yehuda ben Yehiel, known as Messer Leone (fifteenth century), author of the first treatise on rhetoric in Hebrew (*Nofet tsufim*, ca. 1475); Abraham Farissol (1431–ca.1535), a talented geographer; Yehuda (Leone) de' Sommi Portaleoni (1527–1592), playwright and theatre director, author of the first known play in Hebrew, *A Comedy of Betrothal*; Azaria de' Rossi (1511?–1578?), whose name is associated with *Me'or 'enayim* (The Light of the Eyes, Mantua 1573), a book of pioneering essays on history and Jewish erudition; Menahem Azaria de Fano (1548–1620), who contributed to the dissemination of the Kabbalah written at Safed; Yehudah Moscato (ca. 1530–ca. 1593), author of the most famous commentary on Yehuda ha-Levy's Kuzary, *Kol Yehudah*; Yedidiya Samuel Norzi (1560?–1626?), pioneer of the philological examination of the Bible texts; Ya'akov and Immanuel Francés (1615–1667 and 1618–ca. 1710), two of the most remarkable poets in the history of Hebraic profane poetry; Moshe Zakut (1625–1697), kabbalist, juridical authority, poet, one of the most outstanding personalities of European and Mediterranean Judaism of his time. To these famous names one could add a long list of remarkable but lesser-known figures who gained renown in the fields of religious law, thought, and literature. It should also be noted that several protagonists of the city's Jewish community left no written works, or, if these had remained in manuscript state, they have not survived. One should mention in this regard Moshe and Avraham Provenzali, Samuel Raphael Marli, and Moses ben Samuel Cazes. Regarding the latter, the Avraham Portaleone's Hebraic work constitutes one of the rare records.

On the Jewish community in Mantua, see, above all, Shlomo Simonsohn, *History of the Jews of Mantua* (Jerusalem 1964) and, for a later period, Paolo Bernardini, *La sfida dell' uguaglianza. Gli ebrei a Mantova nell'età della rivoluzione francese* (Rome 1996).

2 I have already examined the relevant aspects of the comparison between the two texts in Alessandro Guetta, 'Avraham Portaleone, le scientifique repenti,' *Torah et science: perspectives historiques et théoriques. Etudes offertes à Charles Touati*, ed. G. Freudenthal, J.-P. Rothschild and G. Dahan (Paris and Louvain 2001), 213–27.

3 *De Auro dialogi tres. In quibus non solum de Auri in re Medica facultate, verum etiam de specifica eius, & ceterarum rerum forma, ac duplici potestate, qua mixtis in omnibus illa operatur, copiose disputatur. Abrahamo e Porta Leonis Mantuano Medico Hebræo Auctore* (Venice 1584). The book is dedicated to Guglielmo I Gonzaga, Duke of Mantua and Monferrato, and is possibly a comprehensive survey of Portaleone's scientific and medical opinions. This is how I interpret the quick exchange between Achryvasmus and Dynachrisus on p. 20: 'A.: A few days ago, a person told me your opinion, but in synthesis. But why did you not bring up so many things worth (in my opinion) knowing in your writings? D.: The little time available and the difficulty of the subject mutilated their writing. But I gave the opportunity to many scientists and erudite persons to attain the core of the thing in greater depth, with art and elegance.' Cf. A. Guetta, 'Avraham Portaleone, le scientifique repenti,' 224. The expressions 'the little time available and the difficulty of the subject' and 'the core of the thing' are irresistibly reminiscent of the lexicon of Maimonides in his *Guide for the Perplexed* (1, 34, and introduction respectively). This is probably a rare instance of importation of expressions from Jewish literature into scientific literature.

4 This notion of quintessence was probably inspired by Paracelsus, who in *De Auro dialogi tres*, p. 5, is referred to as 'Paracelsus aureolus' (the golden Paracelsus). Cf. Walter Pagel, *Paracelsus: An Introduction to Philosophical Medicine in the Era of the Renaissance* (Basel and New York 1958), 99–100, who cites Paracelsus, *De vita longa*, ch. 1. Cf. on this subject L. Thorndike's negative view of *De Auro* in *A History of Magic and Experimental Science*, vol. 5 (New York 1929–59), 645–7.

5 As an example, Gabriel de Castaigne published a small book in Paris in 1611 entitled *L'or potable qui guarit de tous maux* (Drinking Gold to Heal All Ills) – which largely consists of a list of attestations by patients healed by drinking gold produced by the author.

6 *De Auro*, 90.

7 Cited in D. Aricò, 'Les "Yeux d'Argos" et les "Étoiles d'Astrée" pour mésurer l'univers. Les Jésuites italiens et la science nouvelle,' *Revue de Synthèse* 120 (1999), 297.

8 Cf. Andrea Battista, *Galileo e i Gesuiti. Miti letterari e retorica della scienza* (Milan 2000).

9 *De Auro*, 36–7.

10 Ibid., 20: 'Achryvasmus: Experientia quidem, rerum omnium naturalium magistra celebratur, quod si denegaris, non repræhensione tantum, sed pœna etiam dignus esse videaris.' The Frenchman Alexandre de la Tourrete's propos are very close to Portaleone's. Cf. his *Bref discours des admirables*

vertus de l'or potable. Avec une apologie de la tresutile [*sic*] *science d'alchimie* (Lyon 1575), 36 recto: 'Their ignorance [that of the Greek and Arab medical authorities] on the one hand, with their incredulity on the other, are the cause, if they know nothing of the said illnesses or of the medicines necessary to heal them, in which the uncertainty of their science is manifestly revealed, since it is founded simply on dead words not on the light of nature, which has its physical reasons and ocular demonstrations for true and certain experiences.'

11 Ibid., 38–9: 'unusquisque nostrum, tunc contumeliose reprehendi debet, quando vel id quod humanus intellectus assequi potest, negligentia quadam ignorat, vel captiosa ratione, & vitiosa seductione, veritatem ipsam occultat.'

12 Ibid., 139, referring to the stupor of Pliny.

13 Ibid., 17: 'Dynachrisus: Id Deus avertat summus, ea quidem stultitia non sum affectus.'

14 Ibid., 140.

15 Ibid., 165.

16 Ibid., 38.

17 Ibid.

18 *Shilte ha-Giborim ve-shelosha meginim le-milḥamta shel Tora 'arukhim, she-ḥamushim 'alu 'im ḥerev pifiyot be-yadam le-have 'avde ha-Shem ha-yere'im le-nafshotam keshe-yishstamshu bam el ha-osher ha-tov ve-ha-nitzhi ha-tsafun be-ḥasdo yitbarakh la-tsadikim kulam* (Shields of the Mighty and three defenders, predisposed for the battle of the Torah, who rise armed, double-edged sword in hand 'to lead the servants of God who are afraid to the eternal felicity prepared for the just by His bounty, blessed be God') (Mantua 1612, 58b). This book is the subject of the excellent monograph by Gianfranco Miletto, *Glauben und Wissen im Zeitalter der Reformation. Der Salomonische Tempel bei Abraham ben David Portaleone (1542–1612)* (Berlin – New York 2004).

19 Ibid., Part I, 58b.

20 Ibid., introduction, 2 verso.

21 Avraham Melamed, 'Wisdom's Little Sister. The Political Thought of Jewish Thinkers in the Italian Renaissance,' (Hebrew) PhD Thesis, Tel Aviv University, 1976.

22 A. Guetta, 'Avraham Portaleone, from Science to Mysticism,' *Jewish Studies at the Turn of the 20th Century*, vol. 2, ed. J. Targarona Borrás and A. Sáenz-Badillos (Leiden 1999), 41–3.

23 *Shilte ha-Giborim*, ch. 48, p. 49a: 'My opinion is somewhat different to theirs [i.e., the philosophical and scientific authorities], since I have my own ideas on the truths of [natural] philosophy. I spoke about them at length in my Latin book printed in Venice on the subject of mineral gold [Hebrew:

mahtzavy, which corresponds to the 'common gold' in *De Auro*] and its supposed medical properties, written at the behest of His Excellence Lord Guglielmo, Duke of Mantua and Monferrato.' One notes the great prudence of tone vis-à-vis *De Auro* with regard to the authorities, even if they are non-Jewish authorities.

24 *Shilte ha-Giborim*, Part 1, 4a.
25 Ibid., introduction, 4a. See also ibid., 42b. Azaria de' Rossi uses the same word, *tzedek* with reference to the contribution of the Jewish and non-Jewish sages to knowledge. See Azaria de' Rossi, *The Light of the Eyes*, trans. Joanna Weinberg (New Haven and London) 409: 'It would be our duty to investigate and search out a solution, applying correct methods and not useless tools [i.e., use all valid sources irrespective of their origin] in order to ensure that faithfulness [*tzedek*] and truth [*emetk*] are met.'
26 The complete absence of reference to *Me'or 'enayim* in *Shilte ha-Giborim*, given that both authors were from the same town and shared the same culture, should be attributed to the misgivings that certain rabbis had expressed concerning the contents of the former work. The Portaleone of the second half of his life probably did not want to be seen to be close to a controversial figure. See Azaria de' Rossi, S*elected Chapters from 'Sefer Meor Einayim' and 'Matzref la-Kessef*,' ed. Robert Bonfil (Jerusalem 1991), with a bibliography on 131–3.
27 *De Auro*, 54.
28 Francesco Roheo, or François de la Rue (Lille 1520–1585), the author of *De gemmis aliquot iis presertim, quarum divus Ioannes in sua Apocalypsi meminit, de aliis quoque, quarum usus hoc aevi apud omnes percrebuit, Libri duo* (Paris 1547 then Zurich 1565). The full information is in Abraham ben David Portaleone, *Die Heldenschilde*, 67, German translation and commentary by Gianfranco Miletto (Frankfurt am Main 2001) and Miletto, *Glauben und Wissen*, 288. See also Samuel S. Kottek, 'Jews between Profane and Sacred Science in Renaissance Italy: The Case of Abraham Portaleone,' *Religious Confessions and the Sciences in the Sixteenth Century*, ed. J. Helm and A. Winkelmann (Leiden 2001), 108–18.
29 *Shilte ha-Giborim*, 46a–b.
30 The sapphire is like the heavens without stars, the ruby like the sphere of the stars, the diamond like the sun; the amethyst and the emerald like the spheres of some stars and the moon. Achryvasmus reacts admiringly to these parallels drawn by Dynachrisus: 'Oh, human intellect, how penetrating you are!' Portaleone reuses exactly the same comparison in *Shilte ha-Giborim*, 80a, with biblical verses to support it.
31 Ibid., 43b.
32 Miletto (*Die Heldenschielde*), vol. 1, 427n466, discovered that the source of this

comparison is the Jesuit Francisco Ribera, *Francisci Riberae Villacastinensis, presbyteri Societas Iesu, Doctorisque Theologi, De Templo, et de iis quae ad templum pertinent, libri quinque* (Antwerp 1602), 241. It is interesting to remark that, in order to satisfy the rabbis, the very orthodox Portaleone drew from a Christian source.

33 Ibid., 49a.
34 Ibid., 51b. This affirmation is reminiscent of the exaltation of experience in *De Auro*, xx: 'Without experience, there would be no real difference between man and the most intelligent animals.'
35 *Shilte ha-Giborim*, 49b.

PART II

INTO MODERNITY

chapter five

Jewish Women, Marriage Law, and Emancipation: The Civil Divorce of Rachele Morschene in Late Eighteenth-Century Trieste

LOIS C. DUBIN

In her petition of 3 December 1795 to the Giudizio Civico e Provinciale of Trieste, Rachele Luzzatto (née Morschene), a twenty-five-year-old Jewish woman, poignantly evoked the 'bitterness and ... anxiety brought on by an ambiguous situation.'[1] Still in doubt was the outcome of her two-year-legal battle to free herself from her husband, the forty-year old broker Lucio Luzzatto, younger brother of one of the most prominent Jews in Trieste.[2] With the help of her wealthy father Anselmo Morschene, Rachele had filed for a civil separation and support for herself and two-year-old daughter Richetta; her aim now was civil divorce. Her case for legal dissolution of the marriage rested on three grounds: her husband had brought the family to economic ruin, he had deserted and dishonoured her, and his venereal disease put her in mortal danger. Lucio Luzzatto blamed the deterioration of their relationship on her selfishness and impropriety, yet he claimed that he would seek appropriate medical treatment and that he wanted to preserve the marriage.

The ambiguities were legal as well as personal, for the road towards legal resolution led through mostly unmarked terrain. The Habsburg state began to regulate marriage as a civil matter only a few years earlier in the context of the Josephinian reform of church-state relations and drive towards centralization, legal codification, and secularization. Joseph II's Marriage Patent (*Ehepatent*) of 16 January 1783 and the 1787 *Josephinisches Gesetzbuch* – the first part of the eventual 1811–12 *Allgemeine Bürgerliche Gesetzbuch* (*Codice Civile Universale*, General Civil Code) – defined marriage as a 'civil contract' (*bürgerlicher Vertrag, Contratto civile*) and asserted the exclusive jurisdiction of state courts for resolving marital issues.[3] The *Ehepatent* left religious ceremonies intact while recasting their validity in civil terms; it thus introduced a civil-religious hybrid of marriage regulation rather than a purely civil system. Given Josephinian civil toleration for religious minorities, the new law in principle pertained to all subjects, Catholic and non-Catholic, Jews included. In practice, however, there was ample room for confusion.

Analysis of Rachele Morschene's civil divorce in the context of the new Habsburg system of marriage regulation helps us approach a well-known process of modern Jewish history, Emancipation, in a novel way: by examining the interplay of public and personal emancipation, or, to express it somewhat differently, the impact of public legal emancipation on personal status and private lives. At its core, Emancipation involved a reordering of the structural relations between states, Jewish communities, and individual Jews, as Jews became subject to general laws and acquired mostly the same civic rights and duties as other citizens. Both the Habsburg monarchy and revolutionary France took significant steps in this direction when, in 1783 and 1792 respectively, they promulgated civil marital legislation to pertain to all. When the state made Jewish marriage and divorce its business, it profoundly affected Jews as communities and as individuals: state law now limited communities' regulation of marriage by Jewish religious law, either replacing it or at the least circumscribing it, and individuals' personal choices were now to be constrained by both Jewish and civil laws, upheld respectively by the Jewish community and by the state. Straddling the public and the private, marriage and divorce afford an important, unique, and relatively neglected avenue through which to study Jewish Emancipation.[4]

In particular, Rachele Morschene's case helps us address the modalities and impact of state intervention in the domain of marriage regulation. How did the modernizing Habsburg state treat existing Jewish law and practice? Did it seek to replace, bypass, or co-opt Jewish marriage law? How did the Habsburg enactment of general marriage laws affect Jewish women in particular? Did it facilitate Jewish women's personal emancipation? How did Jewish women negotiate the new legal and political situation? Through the fascinating story of Rachele Morschene's divorce, this essay seeks to open new perspectives on both Jewish Emancipation and Jewish women's history.

Divorce in Habsburg and Jewish Laws

On Josephinian principles of toleration, the *Ehepatent* recognized confessional differences, particularly in the matter of divorce by non-Catholics.

Civil jurisdiction over specifically Jewish marriage and divorce was established in two steps: first, by the abrogation of separate Jewish courts in 1783–85 and, then, by specific edicts in 1785–86 that formally applied the new marriage laws to Jews, with obvious changes such as rabbi instead of priest. Further adjustments concerning divorce and concerning marriage between relatives were decreed on 18 February 1791.[5] Aiming at standardization, yet resting on confessional bases, the *Ehepatent* and its culminating formulation in the *Allgemeines Bürgerliche Gesetzbuch* provided a three-part marriage law: most of it pertained to all, some of it to non-Catholics generally, and one section to Jews alone.[6] It outlined civil procedures for divorce by Protestants and Jews since their religious laws permitted it, while leaving to the denominations themselves the decision whether a particular marriage was dissoluble and remarriage possible.

The Josephinian marriage reforms created new legal norms, but it was unclear how they would be implemented in practice. Both the civil-religious hybrid and the respect for denominational differences made the system particularly complicated. Moreover, the lack of precedents created ample room for procedural ambiguities. Rachele Morschene's pleas for civil separation and divorce appear to be the first case of a Jewish woman trying to avail herself of the new civil marriage law in Trieste. To put an end to her ambiguous status and to gain personal emancipation, Rachele would have to satisfy both Habsburg and Jewish authorities that her marriage was dissoluble. How exactly would the civil court ascertain whether religious divorce was appropriate in Rachele's case? The Habsburg state had scant experience with Jewish marriage and divorce law, let alone aligning it with civil law. Habsburg and Jewish authorities were not accustomed to bringing their legal minds together to resolve such problems. Indeed, Rachele Morschene was treading on unfamiliar ground: she was surely one of the first Jewish women to seek a civil divorce in Christian Europe. In early modern Europe, marriage and divorce had been largely regulated according to Christian religious norms. Divorce was not widely available. Catholics were permitted separation but not divorce, and while Protestants were theoretically allowed divorce, religious and civil authorities did not readily grant it. Generally Jews had lived subject to their own religious law of marriage and divorce.[7]

There had been little regulation that produced universal civil procedures for marriage; such that existed did not greatly affect Jews. France brought marriage under the umbrella of civil law from the late sixteenth century, but did not include Jews within its purview. (Only during the Revolution did France overturn the Catholic prohibition against divorce, produce a fully secular civil marriage and divorce law, and apply it universally to all citizens, Jews included.) Protestant states had declared marriage a civil matter but their civil regulation usually enforced Protestant marriage law which did not apply to Jews. However, Holland and Hamburg had addressed Jewish marriage and divorce to some degree: from 1580 Holland required civil registration of all marriages including Jewish ones, from 1650 Hamburg stipulated governmental oversight of Jewish divorces, and both applied Protestant norms concerning consanguinity to prohibit the common Sephardic custom of marriage between uncle and niece; yet subsequent reiterations made it clear that in practice these ordinances were often ignored by Jews.[8]

Although Jewish marriages and divorces were generally handled within the Jewish community, some Jewish women did turn to Gentile courts or rulers to pressure Jewish authorities to rule in their favour. Cases have come to light of individual women pressing for inheritance and dowry rights in civil courts in seventeenth-century Holland and mid-eighteenth-century France, as well as in the Holy Roman Empire. Contemporaneous with Rachele was Lady D'Aguilar who brought a separation suit to England's Consistory Court in 1793.[9] Further archival work will no doubt discover other litigious Jewish women and enable us to develop a better sense of how often and under what circumstances Jewish women (and Jewish men) turned to non-Jewish courts in early modern Europe.

In the past, Jewish wives seeking freedom from unhappy marriages had generally turned to rabbinic authorities. To assess the significance of the Habsburg state's providing Jewish women with a civil venue, it is important to remember the unilateral nature of rabbinic divorce law: divorce is not a court decree, but rather the delivery of a writ of repudiation (*get*) by a husband to his wife; a wife cannot issue one to her husband. The textual basis is Deuteronomy 24:1: "A man takes a wife and possesses her. She fails to please him because he finds something obnoxious ('*ervat davar*) about her, and he writes her a bill of divorcement, hands it to her, and sends her away from his house." Properly divorced, a Jewish woman is returned her marriage contract (*ketubah*) and monies, and she is free to remarry. However, without a writ of divorce or with one improperly written, she is bound to her first husband, and any child born of a subsequent union is illegitimate (*mamzer*), a status with long-lasting repercussions.[10]

In different times and places, the unilateral nature of Jewish divorce was somewhat mitigated. Theoretically, rabbinic law stipulated grounds upon which a woman could legitimately seek divorce, such as a husband's refusal to support his wife, or a loathsome physical disease that prevented intercourse or caused revulsion; in such cases, a woman could petition a Jewish court to pressure her husband to grant a divorce such that 'force is applied to him until he says "I consent."'[11] In some ancient[12] and early medieval communities, before rabbinic law became normative and even afterwards, some Jewish women did initiate divorce. Until approximately the eleventh century, marriage contracts written in Palestine allowed a woman to initiate divorce if she 'hated her husband' and did not 'desire his partnership.' From the seventh to the eleventh centuries, a Geonic ordinance was followed in Babylonia and North Africa that allowed rabbis to force divorce upon a husband at a wife's request, with the express reason given to prevent Jewish women from seeking divorce in Muslim courts. The Cairo Geniza shows Jewish authorities' recognition in the late eleventh and early twelfth centuries of 'ransom-divorces,' whereby a woman renounced the monies owed her in exchange for gaining divorce.[13] However, from the twelfth century onward, the view of the tosafist Rabbenu Tam against forced divorce became widespread: a court could apply pressure upon a husband, but not actually compel divorce. Still, Jewish women did gain protection from the generally accepted ordinance attributed to Rabbenu Gershom (960–1028) that largely prohibited divorce without a woman's consent.[14]

The inclination of Jewish courts to act on theoretical grounds for divorce has varied over time and depended on different factors, such as norms concerning women, marriage, and divorce in surrounding Gentile societies,[15] the availability of non-Jewish court action, the jurisdiction permitted Jews by state law, and the general mood of rabbinic self-confidence. However, from the twelfth century, the unilateral character of Jewish divorce was generally reinforced: even when a Jewish court did decide to exert pressure on a husband, a Jewish woman's divorce still depended on the husband's willingness to grant her one.

The Stories Told the Court

The major source for Rachele Morschene's case is the file compiled by her notary-advocate Francesco Saverio Lovisoni. It contains documents that start with her first petition to the court for separation and support on 18 October 1793, up through her formal petition for divorce on 6 January 1796, and the scheduling of the divorce hearing for 27 April

1796.[16] The grounds on which Rachele staked her claim – economic ruin, desertion, and mortal danger – were interwoven throughout.

Starting with her separation petition, Rachele reported with hindsight that she had been an immature seventeen-year-old in 1787 when her parents promised her and a generous dowry to Lucio Luzzatto. She claimed to have seen troubling signs even during their engagement, but that nevertheless she, as an obedient daughter, had resigned herself to her future destiny. The marriage took place in 1788. All went well until the birth of their daughter Richetta in 1790. During nursing, Rachele was stricken with many painful maladies; these she attributed to Lucio's contagious infection, which produced 'a constant flow of discharge.'[17] Her medical experts confirmed her descriptions of his pitiful incontinence, terrible odours, and manifold physical malfunctioning, and they supplied a name: the French disease or venereal disease (*morbo gallico, lues venerea*).[18] She claimed that she had been willing to help care for him though not to share his bed, and that subsequently he became infuriated and mistreated her.

Meanwhile, she charged, Lucio was squandering the family's assets and bringing it to the brink of financial ruin. She had been forced to pawn her jewels and sell many possessions; their servants had left them; by August 1793, Lucio's debts were so great that they were forced to mortgage their house and move to rented quarters. Six weeks later, on 4–5 October 1793, the blow-up occurred. He suffered a fainting spell. His relatives' affidavits attested that she ran to help him, but in his view not quickly enough. Their neighbours' affidavits testified to her husband's cruel behaviour the next day: he and his brother, the prominent Elia Moise Luzzatto, had a nasty confrontation with her about an inventory of household goods, and they returned demonstratively with a third man later that evening. After another scene, Lucio coldly left her, very distraught, 'an exile, abandoned and alone.'[19] Rachele then took refuge in her father's house. Considering her health at risk and herself now deserted, she asked the court – in the name of justice, law, and reason – to grant her a legal separation and to award her weekly support payments from Lucio until her request for a divorce could be decided.

Subsequently, Rachele amplified these basic points to both the court and Chief Rabbi Raffael Natan Tedesco. As a modest woman she had not wanted to be so explicit about certain matters, but she felt compelled to do so by her husband's denials and impugning of her honour. Her later petitions described in graphic detail the mess she was forced to live in, for his lack of muscular control had turned their bed into a latrine. Supporting medical testimony came not only from local doctors including the renowned Dr Benedetto Frizzi, their friend and boarder, but also from Court Physician Lagasius in Vienna.[20] Rachele blamed Lucio for great misery and risk: 'for causing me to be most wretched, and turning my youthful self into a [sacrificial] altar for his capricious whims [and] shameful vices.'[21] If she were to accept his offer to return to him, she would suffer 'an unending martyrdom' that would hasten her death.[22] To Rabbi Tedesco, she acknowledged the gravity of marriage and divorce while pleading the natural duty of self-preservation: 'I too know, though I am a woman, that marriage is a serious matter, as is its dissolution, but I know even more that the first duty of nature is to preserve life.'[23]

In Rachele's final divorce petition, she stated that Lucio's vices and their economic difficulties were matters of public knowledge; further, that her physical avoidance of him was fully justified since every act of coitus could poison her. Rhetorically she asked: how could 'that love, which is the electrical spark of marriage' be awakened? How could she apply herself to the 'task of reproduction' with a broken heart, a battered body, and the worry of producing miserable beings?[24] In sum, Lucio's betrayal had reduced her to a state of economic, physical, and emotional misery, and this marriage that violated reason, nature, and Jewish law should never have taken place. The only solution, dictated by natural reason and Jewish law, was divorce.

For his part, Lucio disputed most of Rachele's charges. He could not deny the sorry economic facts, but he tried to recast them: as a man of honour, he was repaying his debts, which arose from spending for her, not from his own vices. As for his illness, he claimed that it predated their marriage and was curable, and that he was no longer symptomatic. He too brought medical testimony, although not as abundant or distinguished as hers.[25]

Lucio dismissed Rachele's concerns as 'ridiculous female complaints';[26] even if they were true, it was her duty to stay with him, for illness did not give wives the right to withhold themselves from their husbands. These complaints had begun, he charged, only after Dr Frizzi started listening to her too closely 'either as a doctor, or as a friend.'[27] For two years, Dr Frizzi had been a frequent visitor in their home, first as their physician and then as a boarder paying for daily meals. According to Lucio, everything his wife and the doctor said about the couple's medical conditions was suspect because the two had come to enjoy an overly 'familiar relationship.'[28]

Lucio defended himself against the desertion charge by disputing Rachele's version of the move from their house and the fateful quarrel. He claimed they had left their house not to pay off his debts, but rather because of his own stupidity in agreeing to move to Dr Frizzi's building as a way to save money. Lucio had quarrelled with Rachele on 5 October 1793 because he could no longer stand the emotional strain caused by her threats of separation and divorce and by their living arrangements. He explained that he hoped the move to new quarters would give him much-needed peace of mind and distance Rachele from 'advice too tempting from a person too dangerous.'[29] Since she had withdrawn from their conjugal bed earlier and now refused to join him, *she* was the deserter, the one guilty of dereliction of marital duty.

Lucio added other charges. He taunted Rachele for posing as an 'able doctor,' 'philosopher,' and biblical scholar, charging that someone else was feeding her her lines.[30] He also accused her of lying, especially about Dr Frizzi. He had certainly respected Dr Frizzi as 'a man of virtue, physician, and member of my own religion,'[31] and with a sense of the sacred duty of hospitality he had readily invited him to board with them. But, now suspecting that Rachele and Benedetto had become too close, he attributed her divorce action to her desire 'to enjoy her present sweet liberty' and to take a fresh mate, like Cicero who divorced his wife Terenzia.[32] Lucio argued that her desires or claims should not invalidate his rights as husband and family head; if a judge were to sanction wives' disobedience and absolve them from marital dependence and submission, that would cause a 'total revolution in marriage.'[33] Finally, not realizing the requirements of the new law, Lucio protested Rachele turning simultaneously to the civil court and the rabbi.[34] Yet, despite everything, Lucio claimed he wanted Rachele back.

Rachele flatly denied Lucio's charges about an improper relationship with Dr Frizzi, calling them fantasies of his overheated imagination. If Lucio really believed her to be so disloyal, then how could he want her back? He should be ashamed to make such statements to 'an enlightened judge.' His offer of reconciliation was merely an attempt to hold on to her dowry.[35]

Rachele's explicit address to the enlightened judge was a key to her self-presentation. Overall, she wrote as a woman with rights to health and happiness. She asserted a community of enlightenment with the judge by speaking the language of reason, nature, and modern medicine. She appealed to the rabbi's wisdom and humanity to determine an outcome that would satisfy both reason and religion. It is difficult to determine to what degree these documents reflected Rachele's own voice and views, and to what degree her advisers' legal strategy, but at the least, it can be assumed that this was a public presentation of self with which she was comfortable.[36]

The Outcome

How did all this play with the authorities? On 26 September 1794 the Triestine court ruled in Rachele's favour.[37] Citing the relevant provisions of the *Codice Civile Universale* (III: §§47–8, 100–101), the judge declared that Lucio had definitely abandoned her, and that he must support her and Richetta. Rachele thus gained a legal separation. The judge did not credit Lucio's jealousy as valid justification for his conduct, for he deemed his suspicions unfounded and expressly denied by his wife. The court was persuaded by the medical testimony that her illnesses were due to his, and it considered her health fears legitimate. The court discounted Lucio's claims to want Rachele back and stated that she was right to refuse his offer, given his manifest ill will towards her. It faulted him for showing a lack of respect for the marital bond and paternal sentiments, for impugning his wife's honour, and for acting contrary to the obligations of nature. This strongly worded verdict held Lucio liable for both support and court costs. Lucio appealed, but the Court of Appeal in Klagenfurt upheld the judgment on 6 February 1795.[38] Over the next several months, Triestine courts took steps against Lucio's assets, but he still did not pay up.[39]

On 3 December 1795, Rachele finally filed for divorce. On 11 December 1795, the court then instructed her to submit all documents again; it also asked the rabbi to declare whether this marriage was religiously dissoluble, so that ultimately all the proper civil and religious steps would be taken. However, by that point, there was one significant change in this couple's situation: Rachele's final divorce petition of 6 January 1796 referred to 'the amicable agreement' between the two parties, according to which she renounced the court-awarded support payments and her counter-dowry (that is, the part originally contributed by him), while Lucio stated that he voluntarily agreed to divorce her.[40] Lucio's statement of free will was crucial for both Jewish and Habsburg laws. Both parties were summoned to a divorce hearing scheduled for 27 April 1796. I have not yet found records of that court hearing or of the final divorce decree, but Rachele and Lucio were certainly divorced, then or soon thereafter, for by January 1797, Triestine officials were reporting to Vienna about this divorce as an accomplished fact.[41]

Analysis of the Legal Narratives and Arguments

Rachele's legal arguments simultaneously addressed Habsburg and Jewish laws, although she brought different aspects of her case to different legal venues: separation and support to the civil court, and divorce to both civil and Jewish authorities. Although the state had formally abolished Jewish courts, Jewish law did play a role in the civil divorce proceedings. By allowing Jews to divorce because Jewish religious law permitted it, Habsburg law partially incorporated Jewish divorce within a civil framework. Indeed, as an argument to the civil court, Rachele's petitions repeatedly stated that her situation warranted a divorce according to Jewish law.[42]

Habsburg officials were more tentative about the rabbi's role. In 1788 they had sought to exclude rabbis and Jewish writs of divorce, but after Jewish protests, Habsburg law in February 1791 allowed these two elements of Jewish divorce to become integral parts of the civil process. A divorce could proceed in civil court only if husband and wife brought a document from the rabbi attesting to his efforts to reconcile them, and if both parties declared their free will to divorce; then the court could permit the husband to deliver the divorce writ to his wife in its presence.[43]

To all authorities, civil and religious, Rachele's petitions highlighted those elements of the failing marriage that conformed to legal grounds for dissolution. The legal narratives were inevitably a mixture of fact and fiction, of truth stretched to fit legal criteria so as to achieve the desired result.[44] Each of the three major charges – husband's failure to support her economically, desertion, and his venereal disease as threat to her health – was a well-directed arrow in her legal quiver. The court's written opinion on separation affords a partial view of how her arguments were received.

Desertion was the key issue in the separation and support phase. Indeed, the *Ehepatent* specified malicious desertion as one of the grounds upon which a non-Catholic could seek a divorce.[45] Ruling unequivocally that Lucio had in fact cruelly abandoned Rachele, the court invoked *Codice Civile Universale* (*Josephinisches Gesetzbuch* 1787) III: §§47–8 that stipulated a wife's absolute right to support as long as the husband retained her dowry, and a judge's duty to make prompt provision for that support.⁴⁶ Had the judge validated Lucio's allegations that Rachele was an adulterer and the real deserter, then both Habsburg and Jewish laws would have considered her the guilty partner, subject to divorce by her husband, and with no claim to maintenance.⁴⁷ Rather, the court's castigation of Lucio for impugning his wife's honour and displaying 'malicious intent toward his wife'⁴⁸ resonated with the 'mortal hatred or insurmountable aversion' cited in the *Ehepatent* as grounds for divorce of non-Catholics, and with the duty of honour a husband owes his wife according to Jewish law.⁴⁹

Rachele's petitions strongly pressed the charge of economic failure in terms of Jewish law. They cited the relevant passages in the authoritative law code the *Shulhan Arukh* and related sources that state a husband's obligation to maintain his wife, and a wife's right to seek divorce if he unjustifiably refuses to do so – based on Exodus 21:10: 'her food, her raiment, and her conjugal rights shall he not diminish.'⁵⁰ As stated above, the 1787 *Codice Civile Universale (Josephinisches Gesetzbuch)* similarly held a husband responsible for his wife's maintenance, although it did not cite his failure to do so as grounds for separation or divorce. However, such thinking was in the air, for the *Galizisches Gesetzbuch* (drafted 1794, promulgated 1797) allowed separation for Catholics and divorce for non-Catholics if one party endangered a considerable part of the other's property.⁵¹

As the most important ground for divorce, Rachele's petitions stressed the marked deterioration of her health and the mortal threat caused by Lucio's venereal disease. Her divorce petition argued strenuously that his physical condition corresponded exactly to the two loathsome ailments – boils, and chronically foul nasal or mouth odour – cited in rabbinic sources as legitimate grounds for a woman to seek divorce. It also quoted *Be'er Hetev*, a standard commentary on the *Shulhan 'Arukh*, on two points of direct relevance: (1) if a husband and a wife disagree about whether a husband's loathsome disease has been cured, it is the wife who should be believed; and (2) regarding boils, if a husband has 'the French disease' (*holeh ha-tsarfati*) accompanied by disgusting conditions and strong smells, and if doctors deem intercourse inappropriate, then a husband should be made to grant his wife a divorce.⁵² Unfortunately the responsum of the contemporary Rabbi Weill of Karlsruhe that accompanied the petition is now missing.⁵³ Rachele's petition left a clear impression that Jewish law mandated divorce in a case such as hers.

Neither the 1783 *Ehepatent* nor the 1787 Code mentioned venereal disease specifically, but the 'serious abuse' or 'danger ... from depraved morals' stated as grounds for separation might have been considered relevant.[54] It is reasonable to infer that sexually transmitted disease was on Habsburg jurists' minds at the time. Incurable contagious illness had been recognized by some earlier Protestant and Catholic laws as a form of ill-treatment or cruelty that might justify divorce (Protestants) and separation (Catholics), and increasingly by states in the eighteenth century, such as Sweden, Württemberg, Revolutionary France, and Prussia, as grounds for divorce.[55] In the mid-eighteenth century, the natural law theorist Samuel Cocceji and English courts respectively specified venereal disease and wilful communication of it.[56] In Rouen in 1795, two divorces were granted because of husbands' venereal disease.[57] The *Galizisches Gesetzbuch* (drafted 1794, promulgated 1797) referred to endangerment of life and health by a partner as grounds for separation of Catholics, and for separation or divorce of non-Catholics.[58] Only a few years later, the 1811–12 *Allgemeine Bürgerliche Gesetzbuch* specified 'chronic physical disease carrying with it the danger of contagion.'[59] Indeed, in the separation phase of Rachele's case, the court took the threat to health very seriously; subsequently, Rachele and Dr Frizzi referred to 'carnal practices' and 'physical disease' as the main grounds for her divorce.[60]

In general, Rachele's petitions employed the rhetoric of reason, natural law, and medical science to argue the danger of this marriage and its failure to provide procreation or companionship. They bespoke the increasingly influential natural law view of marriage as a contract for the purpose of procreation, as well as a companionate view of marriage as a relation providing affection and emotional support.[61] Rachele's appeals to the judge in the name of justice, law, and reason, and to the rabbi in the name of reason and religion, were remarkably successful. Her tale of misconduct, ill-treatment, and danger was accepted, while her husband's charge of adultery and defence of traditional marriage were not. In general, Rachele seemed to have more facts on her side: economic failure was substantiated by public records, while Lucio's charges of impropriety went unsupported. In a small, closely knit community, the local knowledge of family, neighbours, servants, and business associates was important, and Rachele enjoyed the support of her father, family (including some of Lucio's relatives), neighbours, and the rabbi. Though Rachele and Lucio came from the same social stratum, their respective standings may well have differed at this point. The connections of Dr Frizzi, and perhaps of her other allies, extended further than Lucio's, certainly producing more impressive medical testimony than his. Finally, reflecting the spirit of enlightenment for which a number of Triestine public officials were known, the court proved amenable to arguments based on medical science and natural law.[62]

The legal narratives and arguments can provide only a tantalizing glimpse of this marriage in crisis and the efforts to resolve it. Behind the legal stories lay the deteriorating relationship of this couple, and their evolving individual experiences and outlooks.[63] Even if more material becomes available, the historian will still need to read the legal documents critically as filters that both hide and disclose historical reality.

Procedural Ambiguities

Lucio Luzzatto's complaint in May 1794 – that Rachele was trying to gain conjugal liberty from the rabbi at the same time as support from the civil court – expressed not only his personal frustration, but symbolized the lack of procedural clarity throughout the case. Sometime after the local Triestine court issued the divorce sentence in 1796, Jewish leaders raised post facto procedural questions. It became clear that Habsburg and Jewish authorities had divergent understandings of how their respective divorce laws should work in tandem.

In mid-January 1797, the Triestine governor sought advice from Vienna. Jewish leaders had protested that the court had not acted in accordance with the 1791 law concerning Jewish divorces, claiming that it contravened Jewish religious custom by accepting the husband's divorce letter as sufficient. The court's reply was that 'the rabbi's intervention was to be sure superfluous'; yet, 'to quiet the rabbi's conscience,' it would permit him to issue a divorce decree 'according to Jewish customs,' without this in any way affecting the already decreed civil divorce. For it recognized that 'this formality' was absolutely necessary in order for Jews to consider a civil divorce religiously valid. However, local officials rejected the rabbi's claim of exclusive authority to draft writs of divorce. For their part, the Jews believed that their religious laws and liberties had not been respected.[64]

In May 1797 Vienna responded: there was no need to alter the 1791 law, since it had given Jewish marriage contracts their due religious consideration and no other communities had complained. Jews should not be forced to go to a particular party to write a divorce document; moreover, rabbis should be threatened with punishment if they dared to exercise such compulsion, or if they charged a fee when Jews came to them voluntarily.[65]

How exactly did the Jews think that the 1791 law had not been followed? We must infer the Jews' precise complaint from the government's response. The overtly contested issues were the divorce writ and the role of the rabbi, but underlying them were fundamental questions of timing and definition. Alhough the 1791 law had incorporated two basic features of Jewish divorce – the delivery of the writ by husband to wife, and the possibility that someone besides the husband could write it – it did so in ways that were ambiguous or at variance with Jewish law. For example, it required the husband to deliver the writ to the wife in civil court, whereas Jewish law stipulated that it be done through a very exacting procedure conducted by an expert, that is, rabbi, and that the document itself be written flawlessly and in a prescribed form by a scribe. Jewish law mandated the involvement of experts because the stakes were so high for the woman and any of her future offspring.[66]

The Habsburg drafters of the 1791 law probably had little or no understanding of the subtleties of Jewish divorce law. The 1791 law left several questions open. What kind of divorce writ should the husband deliver in civil court: a letter formulated however he pleased, or one that met the criteria for a valid *get*? What was the rabbi's role to be: to testify to his reconciliation efforts, or to rule on the dissolubility of the marriage according to *halakhah*, or to supervise the preparation of a proper Jewish divorce writ for the husband to bring to the civil court? The answers to these questions would in effect determine the timing and the import of the different civil and religious components. If the husband were to produce a proper Jewish divorce writ for the civil court, then the rabbi would have already been involved in a very serious way, and perhaps the couple would already have undergone a Jewish religious divorce!

In Trieste, expectations seemed to be that the process of obtaining a religious divorce might start during the civil court's proceedings, but that it would not be finalized until those were concluded.[67] We cannot tell if the rabbi felt that his role had been improperly minimized *before* as well as *after* the final civil divorce hearing, but it is clear that Habsburg officials did not concur. They misinterpreted the rabbinic role in Jewish divorce as monopolistic coercion, while to many Jews, it ensured expert supervision of a proper divorce allowing for remarriage and legitimate offspring.[68] They also seemed unaware that it was customary in many Jewish communities to pay rabbis for writing divorce writs. The harsh antirabbinic remarks in the officials' responses of 1797 echoed earlier views of the late 1780s.[69] Both rabbis and Jewish divorce writs were finally included in the 1791 law, but the hesitations and ambiguity regarding them did not fully disappear.

Local officials considered the civil court's decree of divorce to be self-sufficient. Thus they permitted the rabbi to add subsequent religious divorce procedures if he wished, but they asserted that these were superfluous. Whereas earlier they seemed to rely upon the rabbi's expertise as Halakhic decisor that this particular marriage was religiously dissoluble, now in the final stages of the divorce they involved him only in a pastoral capacity. And from the civil perspective, he had no necessary role after the civil divorce was decreed.

For Jewish leaders, the civil-religious hybrid of marriage and divorce legislation looked quite different. Religious divorce was hardly superfluous, for a Jewish woman was not really divorced unless she was divorced religiously. They did not mind adding civil procedures as supplements to traditional Jewish divorce, but they could not serve as substitutes. Regardless of whether or not they stated it, they surely had in mind that rabbinic law had not hitherto recognized divorce writs issued or compelled by Gentile courts.[70]

Although the new marriage and divorce laws left much room for ambiguity of procedure and divergence of views, these did not practically affect the outcome of this case. The civil and religious authorities effectively smoothed over the misunderstandings and worked together at meshing their two kinds of regulation. Rachele was able to navigate the two jurisdictions so as to become legally separated and divorced.

Conclusions: Jewish Marriage, Divorce, and Emancipation

The civil divorce of Rachele Luzzatto Morschene shows how the entry of the state into the business of marriage and divorce could facilitate a Jewish woman's personal emancipation. Civil separation gave Rachele protection and a moral victory: she gained the right to live apart from her husband with her honour and reputation intact, a right not readily available through Jewish law. Court-awarded support also gave her assets that she could use as bargaining chips in negotiating with Lucio for a religious divorce.[71] The state did not create the possibility of divorce, but its civil separation and divorce procedures provided Rachele with new means to pressure her husband to release her.

Still, state action might not have been sufficient to sway Lucio were he determined to deny her a religious divorce. Clearly, the time-honoured method of money remained useful: the resources of Rachele's father, the court-awarded support payments, and the part of her dowry that she could renounce, enabled her to pay for Lucio's agreement to give the *get*.

The state's entry into marriage and divorce regulation gave Jewish women new freedom to manoeuvre. Yet, the state's remedies of civil separation and divorce could not fully resolve a Jewish woman's problems, particularly if she and her community considered *halakhah* binding and deemed a religious divorce necessary. State involvement alone did not lead to full personal emancipation for Jewish women; nonetheless, it created significant new opportunities for them. Most importantly, for resolving messy domestic conflict, it provided a venue in which a Jewish woman was not solely dependent on her husband's unilateral action. In and of itself, this measure was empowering. For individuals, state action could provide a path of legal resolution and a court of public opinion that went beyond the Jewish community and Halakhah. As ChaeRan Freeze's work on nineteenth-century Russia shows, many Jewish women pursued such new civil options once available.[72]

State control, civil marriage, and civil divorce were part of a broader trend of secularization of marriage in modern Europe. All three were often on a continuum, yet state control did not always produce civil institutions and ceremonies. A state's assertion of civil jurisdiction over marriage or even of a civil definition of marriage was not the same as full-fledged civil marriage. A state could claim jurisdiction over marriage and impose certain civil procedures, but leave religious laws or ceremonies relatively intact. (Despite the Habsburg *Ehepatent* of 1783, fully civil marriage did not come into existence in Austria until 1938!)[73] When state entry into the domain of marriage and divorce is analysed, distinctions must be drawn between supervision, jurisdiction, source of law, content of law, procedures of marriage, registration, and the role of officiants as clerics or civil functionaries. Several kinds of mixed civil-ecclesiastical jurisdiction, of secular-religious conflict, and of state-church concordats were possible.[74]

Rachele Luzzatto Morschene's divorce shows some of the complexity of initial state imposition of normative civil regulation for Jewish marriage and divorce.[75] State entry into this domain explicitly presented new opportunities for Jews as individuals and particularly for Jewish women. Moreover, as legal anthropologists have noted, the confusion accompanying state entry into a new legal domain often creates further opportunities for individuals to exploit.[76] Yet, as the procedural post mortem showed, state entry could pose new challenges for Jewish communities seeking to maintain religious law and authority.

Other early examples of state intervention into Jewish marriage and divorce ought to be studied comparatively so that a more detailed and broader picture may emerge. For example, how did the regulations in Protestant Holland (from 1580) and Hamburg (from 1650) really work in practice?[77] The trend accelerated in the late eighteenth century: in Prussia, civil courts began adjudicating certain aspects of Jewish marriages, although still according to Jewish law; in England, civil courts recognized the validity of Jewish marriage law and ceremonies, but decided some Jews' separation and divorce cases on the ground that Jews were entitled to the protection of English law if their marriages were violated.[78]

The most dramatic examples come from the reforming absolutist Habsburg monarchy and Revolutionary-Napoleonic France, for in both places state intervention into Jewish marriage was part of general political and structural changes.[79] On this issue as with so many others, these two states provide a laboratory for observing complex processes in similar, yet different forms. In both places in the 1790s, there in fact existed hybrid systems of civil and religious regulation of marriage. This is obvious in the Habsburg case, but less so in the French.

The usual assumption is that Revolutionary and Napoleonic France quickly produced a strictly civil definition of marriage, and purely civil ceremonies for marriage and divorce. The Sanhedrin's 1807 declarations of the absolute priority of civil marriage are seen as paradigmatic, as the logical consequence of Jewish Emancipation in 1790–91 and the state's embrace of civil marriage and divorce in 1792.[80] However, formal legal equality for Jews as individuals, as well as the end of Jewish corporate autonomy and Jewish jurisdiction, did not immediately bring civil marriage or clarity about the relationship between the civil and the religious. In a few cases during the 1790s and even *after* Emancipation, French courts recognized the validity of Jewish marriage law and did not insist that Jews be subject to French civil marriage law. In one case, in Bordeaux, it was explicitly stated that as citizens Jews were indeed subject to all political laws, but that they retained their religious laws including those pertaining to marriage.[81]

That was precisely the point that Habsburg officials did not concede: when cases involving real conflicts of law between Jewish and Habsburg marriage laws arose in Trieste in the late 1790s, the government stated unequivocally that state law overrode Jewish law, for marriage was now a civil matter. The flashpoints were a clandestine marriage between minors in 1796, and the attempt of Rachele Morschene and Benedetto (Ben-Zion ha-Kohen) Frizzi to marry civilly in 1798, two years after her divorce! Jewish leaders would not marry them in contravention of *hala-*

khah which forbids the union of a *kohen* (priestly descendant) with a divorced woman, and a difficult clash with the Habsburg authorities ensued.[82] At the same time, in early Revolutionary France, the formally civil system produced a de facto civil-religious hybrid, by which Jewish marriage law enjoyed surprising civil recognition. Evelyne Oliel-Grausz has aptly referred to this decade as an 'intermediate period of law' characterized by 'some sort of legal vacuum' and 'transitory vagueness.'[83] This transitional period ended in 1802 when Napoleon ordered that civil marriage and divorce ceremonies must precede Jewish religious ones, a position echoed by the Sanhedrin in 1807.[84]

Comparison of the Habsburg and French routes in the 1780-90s shows two secularizing, centralizing states that declared marriage to be civil and then produced hybrid systems, as they struggled to align the civil and the religious in this sensitive domain. From 1802 their paths diverged: the French declared their marriage law strictly civil and of universal application, while the Habsburg monarchy maintained a measure of confessional diversity even when asserting a civil definition and state jurisdiction over marriage. The Habsburg state overrode Jewish marriage law when it clashed outright with civil law; as Ulrike Harmat has argued elsewhere, the state showed 'consideration for the laws of the tolerated religions, but only where they appeared to be consistent with its own views and purposes.'[85] Yet, Habsburg marriage law – simultaneously civil and confessional – included provisions for divorce by Jews and Protestants even while denying divorce to Catholics, and it did so in accord with their respective religious laws.[86]

Rachele Morschene Luzzatto's civil divorce helps illumine the advantages, ambiguities, and complexities caused by state involvement in Jewish marriage and divorce. Straddling the private and public, her story is a revealing chapter in the histories of Jewish women and of Jewish Emancipation. It shows the potential of the modern state – in this case, a late eighteenth-century reforming absolutist state – to facilitate women's personal emancipation.[87] It also shows how public or legal Emancipation – the reordering of relations between the state, Jewish community, and Jewish individuals – necessarily involved the realigning of civil and Jewish laws. In the domain of marriage law and practice, Emancipation meant the partial incorporation of Jewish law in a civil framework but it did not necessarily mean the full replacement of religious by civil law; rather, it entailed a complex process of one legal system harnessing another. The two were yoked together, with far-reaching consequences for both private and public Jewish life.

Notes

1 Archivio di Stato di Trieste, Archivio notarile, Notaio Francesco Saverio Lovisoni, Atti processuali 1793 no. 38, fasc. Relle Luzzato Morschene contro Lucio Luzzatto, f. 22r (hereafter AST, Lovisoni). I am most grateful to Dr Ugo Cova, former director of the archive, and his colleagues, especially Maria Carla Triadan, for locating this file on the separation and divorce of Rachele (a.k.a. Relle or Bella) Morschene Luzzatto (c. 1770–1844). I refer to her simply as Rachele Morschene since that was her given name, and she bore the name Luzzatto only during the time of her marriage to Lucio Luzzatto. This article forms part of my forthcoming book *Rachele and Her Loves*, on Jewish women, marriage, and the modern state. I also thank the Smith College Neilson Library Reference and Interlibrary Loan staff for their tireless and gracious work on my behalf. Research for this article was funded by Smith College, the Setlow Family Fund, and the Lucius N. Littauer Foundation. I have benefited greatly from the comments of colleagues who heard earlier versions at many venues in the United States, Europe, and Israel. I thank Benjamin Braude, Olga Litvak, Susan Shapiro, Kenneth Stow, and Stephan Wendehorst for their comments on the written text; of course, I alone bear responsibility for remaining errors or shortcomings.

2 Lucio Luzzatto (c. 1755–1801) was the younger brother of Elia Moise Luzzatto, wealthy communal leader, wholesale merchant, and member of the Mercantile Exchange in Trieste.

3 *Costituzione sopra li Matrimonj per tutto cio che riguarda il contratto civile, e li suoi effetti: la quale dovra osservarsi da tutti li sudditi cristiani* (Vienna 1783); also in *Codice ossia Collezione sistematica Di tutte le Leggi, ed Ordinanze emanate sotto il Regno di Sua Maestà Giuseppe II*, trans. Bartolommeo Borroni (Milan 1787), 3: 98–119. For discussions, see Claudio Tosi, 'Giuseppinismo e legislazione matrimoniale in Lombardia. La Costituzione del 1784,' *Critica Storica* 27:2 (1990), 235–301, and Ursula Flossmann, *Österreichische Privatrechtsgeschichte*, Springers Kurzlehrbücher der Rechtswissenschaft, 3rd ed. (Vienna and New York 1996), 82–4.

4 For works that emphasize marriage, law, and the state, see Lois C. Dubin, 'Les Liaisons dangereuses: Mariage juif et état moderne à Trieste au XVIIIe siècle,' *Annales: Histoire, Sciences Sociales* 49:5 (1994), 1139–70, and *The Port Jews of Habsburg Trieste: Absolutist Politics and Enlightenment Culture*, Stanford Studies in Jewish History and Culture (Stanford 1999), 174–97; and ChaeRan Y. Freeze, *Jewish Marriage and Divorce in Imperial Russia* (Hanover, NH 2002). For other studies of Jewish marriage and family patterns in early modern and modern Europe, see also Jacob Katz, 'Family, Kinship, and Mar-

riage among Ashkenazim in the Sixteenth to Eighteenth Centuries,' *Jewish Journal of Sociology* 1 (1959): 4–22; David Biale, 'Love, Marriage and the Modernization of the Jews,' *Approaches to Modern Judaism*, ed. Marc Lee Raphael (Chico CA 1983); Marion Kaplan, *The Making of the Jewish Middle Class: Women, Family, and Identity in Imperial Germany* (New York and Oxford 1991); Steven M. Lowenstein, *The Berlin Jewish Community: Enlightenment, Family and Crisis, 1770–1830* (New York and Oxford 1994).

5 A.F. Pribram, ed., *Urkunden und Akten zur Geschichte der Juden in Wien*, Quellen und Forschungen zur Geschichte der Juden in Deutsch-Österreich 8 (Vienna and Leipzig 1918), 1: 530–48, esp., 530, 543–4, for 3 May 1786 Patent and accompanying discussions; 1: 590–1, 2: 13–17, for 18 Feb. 1791 decree. Later elaborations in Karl Wittig, ed., *Das allgemeine bürgerliche Gesetzbuch für die deutschen Länder der österreichischen Monarchie, mit ... dem Josephinischen und dem für Galizien gegebenen Gesetzbüchern ...* 1 (Vienna 1829), 169–84 (hereafter the *Allgemeines Bürgerliche Gesetzbuch* is referred to as ABGB). On reception of the new laws by Jews, see Dubin, 'Liaisons,' and *Port Jews*, 174–97; Gil Graff, *Separation of Church and State: Dina de-Malkhuta Dina in Jewish Law, 1750–1848* (University, AL 1985), 40–53.

6 *Ehepatent*, §§49–57 on non-Catholics; ABGB, II: §§115–22 on non-Catholic Christians, and §§123–36 on Jews. Flossmann, *Österreichische*, 83, 92–3; Ulrike Harmat, 'Divorce and Remarriage in Austria-Hungary: The Second Marriage of Franz Conrad von Hötzendorf,' *Austrian History Yearbook* 32 (2001), 69–103, esp., 70, 73–4; Ettore Dezza, *Lezioni di Storia della codificazione civile: Il Code Civil (1804) e l'Allgemeines Bürgerliches Gesetzbuch (ABGB, 1812)*, 2nd ed. (Turin 2000), 153–5.

7 The work of Kenneth Stow, Robert Bonfil, and Stefanie Siegmund on Italy highlights the complex relations between Roman law, *ius commune*, and Jewish law, and the recognition of Jewish juridical authority primarily as arbitration. Theoretically, Jewish law was valid insofar as it did not contradict the other prevailing sources of law; practically, how much attention was paid to it by non-Jews varied in different times and places. See Kenneth R. Stow, *Catholic Thought and Papal Jewry Policy* (New York 1977), 102–22; Robert Bonfil, *Rabbis and Jewish Communities in Renaissance Italy*, trans. Jonathan Chipman, Littman Library of Jewish Civilization (Oxford 1990), 207–51; Stefanie B. Siegmund, 'Division of the Dowry on the Death of the Daughter: An Instance in the Negotiation of Laws and Jewish Customs in Early Modern Tuscany,' *Jewish History* 16 (2002), 73–106.

8 For Europe generally, see the wide-ranging surveys of Lloyd Bonfield, 'Developments in European Family Law,' and Jeffrey R. Watt, 'The Impact of the Reformation and Counter-Reformation,' *Family Life in Early Modern Times*,

1500–1789, The History of the European Family, vol. 1, ed. David I. Kertzer and Marzio Barbagli (New Haven and London 2001), 87–125, 125–54, esp. to 143; Lloyd Bonfield, 'European Family Law,' *Family Life in the Long Nineteenth Century, 1789–1913, The History of the European Family*, vol. 2, ed. David I. Kertzer and Marzio Barbagli (New Haven and London 2002), 109–54; and Roderick Phillips, *Putting Asunder: A History of Divorce in Western Society* (Cambridge 1988). On France, see Sarah Hanley, 'Engendering the State: Family Formation and State Building in Early Modern France,' *French Historical Studies* 16 (1989), 4–27, and 'The Jurisprudence of the Arrêts: Marital Union, Civil Society, and State Formation in France, 1550–1650,' *Law and History Review* 21 (2003), 1–40. On Holland, see Daniel M. Swetchinski, *Reluctant Cosmopolitans: The Portuguese Jews of Seventeenth-Century Amsterdam*, Littman Library of Jewish Civilization (London and Portland 2000), 18–19, 48, 239, and Graf, *Separation*, 45–6. For Hamburg 1650 regulations, see M. Grunwald, *Portugiesengräber auf deutscher Erde: Beiträge zur Kultur- und Kunstgeschichte* (Hamburg 1902), 16–17, and Joachim Whaley, *Religious Toleration and Social Change in Hamburg 1529–1819* (Cambridge 1985), 76–7; for 1710 regulations, Peter Freimark and Arno Herzig, eds., *Die Hamburger Juden in der Emanzipationsphase (1780–1870)* (Hamburg 1989), 317 (Art. 23), 321 (Art. 22). On both Holland and Hamburg, see also Salo Wittmayer Baron, *A Social and Religious History of the Jews*, 2nd ed. (New York, London, and Philadelphia 1952–83), 14: 274–5, and 15: 33–4.

9 On D'Aguilar, see H.S.Q. Henriques, *Jewish Marriages and the English Law* (London 1909), 23. For other examples, see Kenneth Stow, *Theater of Acculturation: The Roman Ghetto in the 16th Century* (Seattle, London, and Northampton MA 2001), 78; Vittore Colorni, *Legge ebraica e leggi locali: Diritto ebraico e diritto dello Stato* (Milan 1945), 184; Sherrin Marshall, 'Protestant, Catholic, and Jewish Women in the Early Modern Netherlands,' in *Women in Reformation and Counter-Reformation Europe*, ed. Sherrin Marshall (Bloomington and Indianapolis 1989), 133–5; Swetchinski, *Reluctant*, 240; Frances Malino, 'Resistance and rebellion in eighteenth-century France,' *Jewish Historical Studies: Transactions of the Jewish Historical Society of England* 30 (1987–8), 55–70; and on the Holy Roman Empire, Andreas Gotzmann and Stephan Wendehorst, eds., *Juden im Recht? Neue Zugänge zur Rechtsgeschichte der Juden im Alten Reich* (Berlin 2007), esp., the essays by Anette Baumann and Birgitt Klein.

10 For an overview, see *Encyclopedia Judaica* (Jerusalem 1971), s.v. 'Divorce.' For discussions focusing on women in Jewish divorce, see Judith Romney Wegner, *Chattel or Person? The Status of Women in the Mishnah* (New York and Oxford 1988), 45–50, 129–38; Judith Hauptman, *Rereading the Rabbis: A*

Woman's Voice (Boulder 1998), 102–29; Rachel Biale, *Women and Jewish Law: An Exploration of Women's Issues in Halakhic Sources* (New York 1984), 70–101; Shlomo Riskin, *Women and Jewish Divorce: The Rebellious Wife, The Agunah and the Right of Women to Initiate Divorce in Jewish Law; A Halakhic Solution* (Hoboken 1989).

11 M. Ketubot 7: 1–5, 10; Ketubot 63b on the 'rebellious woman' who says 'he is repulsive to me,' and 77a on boils and polypus, understood as causing offensive odour from nose or mouth; Baba Batra 47b–48a on force; Even Ha-'ezer, Ketubot ch. 70, Gittin ch. 154; Biale, *Women*, 84–101; Irwin Haut, *Divorce in Jewish Law and Life* (New York 1983), 19–20, 23–5.

12 Tal Ilan, *Integrating Women into Second Temple History*, Texts and Studies in Ancient Judaism 76 (Tübingen 1999), 253–62; David Instone Brewer, 'Jewish Women Divorcing Their Husbands in Early Judaism,' *Harvard Theological Review* 92:3 (1999), 349–57; Judith R. Baskin, *Midrashic Women: Formations of the Feminine in Rabbinic Literature* (Hanover, NH, and London 2002), 91–2.

13 On the contracts, Geonim, and ransom-divorces, see Mordecai Akiva Friedman, *Jewish Marriage in Palestine: A Cairo Geniza Study* (Tel Aviv and New York 1980), 1: 312–46; Riskin, *Women*; Mordecai Akiva Friedman, 'The Ransom-Divorce: Divorce Proceedings Initiated by the Wife in Medieval Jewish Practice,' *Israel Oriental Studies* 6 (1976): 288–307.

14 On Tam and Gershom, see Riskin, *Women*, 93ff; summary of medieval developments in Haut, *Divorce*, 49–56.

15 On the differing effects of Islamic and Christian milieus upon rabbinic attitudes, see Howard Tzvi Adelman, 'Law and Love: The Jewish Family in Early Modern Italy,' *Continuity and Change* 16 (2001), 283–303, and the literature cited therein.

16 AST, Lovisoni, ff. 1r–153. Petitions to Court: 18 Oct. 1793 for separation and support, ff. 36r–40v; 3 Dec. 1795 for divorce, ff. 21r–22v (also ff. 45rv); 6 Jan. 1796 for divorce, with accompanying documents, ff. 1r–11r. In the separation suit, see also her 24 Jan. 1794 reply to Court countering Lucio's response, ff. 72r–84v, and her letter to rabbi 24 Jan. 1794, ff. 91r–92r. The 8 Apr. 1796 summons for divorce hearing is on f. 24r. Unfortunately, some important documents from the case are missing, such as Rachele's concluding argument and letters from the rabbi, among others.

17 AST, Lovisoni, f. 37v, 'un rilascio universale.'

18 AST, Lovisoni, ff. 6r–11r, 21r, 43r–45r, 77v–78r, 86r–91v. See Jon Arrizabalaga, John Henderson, and Roger French, *The Great Pox: The French Disease in Renaissance Europe* (New Haven and London 1997); Claude Quétel, *History of Syphilis*, trans. Judith Braddock and Brian Pike (Baltimore 1990), 72–105.

19 AST, Lovisoni, f. 38rv, and in neighbours' and relatives' affidavits, ff. 41r–42r.

Jewish Women, Marriage Law, and Emancipation   141

20 Benedetto (Ben Zion Rafael Ha-Kohen) Frizzi (1756–1844), who lived in Trieste from 1790, was a physician and prolific author on medical, philosophical, and Jewish subjects. Having studied at the University of Pavia and spent time in Vienna, he was well-regarded in Trieste and beyond. For more, see Dubin, *Port Jews*, 238n4, 284n45. Either Frizzi himself or one of his medical colleagues in Trieste must have contacted the distinguished Johann Georg Hasenöhrl von Lagasius.
21 AST, Lovisoni, f. 78v.
22 AST, Lovisoni, f. 83rv: 'aver un martirio continuo con una convivenza tumultuante, acerba, ed inquieta, che terminarebbe col esterminio totale del mio individuo, mandandomi ben presto fra gli Estinti.'
23 AST, Lovisoni, f. 91v.
24 AST, Lovisoni, f. 3v: 'Qual angustia adunque nell'animo di una Sposa tradita! Qual miseria la circonda; qual afflizione la trafige! E come vegliarli in lei quell'amore, che è l'eletrica Sintilla del Matrimonio? Come aplicarsi all'opera della Generazione con un Cuore Stracciato dalle più orribili ristretezze, con una Machina abbattuta da milla [sic] orori, e coll'inquietudine in fine di produrre nel Mondo tanti miserabili?'
25 AST, Lovisoni, Lucio's statements: 30 Nov. 1793, ff. 55r–60v; 20 Feb. 1794 with medical testimony, ff. 145r–153r; 12 Mar. 1794, ff. 108r–125v; 8 May 1794, ff. 140r–143v; 2 Nov. 1794 appeal of 26 Sept. 1794 verdict [f. 28], ff. 129r–137v.
26 AST, Lovisoni, ff. 58v, 110v.
27 AST, Lovisoni, f. 117v.
28 AST, Lovisoni, f. 57v, 'una confidenzial corrispondenza.'
29 AST, Lovisoni, f. 59v.
30 AST, Lovisoni, ff. 117v, 118r, 119r. On criticism of women displaying their learning, see Luciano Guerci, *La sposa obbediente: Donna e matrimonio nella discussione dell'Italia del Settecento* (Turin 1988), 252–3.
31 AST, Lovisoni, f. 117rv.
32 AST, Lovisoni, ff. 123v, 118r, 140v.
33 AST, Lovisoni, f. 135r; cf. f. 130r: 'con ciò verrebbe distrutta affatto la dipendenza delle Mogli alli loro Mariti, il che è contrario a tutte le Leggi civili, sociali, ed ecclesiastiche.' See Guerci, *Sposa*, on the eighteenth-century Italian discourse on wifely obedience.
34 AST, Lovisoni, f. 141rv.
35 AST, Lovisoni, ff. 80r–84v.
36 It is difficult to distinguish Rachele's voice from those of her father, her lawyer, and her friend the doctor; Natalie Zemon Davis advises seeing a collaborative effort among all these parties (oral communication). The classic work

on analysing voice, fact, and fiction in legal narratives is Natalie Zemon Davis, *Fiction in the Archives: Pardon Tales and Their Tellers in Sixteenth-Century France* (Stanford 1987). See also Joanne M. Ferraro, *Marriage Wars in Late Renaissance Venice* (Oxford and New York 2001).
37 AST, Lovisoni, judgment f. 28r; *Rationes decidendi* f. 50r–51v.
38 AST, Lovisoni, N. 8232, f. 29.
39 AST, Lovisoni, ff. 29v–34r, 47r, 49rv.
40 AST, Lovisoni, f. 1r. Robert Bonfil, *Jewish Life in Renaissance Italy*, trans. Anthony Oldcorn (Berkeley, Los Angeles, and London 1994), 258–9, on dowries and counter-dowries in Italy, and their benefits for women; cf. Siegmund, 'Division.' On dowries later, see Luciano Allegra, 'A Model of Jewish Devolution: Turin in the Eighteenth Century,' *Jewish History* 7:2 (1993), 29–58, and Kaplan, *Making*, 85–116.
41 See 'Procedural Ambiguities' below.
42 AST, Lovisoni, f. 21rv: 'un formale Divorzio con perfetta nullità di Matrimonio giusta l'Ebraico Rito ... poichè il Rito Mosaico lo permette e lo vuole.'
43 On the exclusionary regulations of 1788, see Kreisschreiben, 17 Jan. 1788, in Wittig, *Allgemeine*, 182–3: Jews should no longer bring divorce actions to rabbis but henceforth only to civil authorities to be handled in accordance with the ABGB 'so wie auch die Rabbiner unter keinem Vorwande sich in die Ehescheidungssachen einzulassen haben, und von den unter den Juden nach ihren Religionsgesetzen gewöhnlich gewesenen Scheidebriefen keine Frage mehr seyn kann.' Earlier 1785–86 discussions in Pribram, *Urkunden*, 1: 535–7, 541–4. For the 1791 divorce law, see Pribram, ibid., 1: 590–1, 2: 13–17.
44 See n36 above.
45 *Ehepatent*, §51; *Codice ossia Collezione*, 3: 115; Tosi, 'Giuseppinismo,' 271.
46 AST, Lovisoni, ff. 50r–51v, refers to *Codice Civile Universale*, III, §§47–8, 100–1; see Wittig, *Allgemeine*, 109, 150–1. The judge acknowledged that this case did not exactly conform to the provisions in §§100–1 (*Ehepatent* §§45–6), according to which a couple mutually seek separation of bed and board. Perhaps the judge had in mind decrees of the late 1780s and early 1790s that spelled out court procedures for separation cases brought by only one party; ibid., 143, 145–6, 149.
47 *Ehepatent* §50, in *Codice ossia Collezione*, 3: 114–15, and Wittig, *Allgemeine*, 162; ABGB, II: §§109, 115, 121, 135; *Encyclopedia Judaica*, s.v. 'Divorce,' 6: 129.
48 AST, Lovisoni, f. 51r.
49 *Ehepatent*, §52, in *Codice ossia Collezione*, 3: 115, and in Wittig, *Allgemeine*, 162: 'Hauptfeindschaft oder eine unüberwindliche Abneigung' or 'odio capitale, o di avversione invincibile.' The classic phrase in the Jewish marriage con-

tract: 'I will work, honour, support and maintain thee'; Haut, *Divorce*, 8, and *Encyclopedia Judaica*, s.v. 'Divorce,' 6: 128.

50 AST, Lovisoni , f. 2v-6r, citing *Shulhan Arukh*, Even Ha-ezer, Ketubbot ch. 70.

51 *Galizisches Gesetzbuch* §§108–9, in Wittig, *Allgemeine*, 151–2, 163: 'wenn ein Ehegatte von dem andern gröblich misshandelt worden, und wenn sein Leben, seine Gesundheit, ein beträchtlicher Theil seines Vermögens, oder wegen schlechten Beispiels auch die guten Sitten in Gefahr gesetzt werden.' On this code, see Henry E. Strakosch, *State Absolutism and the Rule of Law: The Struggle for the Codification of Civil Law in Austria 1753–1811* (Sydney 1967), 187–8; Dezza, *Lezioni*, 132–7.

52 AST, Lovisoni, ff. 6r–10v, especially 9r–10v, quoting *Shulhan Arukh*, Even Ha-ezer, Gittin ch. 154, in Hebrew and Italian translation. See n11 above for M. Ketubbot 7: 10 and other sources.

53 Yedidiah Tiah Weill (1721–1805) served as rabbi in Karlsruhe and as *Oberlandrabbiner* for Baden.

54 *Ehepatent* §45, in *Codice ossia Collezione*, 112, 'gravi ingiurie' and 'pericolo ... di depravati costumj'; Wittig, *Allgemeine*, 150: 'Wenn ein Ehegatte von dem andern gröblich misshandelt; oder der Verführung zu Lastern und verderbten Sitten ausgesetzt wird.' The corresponding III: §100 in the *Josephinisches Gesetzbuch* is not quoted directly in Wittig; I thank Miriam Levy for tracking down this rare material and verifying its wording. The Triestine judge did cite §100, although only with regard to procedure; AST, Lovisoni, f. 50v.

55 On Protestants, see Merry E. Wiesner-Hanks, *Christianity and Sexuality in the Early Modern World: Regulating Desire, Reforming Practice* (London and New York 2000), 78; Thomas Max Safley, *Let No Man Put Asunder: The Control of Marriage in the German Southwest, A Comparative Study, 1550–1650* (Kirksville 1984), 131, 159 (1586 case in which divorce was granted because of husband's venereal disease). On Catholics (Tametsi 1563), Diego Quaglioni, '"Divortium a diversitate mentium." La separazione personale dei coniugi nelle dottrine di diritto comune (appunti per una discussione),' in *Coniugi nemici. La separazione in Italia dal XII al XVIII secolo*, Annali dell'Istituto storico italo-germanico in Trento, Quaderni, 53), ed. Silvana Seidel Menchi and Diego Quaglioni (Bologna 2000), 95–118, esp. 114, 116. Venereal disease figured among other factors in two Venetian cases, 1619 and 1623, with different outcomes; Ferraro, *Marriage Wars*, 97–102, 126–7. On states, Phillips, *Putting Asunder*, 173, 179, 202–3.

56 John M. Biggs, *The Concept of Marital Cruelty* (London 1962), 131; Phillips, *Putting Asunder*, 215.

57 Roderick Phillips, *Family Breakdown in Late Eighteenth-century France: Divorces in Rouen 1792–1803* (Oxford 1980), 131–2.

58 'Leben' and 'Gesundheit'; see n51 above.
59 ABGB, II: §109, 'anhaltende, mit Gefahr der Ansteckung verbundene Leibesgebrechen.'
60 Archivio di Stato di Trieste, Cesareo Regio Governo in Trieste (hereafter AST, C. R. Gov.), 1776–1809, busta 621, Ebrei, 16 July 1798 petition to Vienna.
61 AST, Lovisoni, f. 3v: 'Matrimonio, che Dio ha istituito per il bene della Società, e per il mutuo Soccorso delle parti, che vi si dedicano!' On changing views of marriage, see, e.g., Alfred Dufour, *Le mariage dans l'Ecole allemande du Droit naturel moderne au XVIIIe siècle* (Paris 1972), esp. 253–310; Lawrence Stone, *The Family, Sex and Marriage in England, 1500–1800* (London 1977); James F. Traer, *Marriage and the Family in Eighteenth-Century France* (Ithaca and London 1980); Phillips, *Putting Asunder,* 159–225; Isabel V. Hull, *Sexuality, State, and Civil Society in Germany, 1700–1815* (Ithaca and London 1996); Giacomo Francini, *Moralia Coniugalia ou de l'impossible sacralité du mariage à l'époque de la raison 1750–1792,* Thèse de doctorat en Histoire, École des Hautes Études en Sciences Sociales 1997–98 (Villeneuve d'Ascq 1999); Daniela Lombardi, *Matrimoni di antico regime,* Annali dell'Istituto storico italo-germanico in Trento, Monografie 34 (Bologna 2001), esp. 359–468.
62 The court was headed by Baron Ferdinando d'Argento, a member of a venerable patrician family of Trieste. From the documents at my disposal, I cannot tell whether the decision was his alone or a collegial one taken by all the court members. Karl von Zinzendorf, Governor of Trieste 1776–82, and Pietro Antonio Pittoni, who served as Chief of Police 1766–1801 among other posts, were two well-known proponents of Enlightenment in Trieste. Zinzendorf's voluminous journals, which reflect his wide-ranging travel and research, constitute a major source on Enlightenment and reform in eighteenth-century Europe; an international research team headed by Grete Klingenstein and sponsored by the Austrian Academy of Sciences, is preparing a critical edition for publication.
63 I plan to address the fascinating theme of Rachele's 'sentimental education' in future work (I thank Olga Litvak for this formulation). For example, assuming the views in Rachele's petitions were not merely legal ploys, how did she come to express companionate and natural law views of marriage? What was the interplay between economic failure, personal distress, friendship, and ideology?
64 Österreichisches Staatsarchiv, Hofkammerarchiv, Kommerz. Littorale. 1749–1813 (hereafter HKA, Komm. Litt.), rot 502, Akatholiken und Juden im Littorale 1750–97, ff. 709–715, Bericht des triester k.k. Guberniums 14 Jan. 1797; also in AST, C.R. Gov., b. 621. Unfortunately I have found only the governmental report and response, not the Jews' original complaint.

65 HKA, Komm. Litt., rot 502, ff. 707r–708v, 714rv, Dekret an das Triester Gouvernement 11 May 1797, formulated by the noted jurist and justice minister Karl Anton Martini.
66 Maimonides, *Mishneh Torah*, Book of Women, Divorce, chs. 1–9; Seder ha-get (The get procedure), in Even Ha-ezer, ch. 154, translation in Haut, *Divorce*, 31–41.
67 AST, Lovisoni , f. 22r,: Dec. 3, 1795 divorce petition: 'perchè venga dichiarato nullo il Matrimonio ... onde possa poi il Rabino stesso More Hebreorum passare a' quelle ulteriori formalità proprie del suo Rito.'
68 Criticism of rabbinic punctiliousness with regard to the details of Jewish divorce procedures was voiced a few decades later by *maskilim* (adherents of the Enlightenment): e.g., Judah Leib Gordon's classic poem 'Kotzo shel Yud' ('The Tip of the Yud'); also Nancy Sinkoff, 'The *Maskil*, the Convert, and the '*Agunah*: Joseph Perl as a Historian of Jewish Divorce Law,' *AJS Review* 27:2 (2003), 281–99.
69 See above, and n43.
70 M. Gittin 1: 5, 9: 8; Gittin 10b-11a; Baba Batra 47b-48a. Compulsion by a Gentile court was acceptable if its purpose was to tell a Jew to obey Jewish authorities; Maimonides, *Mishneh Torah*, Book of Women, Divorce, 2: 20.
71 In a sense, the state made it even easier for Rachele to 'ransom' herself; see above, n13.
72 Freeze, *Jewish Marriage*.
73 Harmat, 'Divorce'; Flossmann, *Österreichische*, 83–7.
74 Bonfield, 'Developments,' and Watt, 'Impact'; Phillips, *Putting Asunder*, 191–226. Joel F. Harrington, *Reordering Marriage and Society in Reformation Germany* (Cambridge 1995), sees the mixing of secular and ecclesiastical control of Christian marriage in pre-Reformation medieval Europe.
75 State imposition of civil law for marriage was quite different from exceptional instances in the past when Jewish individuals requested Gentile intervention to support one party in a dispute over a contentious Jewish marriage or divorce; see, e.g., Shlomo Simonsohn, *History of the Jews in the Duchy of Mantua* (Jerusalem 1977), 501–4, on the Tamari-Venturozzi 'divorce scandal' in sixteenth-century Italy.
76 Simon Roberts, 'The Study of Dispute: Anthropological Perspectives,' in *Disputes and Settlements: Law and Human Relations in the West*,' ed. John Bossy (Cambridge 1983), 5–6, and Nicole Castan, 'The Arbitration of Disputes under the "Ancien Régime,"' ibid., 258–60.
77 See n8 above.
78 On Prussia, Michael A. Meyer, ed. and Michael Brenner, assistant ed., *German-Jewish History in Modern Times*, vol. 1, *Tradition and Enlightenment 1600–*

1780, by Mordecai Breuer and Michael Graetz, tr. William Templer (New York 1996), 254. On England, Israel Finestein, 'An Aspect of the Jews and English Marriage Law during the Emancipation: The Prohibited Degrees,' *Jewish Journal of Sociology* 7:1 (1965), 3–21, esp. 4–6, 16–17. Several of the celebrated salon hostesses in late eighteenth-century Berlin were divorced from their Jewish husbands, presumably by Jewish divorces, but how exactly they were handled merits further investigation; see Deborah Hertz, *Jewish High Society in Old Regime Berlin* (New Haven and London 1988).

79 Werner Ogris, 'The Habsburg Monarchy in the Eighteenth Century: The Birth of the Modern Centralized State,' *Legislation and Justice*, ed. Antonio Padoa-Schioppa (Oxford and New York 1997), 313–33.

80 M. Diogene Tama, *Transactions of the Parisian Sanhedrim, or Acts of the Assembly of Israelitish Deputies of France and Italy*, trans. F.D. Kirwan (London 1807; repr., Brown Classics in Judaica, Lanham MD 1985), 149–56.

81 Zosa Szajkowski, 'Marriages, Mixed Marriages and Conversions among French Jews during the Revolution of 1789,' *Jews and the French Revolutions of 1789, 1830 and 1848* (New York 1970), 826–47, esp. 826, 832–4, 847; Evelyne Oliel-Grausz, 'Divorce mosaïque et legislation révolutionnaire,' in *Les Juifs et la Révolution française: Histoire et Mentalités*, ed. M. Hadas-Lebel and E. Oliel-Grausz (Paris 1992), 71–84, esp. 81–4.

82 On these cases, see Dubin, 'Liaisons,' and *Port Jews*, 174–97. I will explore the relationship of Morschene and Frizzi more fully in my book *Rachele and Her Loves*.

83 Oliel-Grausz, 'Divorce,' 83.

84 Some rabbis provided a novel Halakhic justification for the sequence of civil, then religious divorce: since *halakhah* stipulates that a *get* must completely sever the marital relationship, the civil divorce ought to precede the religious divorce in order for the giving of the *get* to be the final act of divorce; Tama, *Transactions*, 153–4; Graff, *Separation*, 75–85, 91–2, 102–3. This was the first application of the Talmudic dictum 'the law of the kingdom is law' (*dina de-malkhuta dina* in Nedarim 28a, Gittin 10b, Baba Kama 113, Baba Batra 54b–55a) to marriage and divorce law. It was not used for the *Ehepatent*; Graf, *Separation*, 51, 88–9. More generally on civil marriage and Judaism, see Abraham Hayim Freimann, *Seder kidushin ve-nissu'in ahare hatimat ha-Talmud: Mehkar histori-dogmati be-dine Yisrael* (Jerusalem 1945), 362–84.

85 Harmat, 'Divorce,' 73–4.

86 Ibid., 70; Dezza, *Lezioni*, 153–5; Flossmann, *Österreichische*, 83, 85; Annamaria Galoppini, 'Profilo storico del divorzio in Italia,' *Commentario sul divorzio*, ed. Pietro Rescigno (Milan 1980), 2–14.

87 Heide Wunder, *He Is the Sun, She Is the Moon*, trans. Thomas Dunlop (Cam-

bridge MA and London 1998), 197–9, argues that women attained considerable rights in the estate-based, late absolutist societies of Prussia and the Habsburg monarchy; cf. Edith Saurer, 'Il Matrimonio fra obbligo e privilegio (Veneto e Bassa Austria, sec. XIX),' *Venezia e l'Austria*, ed. Gino Benzoni and Gaetano Cozzi (Venice 1999), 161–2, and Hull, *Sexuality.*

chapter six

The Jews of Italy in the *Triennio Giacobino*, 1796–1799

GEOFFREY SYMCOX

The French Invasions, 1796–1800

In this essay I will examine what happened to Italy's Jewish communities during the *Triennio Giacobino*, the three years of Jacobin rule between 1796 and 1799. During this short, dramatic period Italy's Jews would experience what has come to be called their 'first emancipation.' The victorious French armies and their Italian Jacobin allies proclaimed the revolutionary ideal of civil equality, irrespective of race or creed. In the new republics they established, they opened up the ghettoes and promulgated laws that for the first time granted Jews the rights – and imposed the duties – of citizenship. But this emancipation did not last, for it depended on the military ascendancy of France and the political domination of the Jacobin regimes it had called into being. The defeat of the French armies in 1799 doomed the Italian Jacobin republics, which were too weak to stand on their own; a counter-attack by the armies of an anti-French coalition and a tidal wave of 'throne and altar' revolts swept them away and restored the old governments. The Jews, who were identified in the popular mind with the fallen Jacobins, were persecuted, the ghettoes restored, the old discriminatory laws reinstituted. Not for long, however: in June 1800 the French armies returned, this time to win a more lasting victory, install the Jacobins in power once more, and resume the interrupted process of Jewish emancipation.

To make sense of this chaotic period I must briefly recapitulate the key events. Early in April 1796 the French Revolutionary Army of Italy, commanded by the young Napoleon Bonaparte, advanced from the coast near Genoa into the north Italian plain, quickly defeating the Austrian and Piedmontese armies in its path. By the end of the month the Piedmontese government had concluded an armistice with France, leaving Bonaparte free to push the Austrian forces out of Lombardy. He entered Milan on 14 May; the Austrians fell back on their stronghold at Mantua, where Bonaparte besieged them. French detachments then fanned out across the small duchies of the Po valley and into the northern Papal States. Bonaparte's whirlwind invasion shattered the old regime states of northern Italy. Italians who sympathized with the revolutionary cause, who for some time had been calling themselves 'patriots' or 'Jacobins' after the French model, pressed for the establishment of democratic, constitutional republics in their place. In April 1797, Bonaparte expelled the Austrian army from Italy and concluded a provisional armistice, which was confirmed in a final peace treaty at Campo Formio in October of that year. It left the French in control of northern Italy and guaranteed the new republics they had established there. The most important of these was the Cisalpine Republic in Lombardy, created with Bonaparte's approval in 1796 and endowed with a French-style constitution a year later. A second, smaller republic was established in Liguria, with its capital at Genoa.

Having concluded his treaty with Austria, late in 1797 Bonaparte departed from Italy, already planning the conquest of Egypt that he would attempt – unsuccessfully – the following year. But his departure did not halt the revolutionary ferment spreading through the peninsula. In February 1798 a small group of local Jacobins established a republic at Rome, backed by French troops. They declared all citizens free and equal, opened the Roman ghetto, deposed Pope Pius VI, and later imprisoned him. Meanwhile the French gradually extended their control over the Papal States and Tuscany, occupying Florence early the next year, and declaring the local Jewish communities free and equal. But these events triggered a powerful backlash. From the early summer of 1798 a peasant insurrection spread across central Italy; marching to the cry of 'Viva Maria,' the rebels declared their hatred for the godless French, the godless Jacobins, and the Jews, whom they perceived to be their allies.

External events soon combined with this insurgency to make the situation of the Roman Jacobins and their French allies increasingly precarious. Bonaparte's Egyptian campaign miscarried. The destruction of his fleet at Aboukir in August 1798, marooning him and his army in Egypt, led to the formation of a new coalition against revolutionary France, made up of Britain, Austria, Russia, and the Bourbon Kingdom of Naples. In November 1798 a Neapolitan army took Rome and overthrew the

Jacobin republic there. A month later the French army counterattacked, restored the republic, and in January 1799 went on to conquer Naples, where it installed yet another republic led by local Jacobins.

This triumph proved very short-lived. In February 1799, a peasant 'Army of the Holy Faith' (*La Santa Fede*) formed in Calabria. Led by a cardinal, the *Sanfedisti* advanced on Naples; in June they crushed the Jacobin republic and restored the Bourbon monarchy. The small French garrison that had occupied Naples withdrew northwards. Meanwhile in March an Austro-Russian army had invaded Lombardy, extinguished the Cisalpine Republic, and advanced into Piedmont. Spurred by the success of the *Sanfedisti* and the Austro-Russian advance, the 'Viva Maria' insurgency in central Italy sprang up again with renewed ferocity, while other 'throne and altar' insurrections spread across Lombardy, Piedmont (the 'Massa Cristiana'), and Liguria (where the rebels also adopted the title of 'Viva Maria'). The beleaguered French armies retreated to Genoa and into Switzerland. In the ensuing anarchy the peasant rebels wreaked atrocities against local Jacobins and a number of Jewish communities. The Triennio Giacobino was over, and the 'first emancipation' had ended in blood and chaos. Order was gradually reimposed by the Austrian armies. Through these three turbulent years the fate of Italy's Jews had been inextricably and tragically intertwined with the fate of its Jacobins; together they had tasted ephemeral liberation, and together they were overwhelmed by counter-revolution.

But the French were only temporarily beaten. In the spring of 1800 Bonaparte returned to Italy and defeated the Austrians at Marengo. He restored the Jacobin regimes in northern Italy, under his own firm tutelage, and the emancipation of Italy's Jews recommenced. Let us now briefly examine the various Italian Jewish communities on the eve of the revolution in order to assess how they were affected by the cataclysmic events of the Triennio Giacobino.

Italy's Divergent Jewish Communities

We must begin by noting that Italy's Jewish communities were located only in certain regions of the north and centre of the peninsula; two centuries of Spanish rule had left the Duchy of Milan, southern Italy, Sicily and Sardinia *Judenrein*. Reflecting the diversity of the patchwork of Italy's Old Regime states, in which they were embedded, Italy's variegated Jewish communities differed widely in size, culture, juridical status, and economic prosperity. Some were tiny, somnolent rural enclaves; others were large, vibrant urban communities, frequently beset by divisions of class and culture. Their responses to the events of the Triennio Giacobino and to the promise of emancipation that it offered were therefore far from uniform. We must be careful always to think of them in the plural: Italy's multifarious Jewish communities did not constitute a single monolithic bloc.

In aggregate the Jewish population of Italy in the 1790s was very small; around 31,000 persons out of a population of perhaps sixteen million for the whole peninsula.[1] As was customary in the corporative structure of the Old Regime, the local communities of Jews were organized in self-governing entities – called the *Università degli Ebrei* or *Nazione Ebrea* – whose rights, taxes, and duties were defined by a *condotta* or contract of privileges, renegotiated periodically with the governments of the states in which they lived. From the sixteenth century onward, in a gradual, piecemeal process, most of these communities had been confined to ghettoes. By 1790 perhaps three-quarters of Italy's Jews lived in ghettoes, with some notable exceptions; the rest were scattered in nuclei too small for formal ghettoization.

The largest ghetto was in Rome, with over 5,000 inhabitants. Other substantial ghettoes were at Venice, Mantua, and Turin, each with its specific social structure and administrative machinery. The big Jewish community of Livorno, by contrast, was not ghettoized. It had a population of over 4,300 in 1784, and was dominated by an oligarchy of wealthy Sephardic merchant dynasties, which kept a tight hold on the communal administration despite the efforts of Grand Duke Peter Leopold of Tuscany to open it up to other elements of the Jewish population.[2] This was the most prosperous Jewish community in Italy; it enjoyed a privileged status, and unlike the other large Tuscan communities at Florence and Siena, its population was expanding. But the fastest-growing Jewish community in late-eighteenth century Italy was that of Habsburg Trieste – like Livorno, a free port dominated by a mercantile elite. The Jews there had benefited – as had their fellows in the Austrian-ruled Duchy of Mantua – from Joseph II's Toleration Patents of 1781–82, and from the abolition of the ghetto three years later.[3] Sustained by their relatively buoyant mercantile economies, Livorno and Trieste had become the twin poles of Jewish cultural life in the peninsula, with an array of schools and polyglot publishing houses.

The other communities were less prosperous, and less culturally open. The Roman ghetto is a case in point. It could not match the cultural florescence of Trieste or Livorno, for its economy was in decline, and the communal administration was effectively bankrupt.[4] A few of its elite families prospered in long-distance trade and government contracting, but most of the inhabitants eked out a meagre living as artisans and secondhand dealers. Rome in fact offers a good example of the political and economic fissures that ran through the larger Jewish communities in the later eighteenth century: the communities at Venice or at Turin were similarly divided between a narrow, affluent elite and a large, impoverished proletariat.[5] The disparity between rich and poor generated resentments, exacerbated by the better-off Jews' ability to obtain privileges that exempted them from many disabilities, and allowed them to reside outside the ghetto. But in the small rural communities of Tuscany and the Po valley, such social divisions were hardly evident: something closer to shared penury prevailed.[6] The inward-looking, traditional culture of these isolated communities was very different from that of cosmopolitan centres like Venice or Livorno or Trieste, where some of the leading spirits were in touch with the new currents of Enlightenment thinking.

These social and cultural divisions were compounded by political divergences, because of the wide variations in juridical status between Italy's heterogeneous Jewish communities from state to state, and even within the confines of a single state (for instance, in Tuscany). So when the revolution burst upon them their responses inevitably differed from one place to another. Nevertheless it is probably true, as some scholars have argued, that the general reaction was favourable from the first. As revolutionary agitation spread through the peninsula in the early 1790s, Jews were to be found here and there among the Italian Jacobins and patriots, joining Masonic lodges and political clubs, and after the French invasion they seem in the main to have supported the new Jacobin regimes.[7] But their reaction was not one of simple, univocal approval. In many communities, for instance, the new freedom offered by the revolution evoked a guarded or lukewarm response.[8] Emancipation offered benefits, true, but also risks and uncertainties. Its secular ideology posed a direct threat to the religion that underpinned the community and did so much to define its identity, especially for the Orthodox.[9] The revolution offered the Jews emancipation and civil equality, but it also dissolved the familiar corporate structures and social hierarchies that had governed their lives for centuries, and precipitated them into an entirely new relationship with the outside world, a relationship for which they were totally unprepared. This ambivalence replicated the mixed feelings with which these communities had previously greeted the new ideas propagated by the Enlightenment. Thus in 1797 the Jews of Ferrara rejected a proposal to abolish their *Università degli Ebrei*, preferring to maintain the old social and political structure that had long governed their lives. The Jews of Rome were reluctant to join the revolutionary National Guard, in which they would have had to serve alongside non-Jews.[10] The revolution also heightened the existing social and political tensions within the Jewish communities: the Jewish patricians at Livorno, for instance, showed little or no enthusiasm for the revolution, but those lower down the social scale joined the new National Guard when it was formed, while one or two bold spirits among them even dared to criticize the 'despotism' of the ruling oligarchy, and called for democratic governance.[11]

Before the Revolution: Tension and Coexistence

The revolutionary events of 1796–99 came as a sudden, traumatic shock. But these events must also be understood as the continuation, compressed into a brutally short interval, of a process long under way: the struggle against the traditional order in Church and State, waged by intellectuals and reforming rulers inspired by the Enlightenment, which Franco Venturi has charted so magisterially.[12] The central element in this conflict, the steady whittling away of ecclesiastical jurisdiction and fiscal privilege by secular rulers bent on extending their authority, had vital implications for Italy's Jews, for the Catholic Church was a virulent source of anti-Semitism. The clergy, and the Mendicant Orders in particular, were always ready to whip up popular hostility against the Jews or encourage forced baptisms of Jewish children, a practice that Pope Benedict XIV (1740–58) explicitly favoured. This pope also blocked the efforts of the new Bourbon ruler of Naples, Charles III, to allow some Jews to settle in his kingdom in the 1740s.[13] And although Clement XIV (1769–74) relaxed some of his predecessors' measures against the Jews in the Papal State, his successor Pius VI (1775–99) restored them. Any weakening of the Church's authority would therefore tend to benefit the Jews.

It is important to note, however, that the Catholic clergy were not uniformly hostile to the Jews. The Jansenist reform movement in particular, which gathered momentum in the later eighteenth century, thanks in part to the support of the reforming sovereigns in Lombardy and Tuscany, had begun to change the intellectual climate within the Church. Jansenist theologians were highly critical of papal power and of the Jesuit Order which strenuously upheld it. The Jansenists were also hostile to the forms of popular piety that the Jesuits propagated, which they deemed extravagant and insincere, in contrast to the more austere, internal devotional life they themselves advocated. The Jansenists were determined to rid the Church of this type of corrupting influence, and they played an important part in forcing the pope to dissolve the Jesuit Order in 1773. Their program of reform sought to return Catholicism to the simplicity of the early Church. This led some of them into an investigation of Christianity's Jewish roots, and thus to a more positive evaluation of Judaism.

But despite the secular rulers' offensive against Church power in Piedmont, the Habsburg states, and some of the lesser principalities, and despite the philosemitism of a few Jansenist divines, the condition of Italy's Jews was still far from enviable, although it was perhaps not as gloomy as earlier writers like Attilio Milano and Renzo De Felice have suggested.[14] Although the status of the Jewish communities varied considerably from one state to another, everywhere the Jews were hedged about with different kinds of discriminatory legislation. Their economic opportunities were gravely limited, and they were subject to day-to-day vexations interspersed by occasional bouts of persecution. The bigoted Savoyard monarchy in Piedmont, and the governments of the Papal State and Venice were particularly restrictive. In a number of states the activities of Jewish loan banks – an important resource for many communities – were curtailed or forbidden outright, with serious effects on the economic life of those communities.[15] Everywhere there was friction between Jewish artisans and the local guilds, eager to limit possible competition. At Rome, Turin, and elsewhere a trickle of conversions was abetted by the local *Case dei Catecumeni* (Houses of Converts), and by the blandishments of the clergy.[16] The forced or surreptitious baptism of Jewish children provoked periodic protests from their communities.[17] The process of ghettoization continued: in the course of the eighteenth century the total number of ghettoes in Italy rose from twenty-nine to forty-one, the last being established at Correggio in 1779.[18] But at the same time the absolutist rulers and republican oligarchies of Old Regime Italy were generally successful in suppressing any outbreaks of popular hostility against their Jewish subjects. Pogroms and anti-Semitic riots were largely a thing of the past – not so much because these rulers were moved by an enlightened spirit of toleration, but from their firm desire to suppress any challenge to their authority and to maintain public order against any forces that might threaten it.

Yet change was in the air. Only two years after the last ghetto of the Old

Regime was established at Correggio, the Emperor Joseph II would sign the Toleration Edicts extending the rights of the Jews of Mantua, Trieste, and the lesser communities he ruled in Italy, and in 1785 he would abolish the ghetto at Trieste.[19] His reforms, and those of his brother Peter Leopold, Grand Duke of Tuscany, mark the high point of the Enlightenment attack on clerical power. Both were strongly influenced by the Jansenist vision of a simpler, more personal piety, purged of baroque emotionalism, and of a clergy devoted to the service of the state rather than the pope. But these successes helped stimulate a revival of traditional anti-Semitism. In 1772 the Venetian government negotiated a new *condotta* that imposed harsher conditions on its Jewish subjects. In 1775 Pius VI issued a sweeping edict reimposing the restrictions on the Jews in the Papal State that his predecessor, Clement XIV, had relaxed.[20] In the same year Francesco Rovira Bonet – director of the *Casa dei Catecumeni* at Rome – published a *Life* of the boy-saint Simon, supposedly the victim of ritual murder by Jews in 1475 at Trento. Twenty years later, during the revolutionary period, Bonet would go on to publish *L'armatura dei forti*, in which he collectively indicted Freemasons, *philosophes*, Jansenists, and Jews as enemies of the Church. His literary trajectory demonstrates how the Catholic reaction against the Enlightenment led seamlessly into the anti-Jacobin and anti-Semitic reaction of the 1790s.[21]

The religious innovations decreed from above by reforming rulers and their clerical supporters also stirred popular opposition, paving the way for the 'throne and altar' uprisings of the revolutionary period. In Tuscany, the efforts of the Jansenist bishop Scipione de'Ricci (explicitly supported by Grand Duke Peter Leopold) to limit processions, feast days, and the cult of the Sacred Heart in 1786 provoked riots, for the lower classes remained deeply attached to these hallowed devotional practices. In the same way, Joseph II's Jansenist-inspired reforms in Lombardy aroused an undercurrent of opposition. The attack on traditional forms of piety by reforming clergy and enlightened rulers began to create a feeling that Christianity itself was threatened, and would help fuel the violent popular movements a decade later directed against all those who were seen as the foes of traditional religion: free-thinkers, Jansenists, Jacobins, and its most ancient enemies, the Jews.

Revolution and Counter-Revolution

Bonaparte's invasion overthrew the old structures of Church and State, and set out to create a new order in their place, based on the ideals of the

Enlightenment and the Declaration of the Rights of Man. As his victorious troops advanced across northern Italy in 1796 they proclaimed the revolutionary creed of freedom, equality, and religious toleration. In June the Jews of Lombardy were freed, followed by those of Ferrara and Bologna in the northern Papal State, then those of Modena and Piacenza. (The Jewish communities in Piedmont would not be liberated until the French occupied the region in 1798.) In February 1797 it was the turn of the Jews of Mantua, then of Ancona, then of the Venetian Terraferma, and finally of Venice itself in mid-May. There the gates of the ghetto were ceremoniously destroyed and a liberty tree planted.[22] Trieste was briefly occupied by the French, but without eliciting enthusiasm from its Jewish community, content with the privileges it enjoyed under Habsburg rule. The 'first emancipation' thus developed as a piecemeal process, contingent on the success of the French army, and only extending into the areas that the French conquered in the Po valley and the northern Papal State. And the new freedoms proclaimed by the French armies immediately provoked a backlash of popular hostility: the 'godless' Italian Jacobins and their 'godless' French allies were feared and distrusted, along with the 'godless' Jews they were liberating.

The behaviour of the French invaders lent credence to this belief. They desecrated churches, confiscated sacramental vessels, and sold off Church lands as *biens nationaux*. Often it was Jewish merchants who handled the sale of the church plate, since Christians would not touch it.[23] The laws of the most important French-supported republic, the Cisalpine, aroused Catholic hostility by placing Christianity on an equal footing with all other creeds. The constitution promulgated for it by Bonaparte in July 1797, modelled on the French Directorial constitution of 1795, stipulated the equality of all faiths and freedom of worship for all.[24] The foundation of the Jacobin republic at Rome in February 1798 further outraged Catholic feelings. Pope Pius VI was deposed, and then imprisoned. When General Berthier's troops and the Roman Jacobins opened the ghetto, which they renamed the *Piazza della Concordia*, the *basso popolo* responded by assaulting it.[25] In this highly charged atmosphere the French moved on to occupy much of Tuscany and then Piedmont, proclaiming the Jewish communities free and equal wherever they went. Everywhere it seemed that the Jews were among the chief beneficiaries of the French conquerors and the Jacobin regimes they installed.

A reaction now set in. The arrest of Pius VI touched off a wave of 'throne and altar' rebellions across central Italy. Peasant bands, led by priests and nobles, and encouraged by a spate of miracles associated with the Madonna, rose up to do battle against the Jacobins and the well-to-do with the rallying-cry of 'Viva Maria.'[26] The desperate economic situation, caused by a series of bad harvests further exacerbated by the disruption brought on by the war, did much to stoke these insurgencies. In Tuscany, the epicentre of the revolts, grain prices rose by 271 per cent between 1791 and 1801.[27] The peasants attributed the high prices to the economic reforms enacted by Grand Duke Peter Leopold over the preceding decades, which had abolished price controls and traditional provisioning mechanisms in order to create a free market in grain, according to physiocratic principles. The insurgency thus formed part of a generalized reaction against every aspect of Enlightenment reform: the rural masses were rejecting the brave new world of rational piety and laissez-faire economics imagined for them by Peter Leopold and his Jansenist and physiocrat advisers.[28] This wave of revolts would climax the following year in a massive *jacquerie* that destroyed the fragile Jacobin republics and led to atrocities against a number of Jewish communities.

It is important to note, however, that although the Jews of central Italy became a target of the 'Viva Maria' insurgency, they were neither its sole nor its primary objective. The revolt was fundamentally a *jacquerie* directed against the better-off, triggered by famine and by the breakdown of social and political authority that followed the French invasions. Thus in Liguria, where there were few, if any Jews, the 'Viva Maria' rebels attacked the local landowners and their representatives.[29] Similarly, the targets of the peasant Sanfedisti in southern Italy – where there were no Jews – were the local bourgeoisie and the Jacobins, who came from that social class. To the rebels everywhere, in the Kingdom of Naples or Tuscany or Piedmont, the predominantly middle-class Jacobins were identified with the rural bourgeoisie that oppressed and exploited them. And insofar as the Jews were stereotyped as wealthy (most of course were not), and traditionally seen as usurers battening on the Christian population, they too became the objects of this economic resentment. In this sense it could be said that, in those places where Jewish communities existed, the insurgencies were also driven by a recrudescence of deeply rooted anti-Jewish feelings. After being held in check for a century and more by the governments of the Old Regime states, this traditional popular hostility now erupted with renewed vigour. The explicitly Christian appellations and battle-cries that the rebels adopted indicate the extent to which they were motivated by traditional religious animosities, among which anti-Semitism of course bulked large.

Events reached a climax in the early months of 1799. In the autumn of

1798, as counter-revolutionary insurrections spread through central Italy, a second coalition formed against revolutionary France, sparked by the news of Bonaparte's defeat in Egypt. It consisted of Britain, Austria, Russia, and the Bourbon Kingdom of Naples. In November 1798 a Neapolitan army captured Rome, overthrew the Jacobin republic, reimposed the old restrictions on the Jews, and walled the ghetto up again.[30] The French quickly counterattacked, expelled the Neapolitan army from Rome, restored the republic, and reopened the ghetto. Having secured Rome, in January 1799 the French marched south to conquer Naples and expel its Bourbon rulers. With French military backing, the Neapolitan Jacobins established yet another republic, the Parthenopean, destined to have a short and tragic life. Within a month Cardinal Ruffo's counter-revolutionary peasant army of the Sanfedisti had formed in Calabria and was on the march northwards, attacking all those it deemed to be Jacobins along its route. The French soon withdrew from Naples, and in June the Sanfedisti took the city and extinguished the Parthenopean Republic. The collapse of French power in the south encouraged the 'Viva Maria' insurgency in central and northern Italy; in both regions the clergy and nobles mobilized the peasantry in defence of the traditional order. Meanwhile an Austro-Russian army was advancing into Lombardy. It defeated the French at Cassano d'Adda on 27 April, overthrew the Cisalpine Republic, and went on to occupy Piedmont in May. This threat to their rear forced the French troops in central Italy to retreat northwards, harassed by the 'Viva Maria' bands, leaving the local Jacobins and Jews unprotected. The insurgency in central Italy now entered its most violent phase.

On 6 May a supposed apparition of the Madonna touched off a revolt at Arezzo.[31] The rebels imprisoned the local Jacobins and a number of Jews along with them.[32] Here, as elsewhere, the local notables and clergy took the lead in stirring up the revolt.[33] From Arezzo the 'Viva Maria' bands marched out to capture the nearby towns, some of which harboured small Jewish communities, as at Monte San Savino and Montepulciano. Encouraged by the insurgents' success, revolts sprang up again in the Papal State: they followed the now-familiar pattern of attacks on local Jacobins and on Jewish communities, where these were to be found. On June 18 the rebels massacred thirteen Jews at Senigallia. But their attacks were not always successful: at Pitigliano the citizens fought off the rebels and protected their Jewish neighbours.[34] Likewise in Tuscany the violence was partially contained. At Livorno the authorities bought off the rebels with a hefty contribution levied from the Jews.[35] At

Florence, Archbishop Antonio Martini intervened in person to halt the rebels' assault on the ghetto.[36]

But at Siena the Jews were subjected to the full violence of the insurgency. The 'Viva Maria' rebels from Arezzo entered the city on 28 June. Some townspeople joined them in a rampage of plundering and in attacking the Jews, whom they branded as supporters of the French and the Jacobins, although in fact the Sienese Jews seem to have shown scant enthusiasm for the revolutionary cause.[37] Jewish houses were pillaged, the synagogue was desecrated, and a dozen Jews, male and female, were wounded or killed, along with a French soldier. The victims were cast, dead or still alive, onto pyres in the Campo and burned.[38]

The massacres at Senigallia and Siena marked the hideous climax of the 'Viva Maria' insurrections. In July the first Austrian troops arrived in Tuscany and the Papal State, and began slowly to re-establish order.[39] And with the Austrian army came the restoration of the Old Regime. The 'first emancipation' was over. Or perhaps not. In June 1800 Bonaparte defeated the Austrians at Marengo and reasserted French hegemony over the north and centre of the peninsula. The emancipation of Italy's Jews resumed, this time less fleetingly, until the collapse of the Napoleonic regime in 1814.

Experiencing the 'First Emancipation'

In a leap of historical imagination, I should like to pose what I consider a crucial question: how did Italy's Jews react to these tumultuous events? What did it feel like to experience this chaotic, piecemeal emancipation? One reaction must have assuredly been disorientation and shock. Consider, for instance, the Jews of Rome, buffeted hither and thither by revolution and counter-revolution, invasion and counter-invasion. In February 1798, after the Jacobin Republic was established, the French dismantled the Roman ghetto, planted the customary liberty tree, gave the Jews tricolour cockades to wear in exchange for their yellow badges, and told them to enrol in the National Guard. Seven months later, in October, the Neapolitan army took Rome and closed them back into the ghetto. But after an interval of just over a month the French returned, declared the Jews free and equal, and opened the ghetto once more. Six months later, however, in the spring of 1799, the French garrison was forced out of Rome by the armies of the coalition, and the Jews were consigned to the ghetto for a third time.

Then from an existential standpoint, what did it actually mean for

Italy's Jews to be told that they were 'free,' that they were 'citizens,' with equal rights? I am reminded, mutatis mutandis, of the reaction of Booker T. Washington's family when told by a Union officer at the end of the American Civil War that they were no longer slaves: a tumultuous mixture of elation, bewilderment, and foreboding.[40] We should perhaps not push this parallel too far: the disabilities imposed on Italy's Jews, dire though they may have been, were in no way equivalent to the total bondage of slavery. But I would hypothesize that the Jews' reaction may well have been a similar mixture of joy and foreboding. The promise of freedom and equality opened up for them by the Triennio Giacobino was an obvious blessing, but it entailed heavy new responsibilities and came at a considerable price: the dissolution of the familiar structures and routines that governed everyday life, the potential subversion of religious faith, the pressure to participate in the strange new world that the revolution was creating. Without any preparation, the erstwhile inhabitants of the ghetto now had to face a bewildering new world, rich with opportunities but also bristling with dangers. How were they to preserve their culture now that they were ostensibly equal members of civil society and free to move in the wider world without restrictions? Would emancipation entail assimilation and acculturation? These were fundamental questions that the events of the Triennio Giacobino forced Italy's Jews to confront. Their history offered few answers to these questions: those answers would have to be invented.

Notes

1 Sergio Della Pergola, 'La popolazione ebraica in Italia nel contesto globale,' *Storia d'Italia: Annali. Gli ebrei*, vol. 2, ed. Corrado Vivanti (Turin 1997), 897–936. Cf. Marina Caffiero, 'Tra Chiesa e Stato. Gli ebrei italiani dall'età dei Lumi agli anni della rivoluzione,' ibid., 1089–1132; reference here is to 1094–8.
2 Jean-Pierre Filippini, 'La nazione ebrea di Livorno,' Vivanti, *Storia d'Italia*, vol. 2, 1047–66; see esp. 1052–4.
3 Lois Dubin, *The Port Jews of Habsburg Trieste: Absolutist Politics and Enlightenment Culture* (Stanford CA 1999), ch. 6.
4 Attilio Milano, *Storia degli ebrei in Italia* (Turin 1963), 288 ff. By 1755 the community's debt stood at 280,000 scudi, while the total value of Jewish property was 75,000 scudi, down from 189,000 scudi in the 1680s. Cf. Mario Rosa, 'La Santa Sede e gli ebrei nel Settecento,' Vivanti, *Storia d'Italia*, vol. 2, 1067–87.

5 Renata Segre, 'Gli ebrei,' *Storia di Torino*, vol. 5, ed. Giuseppe Ricuperati (Turin 2002), 453–73; see esp. 466–7.
6 For instance, Gabriele Fabbrici, 'Le comunità ebraiche nello Stato estense. Il caso di Reggio Emilia,' *Vita e cultura ebraica nello Stato estense. Atti del primo convegno internazionale di studi, Nonantola, 15–16–17 maggio 1992*, ed. Euride Fregni and Mauro Perani (Nonantola 1993), 286–98.
7 As argued by Renzo De Felice, 'Per una storia del problema ebraico in Italia alla fine del XVIII secolo e all'inizio del XIX. La prima emancipazione,' *Movimento Operaio* n.s. vol. 5 (1955); Franco Della Peruta, 'Gli ebrei nel Risorgimento fra interdizioni ed emancipazione,' Vivanti, *Storia d'Italia*, vol. 2, 1133–67; reference here is to 1135–7.
8 Roberto Salvadori, 'Gli ebrei in Toscana nel passaggio dal Granducato al Regno d'Etruria,' *La Toscana e la rivoluzione francese*, ed. Ivan Tognarini (Naples 1994) 475–98; reference here is to 476–8.
9 Milano, *Storia degli ebrei*, 345.
10 Caffiero, 'Tra Chiesa e Stato,' 1129; Della Peruta, 'Gli ebrei nel Risorgimento,' 1137.
11 Roberto Salvadori, *Breve storia degli ebrei toscani. IX-XX secolo* (Florence 1995), 90–1; idem, 'Gli ebrei in Toscana,' 484–6; Filippini, 1060.
12 See esp. his *Settecento riformatore. Da Muratori a Beccaria* (Turin 1969), and *La Chiesa e la repubblica dentro i loro limiti, 1758–1774* (Turin 1976).
13 On the failed attempt to introduce Jews to Naples, see Caffiero, 'Tra Chiesa e Stato,' 1099–1100; Venturi, *Settecento riformatore*, 75–7. Rosa, 'La Santa Sede,' 1074–5 notes that Benedict XIV in 1747 authorized the 'offering' of Jewish children for baptism under certain circumstances.
14 Rosa, 'La Santa Sede,' 1086; Caffiero, 'Tra Chiesa e Stato,' 1092. She notes that Milano entitled the chapter of his work dealing with this period, 'L'età dell'oppressione.'
15 E.g., at Rome in 1682, or in the Venetian Terraferma after 1714.
16 Luciano Allegra, *Identità in bilico. Il ghetto ebraico di Torino nel Settecento* (Turin 1996), 64, table 3, lists only 320 Jewish conversions at Turin between 1720 and 1902. The *Case dei Catecumeni* were institutions founded during the Counter-Reformation expressly to convert heretics and Jews.
17 Ibid., ch. 1.
18 Caffiero, 'Tra Chiesa e Stato,' 1092.
19 Dubin, *Port Jews*, 67–92, 139–48.
20 This 'Editto sopra gli ebrei,' inter alia, restricted the study of the Talmud, placed controls on the sale of books, and ordered the Jews to wear yellow badges.
21 Rosa, 'La Santa Sede,' 1084. The *Life* was published in 1775. In 1759 Rovira

Bonet had published three devotional tracts: *Breve, e divota notizia della vita, martirio, virtù e miracoli di alcuni santi dell'Anfiteatro Flavio, volgarmente detto il Colosseo; Metodo pratico per venerare Maria vergine addolorata;* and *Metodo pratico della via crucis.* These works were reissued in 1796.

22 The Habsburg Emperor Francis II did not restore the ghetto when Venice was ceded to Austria in October 1797.

23 E.g., at Rome: Attilio Milano, *Il ghetto di Roma. Illustrazioni storiche* (Rome 1988), 407.

24 See Art. 355 of the Cisalpine Republic's constitution of 1797, and Art. 349 of that of 1798, A. Aquarone, M. D'Addio, and G. Negri, eds., *Le costituzioni italiane* (Milan 1958), 117, 151. However the constitutions of the short-lived Cispadane and Ligurian Republics did enshrine the Catholic faith as the only legitimate public cult: ibid., 43, 170.

25 Milano, *Il ghetto di Roma*, 397.

26 Michael Broers, *The Politics of Religion in Napoleonic Italy 1801–1814: The War against God* (London 2002), 55: 'When a Madonna cried, moved, fell over or worked a miracle, French officials and the local *giacobini* reached for their guns.'

27 Figures in Furio Diaz, Luigi Mascilli Migliorini, and Carlo Mangiò, *Il Granducato di Toscana. I Lorena dalla Reggenza agli anni rivoluzionari* (Turin 1997), 435.

28 This is the basic argument of Gabriele Turi, *'Viva Maria.' La reazione alle riforme leopoldine (1790–1799)* (Florence 1969).

29 Giovanni Assereto, 'I "Viva Maria" nella Repubblica ligure,' *Studi Storici* 39:2 (1998), 449–71. The Republic of Genoa had expelled its small Jewish community in 1743, but allowed a few families to return a decade later: see Rossana Urbano and Nathan Zazzu, *The Jews in Genoa*, vol. 1 (Leiden 1999), c–cxi.

30 Milano, *Ghetto di Roma*, 407–8.

31 Turi, *'Viva Maria.'* 248 ff. gives a detailed account of the revolts in Tuscany.

32 Salvadori, 'Ebrei in Toscana,' 489.

33 Claudio Tosi, 'Il marchese Albergotti colonello delle bande aretine del 1799,' *Studi Storici* 39:2 (1998), 495–531. Salvadori, 'Gli ebrei nell'Aretino,' 73, notes the role in these events of Mgr Passeri, titular bishop of Larissa, then residing at Siena with the archbishop, and of Giuseppe Romanelli, a priest from Arezzo.

34 Salvadori, *Breve storia*, 93.

35 Ibid., 91.

36 Ibid., 94. Antonio Martini (1720–1809) was a renowned biblical scholar who produced the first Italian translation of the Vulgate between 1769 and 1781.

Appointed to the see of Florence by Pius VI in 1781, he showed little sympathy for the local Jansenist clergy and did not support Grand Duke Peter Leopold's reforms.
37 Diaz, Migliorini, and Mangiò, *Il Granducato*, 475.
38 Salvadori, 'Gli ebrei nell'Aretino,' 73–4.
39 Renato Giovagnoli, 'Il conflitto tra il Senato fiorentino e la Suprema Deputazione di Arezzo,' Tognarini, *La Toscana*, 421–47.
40 Booker T. Washington, *Up from Slavery, An Autobiography* (New York 1901), 15: 'For some minutes there was great rejoicing, and thanksgiving, and wild scenes of ecstasy ... The wild rejoicing on the part of the coloured people lasted but for a brief period, for I noticed that by the time they returned to their cabins there was a change in their feelings. The great responsibility of being free, of having charge of themselves, of having to think and plan for themselves and their children, seemed to take possession of them.'

chapter seven

Singing Modernity: Synagogue Music in Nineteenth- and Early Twentieth-Century Italy

EDWIN SEROUSSI

Liturgical music is slowly but surely emerging as a rich field of enquiry contributing, among other aspects, to a deeper understanding of the Jewish responses to modernity in Western Europe and elsewhere. The performance of prayers in the synagogue has always been a locus for the public display of communal identity, the representation of its aesthetic ideals, and the construction and exposition of its historical memory. Modernity therefore could be 'heard' in nineteenth-century synagogues in Western Europe, resonating in its musical choices the diverse Jewish stances towards the quandaries of new, unprecedented times.

The narrowing of formal Jewish identity to its religious component in nineteenth-century Germany, and eventually in other Western European countries, transformed the synagogue into an awe-inspiring sacred space where the dimension of sound became a crucial element. Bearing in mind that the music of the Jewish liturgy has always been an open system, that is, its musical dimension was potentially open to innovation (even in the most traditional synagogues), one can understand why choices of repertoire and performance practices at synagogues during the modern period can be interpreted as signifiers of Jewish mentalities in specific times and locations.

We are far from taking full advantage of the wealth of information that synagogue music has to offer to studies of modern European Jewry. Research in this area has often focused on the content of selected traditional or 'authentic' repertoires rather than on interpretations of the overall practices of Jewish liturgical music in their proper historical and social context. Put differently, the deadlock created by the essentialist concept of Jewish music, the term widely employed to refer to studies of music in Jewish culture and society, has limited the scope of the field.

Music of the Italian synagogues in the nineteenth and early twentieth centuries is one of the classic 'victims' of the failure of Jewish musicology to tackle the issue of liturgical musical practices that were, on the surface, evidently influenced by exposure to the music of the non-Jewish surroundings. Avoiding the treatment of seemingly strong acculturating tendencies, as if they were a symptom of the disintegration of 'authentic' Jewish identity, is a residual of modern Jewish nationalistic trends in Jewish musicology. This chapter proposes, in the footsteps of recent research on Italian Jewish liturgical music after 1848, new readings of the processes that led to a unique era in the history of synagogue music.[1]

On July 1797 the army of Napoleon Bonaparte entered Venice and brought down the gates of the old Venetian ghetto. The Napoleonic conquest of the Veneto was short-lived and, from the Jewish viewpoint, not positive.[2] Once the news of the return of Mantua to Austrian rule following the Treaty of Campo Formio (18 January 1798) reached Venice, the Jews led by Rabbi Abraham Jona (c. 1745–1814), the last rabbi of the Venetian ghetto, held a special synagogue service. Although there was official pressure not to display publicly the local Jews' satisfaction with the turn of events, a genuine pro-Austrian feeling was in the air during this service. In his autograph diary, Rabbi Jona describes in detail this performance, which he conducted at the synagogue on the Fourth of Shevat (21 January 1798).[3] After he recited Psalm 18 in a simple style (*pashut*), 'a choir (*kat ha-meshorerim*) sang *Halleluyah odeh ladonay be-khol levav* [Psalm 111] with a composed melody (*be-nigun ha-musika*) with the additions that were added [as required] by the event.' Then Rabbi Jona 'sang with the congregation *Hodu l'adonay kir'u bi-shemo* [1 Chronicles 8: 16; opening verses of the Sabbath and Holiday morning services] to the tune of Simhat Torah (*be-nigun kemo yom Simhat Torah*), and the entire congregation joined him in the *Hallel* [Psalms 113–118], followed by an appeal for alms-giving ... The musicians then started all over again with singing and instrumental music.' As it grew dark, all the lights of the ghetto were lit and the festivities continued outdoors. Part of the celebration included solemn prayers for the well-being of the Austrians.

This description of the musical repertoire of this festive event reveals a complex musical heritage that intertwines traditional liturgical melodies (*lehanim*), performed by the rabbi and the congregation in unison (Jona goes into detail describing the name of the melodies for each text), with original music, perhaps polyphonic, performed by a choir accompanied by unspecified musical instruments. This kind of musical setting is not a minor detail, for it discloses the rooted Venetian tradition of embellishing synagogue rituals with elaborate musical performances. Rabbi Jona was not a liberal rabbi at all. On the contrary, he was a stiff opponent of the younger and more open-minded rabbi of the city at the time, Rabbi Jacob Emanuel Cracovia, who flirted with the liberal ideals originating in Germany and represented the Italian Jewry in the Sanhedrin, which was convened by Napoleon in Paris in 1807.

The character of Venetian synagogue music that emerges from the description of this late eighteenth-century event, with its mix of old liturgical traditions and music inspired by and arranged according to the contemporary musical taste of the surrounding society, shows the complex attitude of Italian Jews to autochthonous traditions and cultural integration. This attitude had been developing since the late Renaissance as the result of ghettoization, a profound social shift that many historians of Italian Jewry, such as Robert Bonfil, Benjamin Ravid, and David Ruderman, perceive as the cause for a major restructuring of Italian Jewish identity and mentality.[4] Religious notions of space and time, the separation of the sacred from the secular, and attitudes to Jewish mysticism were reshuffled. In short, this case of Italian Jewry ghettoization was paradoxically an agent of incipient modernization.

Changes in the liturgical music of the Italian Jews during this critical period have been frequently mentioned as a clear reflection of this mental shift.[5] From the seventeenth century onwards, the Italian Jews had, as Israel Adler has argued, 'a long tradition of fruitful coexistence with the culture of their Christian neighbours which was never completely disrupted by the segregation of the Ghetto. It was normal for them to put their musical education at the service of their religious needs. Yet, no intention of "reform" lay behind this [practise]. They were certainly ready to imitate the uses of their neighbours, but such [practise] was never carried out with the conscious intention of removing traditional practises.'[6] The tension between the constituent forces behind the liturgical music of the Italian Jews, namely, traditional versus non-Jewish practices, intensified as the nineteenth century unfolded. Major catalysts of this process were the new spirit blowing in from Germany after the dawning of the Jewish Reform movement and the Jewish responses in the wake of modern Italian nationalism that culminated with the Edict of Emancipation (29 March 1848).

Expressions of modernity in the synagogue music of the Italian Jews can be considered a unique phenomenon within the many variants of European Jewish liturgical music after the emancipation. Following

Jacob Katz, we can state that 'local conditions determined everywhere not only the time of absorption [of cultural patterns from the Gentile society] but also the extent of emulation, adapting it to the needs and possibilities of the locality.'[7] For this reason, the inclusion in synagogue services of musical patterns deriving from the surrounding Italian Christian society was not perceived in Italy as a breakthrough, as it was in Central Europe, the Netherlands, France, and England, but rather as a continuation of latent tendencies that had been developing since the late Renaissance. Reform German Jews frontally challenged traditional forms of liturgical music (in extreme cases, even the revered practice of biblical cantillation) not as a result of accommodation, but rather out of a full awareness of the symbolic significance of their acts.[8] In early nineteenth-century Germany, synagogue services were adapted to the contemporary sensibilities of good taste (linguistically represented in discourses about liturgical performances by the term *decorum*), characteristic of the aspirations of the new Jewish urban bourgeoisie. The aesthetics of older liturgical music, such as highly embellished recitative improvisations, indeterminacy of form and timing, three-part extemporized vocal polyphony that awkwardly imitated contemporary instrumental music, and so forth, were declared irreconcilable with the ideals of control, predetermined timing, the perfect harmony of voices, orderly congregational participation, and the use of 'pure,' that is, instrumental, music as a means of spiritual elevation and meditation that characterized the bourgeois conception of ritual.

Against this background, it is not surprising that at the outset of the German Jewish Reform, the Italian 'model' of synagogue music, especially the use of instrumental music in the synagogue (for organ or harmonium), was for a very short period perceived as a source of inspiration for the reformers from the north. Superbly analysed by Lois Dubin in her study, the series of written exchanges regarding the use of the organ and harmonized vocal music, which took place from 1816 to 1819 between rabbis from Livorno, Verona, and Padua, and reformers from Hamburg, shows the extent of the misunderstanding between the Italian Jewish perceptions of permissible musical innovation and their German-Jewish interpretations.[9] The Italian rabbis' denunciation of the German reformers in 1819 illuminates not only the politics of the German Reform controversy, but also the Italian Jewish spiritual leaders' assessments of their own identity. As Dubin states, the Italian Jews in 1819 'were willing to be depicted as cultural progressives, not as religious radicals ... In 1819 they spoke plainly in terms of custom, continuity, and tradition ... What confused the German modernizers was that they failed to see that the Italians were speaking from a different context and a different tradition. What was customary in one locale was innovative in the other.'[10]

Returning to the formal abolition of the oldest ghetto in Italy, in Venice, we may consider it the beginning of a new era in the history of Italian Jewish culture. Although a rapid return to the more restrictive policies of the Austrians followed, the Jews of Italy were soon to experience novel challenges. The incidents of 1816–19 were, from this perspective, among the first tangible experiences that forced them to redefine their identity, reread their history, and display their positions regarding modernity. Expressing themselves within discourses of Jewish emancipation, on the one hand, and of Italian national unity, on the other, Italian Jews in the first decades of the nineteenth century had to cope with new and often uncertain political, social, and cultural circumstances. Yet, a simplified, binary analytical model based on the contrast between 'old/orthodox' and 'modern/reformed' paradigms of Italian Jewish cultural practices, including the traditions of liturgical music, is rather unhelpful. Moreover, the atomized character of the Italian Jewish community since its inception does not allow for a uniform appreciation of processes of change in synagogue music throughout the peninsula. Each community developed it own practices, in its own rhythm, of liturgical music in accordance with local constellations, that is, following the ideals, tendencies, aesthetic concerns, and economical means of the lay and religious leaders of each congregation. Patterns, which were distinct from those of Rome, Livorno, and Florence in the south, developed in the communities of Piedmont and the Veneto in the north. Add to this complex picture of Italian culture the persistence of ethnic variants of Jewish identity (Italian, Sephardi, Ashkenazi), as well as the gaps between Jews of different social classes.[11]

Yet, the 'successful' amalgamation of tradition and innovation in Italian Jewish liturgical music of the pre-modern period, much admired by the German Reform (as well as by historians of Jewish music), should not be automatically perceived as a direct forerunner to new practices of synagogue music in nineteenth-century Italy, especially after 1848. By introducing new musical styles borrowed from the secular (meaning, in this context, mainly operatic) and even religious strands of Gentile culture, Italian Jews in the second half of the nineteenth century employed liturgical music to articulate their ambivalent and shifting attitudes towards modernization. Colliding tendencies latent among Italian Jews, such as assimilation and acculturation, on the one hand, and a return to their roots in the face of the disintegration of their identity, on the other, are well represented in the various approaches to liturgical music that developed between roughly 1840 and the First World War.

Manifestations of these predicaments in the field of liturgical music are substantially documented in the large collections of musical scores from diverse Italian communities that for the most part have remained untouched in archives until the present. Additional and indispensable literary sources documenting these processes are found in the modern Italian Jewish journals that first appeared in the mid-nineteenth century, as a further symptom of the new period.[12] These journals recorded, sometimes in vivid detail, liturgical musical events of significance, such as lavish performances, the premières of new works, the hiring of musicians by the synagogues, the installation of organs, and so forth. *L'educatore israelita*, which appeared in Vercelli (1853–74) and later became *Il vessillo israelitico* (1874–1922), is one of the best examples.

By studying the rich and still largely under-researched body of music from Italian synagogues of the nineteenth and early twentieth centuries, one can get a more refined sense of the complex social and cultural processes underlying Italian Jewry during this thrilling period of its history.[13] While the efforts dedicated to the study of the relatively meagre corpus of synagogue music from Italy prior to the emancipation are remarkable, the nineteenth century has, until very recently, remained an unexplored space. As Massimo Torrefranca states,

> after the emancipation and the unification of Italy ... new chants were added to the synagogue services. This is a chapter [of the history of Italian synagogue music] about which no one has yet written. The fruit of the patient work of choir masters who were very often dilettantes, but always conscientious, sometimes even non-Jewish, the pieces of this repertoire are today almost absolutely forgotten, kept in the archives of the [Jewish] communities and recorded in manuscripts that are not always in good condition. These are harmonizations of traditional melodies, mostly for four voices usually arranged in a homophonic setting and with an accompaniment of chords, that for the most part reveal a tendency to deliver the melodic and basic motifs in a tonal manner.[14]

Torrefranca's assessment is only partially correct, for what emerges from the archives of the Jewish communities that he mentions is a wealth of mostly original musical compositions, together with arrangements of traditional melodies, set for a variety of vocal ensembles with or without instrumental accompaniment (usually for organ or harmonium). The Department of Music of the Jewish National and University Library in Jerusalem houses substantial collections of music manuscripts from the nineteenth-century (originals or copies) from the communities of Asti, Alessandria, Vercelli, Casale Monferrato, Turin, Rome, Florence, Venice, Livorno, and others. Most of these collections were brought in by the founder of the Jewish Music Research Centre at the Hebrew University, Professor Israel Adler, as part of an enterprise to save the musical memory of European Jewish communities after the Holocaust.

The stream of discoveries in this field has not ceased. Recently Marco Iona uncovered the musical archive of the Ashkenazi synagogue of Padua, containing music performed there around the mid-nineteenth century, when the renowned scholar Rabbi Samuel David Luzzatto (Shadal) was active in that community.[15] These materials were found lying unnoticed in the cabinets of the Jewish community of Padua. The collection includes materials (scores and parts) from the community of Rovigo, which ceased to exist after the Second World War. The scores bear the names of the composers and the performers of the premières. The materials were found in poor condition and in disarray, perhaps because they were hastily removed during the fire of the *Sinagoga tedesca* of Padua in 1943.

What this wealth of music manuscripts and journalistic accounts on liturgical practises in Italian synagogues tells us is the story of a society in an intense period of fermentation. Diverse, sometimes opposing forces were at play in defining new variants of Jewish identity that were modern, responsive to Italian national feelings while also remaining, in certain aspects, committed to the venerable (and sometimes imagined) practices of the premodern period.

To understand the changes in liturgical music in modern Italy in their proper context, we must differentiate between the early attempts, occurring roughly from the fall of the ghetto walls after the Napoleonic invasions up to the early 1840s, and from that period up to the Second World War. In the 1840s a new generation of Italian rabbis, mainly trained in the new rabbinical seminary of Padua, which opened in 1829, faced the challenge of reconciling traditional Judaism with the 'spirit of the time,' by applying scientific enquiry in a more vigorous manner than their predecessors. The Jews' growing participation in the Italian national project also contributed to the generation's new attitudes. As early as 1832, the liberal lawyer Giuseppe Consolo from Verona proposed the introduction of new liturgical music into the synagogue of his city in order to express these new 'sentiments.'[16]

Moreover, notices arriving from the Reform movement's councils held in Germany in the mid-1840s (especially the Frankfurt meeting of 1845) led to a new round of arguments regarding the reform of Jewish ritual in Italy, including the role of music. The variety of the responses shows a growing fragmentation, if not disorientation and even disarray, among rabbis and lay leaders, in their attitudes towards the reforms. In general, their approach was to address the external, aesthetic shortcomings of the traditional rituals rather than their substance, such as the theological content or even the canonical selections of the liturgical texts. For example, the exclusion of liturgical references to the coming of the Messiah, a hallmark of the new Reform liturgy, was rejected because of fierce opposition from the rabbis of Livorno and Florence.[17]

Musical innovations also had a parallel in the spatial and visual realms of ritual. In these realms, too, the concern was with form rather than with content. For example, a new style of synagogue architecture surfaced in nineteenth-century Italy, in many cases drawing from Moorish themes. In these new buildings, the *bimah* and the *aron ha-kodesh* were unified, creating a sort of altar, as found in churches. In the new synagogues, a space was provided for the choir and the organ. Rabbis and cantors started to dress in solemn garments and hats.

The new synagogue music of mid-nineteenth-century Italy that emerges from the archives is marked by the commission of original compositions, a sharp increase in the role of choral music, the creation of new rituals to commemorate national and other local events, changes in the functions of the performers of the liturgy, and the intervention of lay authorities in the content and the maintenance of the new musical apparatus.

The community members' participation in the synagogue rituals was an issue frequently debated in the context of liturgical musical reforms. This most tangible behavioural pattern, attesting to the decreasing adherence to tradition, was not solved by the attempts to shorten or to beautify the services. Beautifying the services with choral music, professional musicians, and new compositions did not always remedy the chronic decrease in attendance, for the modernized services were not always shorter than traditional ones. The increased use of the vernacular language in the services (a feature found in premodern Italian synagogues, too) was not enough to entice participation either. Moreover, the quandary of maintaining the ritual cycle of the traditional premodern society, unchanged at all costs, while at the same time adapting it to the necessities of the modern civil society (e.g., opening businesses on the Sabbath) led the lay leadership (e.g., the upper classes) to pay poorer members of the community to fulfil religious duties on their behalf. In Venice the Jewish community in the mid-nineteenth century even paid to maintain some semblance of activity through the venerable religious confraternity *Shomrim la-boker*, the 'early morning watchers,' although it was clear that such a pietistic society originating in the seventeenth-century ghetto was far removed from the concerns of the modernized Jewish civil society of the time.[18]

Another illuminating issue is the changing attitudes to female voices in synagogue choirs. As it is known, listening to the voice of women in general, let alone in the ritual space, was banned by Orthodox Judaism. Higher voices in premodern Italian synagogues were sung by children. In the course of the nineteenth century, one can perceive a gradual increase in the participation of women, reaching a peak with the inclusion of female performers in the liturgy of the High Holidays in communities such as Ferrara and Senigallia.

Controversies on this topic, also related to the issue of counting women in a *minyan* (prayer quorum), reveal diverse opinions suggesting a variety of attitudes to the dilemma of maintaining tradition (banning women's voices) while succumbing to modernization (allowing female participation in choirs). An increase in the power and independence of European Jewish women, which from the start was relatively stronger in pre-modern Italy than in other Jewish centres, emerges as an additional factor in the relatively receptive attitudes of the (male) leadership to the female voice.

An interesting and unique aspect of the changes in the liturgical music practices in Italy relates to the function of the *hazzan* (the cantor).[19] Unlike the professional cantor's rise to prominence in modernized Western European synagogues – evident in the development of special training schools, the establishment of professional associations and journals, and the system of the 'star cantor' – the cantor's position in nineteenth-century Italy remained relatively subdued. When the position was appointed by the community, it was dependant (as it was in the pre-modern period) upon other assignments, such as teaching, ritual slaughtering, performing circumcisions, or serving as substitute to the rabbi. In many cases, volunteers from among the membership of the community fulfilled the role of leaders of the prayer, while, on the prestigious High Holidays, it was the prerogative of the rabbis to conduct services. Few names of distinguished Italian cantors arise from the available sources, a notable feature considering the fact that we are talking about the cradle of opera. Alberto Della Pergola (1884–1942) from Florence, who made most of his career serving at the great Sephardi synagogue in Bucharest, as well as working as an opera singer and producer in the Rumanian capital, is one notable exception.

Musical directors of synagogues emerge, on the other hand, as key figures in the setting of the new liturgical music. Jewish or not, these individuals were in charge of training and conducting the choir, preparing the repertoire (for the choir and soloists) by collecting pieces from extant sources, arranging traditional melodies and, if they were also composers, producing new works. The study of the background, skills, and activities of these key figures in the shaping of the *musica sacra*, a new concept that evolved along with the development of new Italian synagogue music in the late nineteenth century, is a desideratum for future research.

Another result of the incorporation of the new musical apparatus into Italian synagogues was the need to coordinate and produce these activities efficiently. For this purpose, community regulations that stipulated the support and organization of the musical aspect of the ritual, stressing the rules for the engagement of musical officials, were published.[20]

A brief glimpse into the repertoire of the synagogue of Padua mentioned above reveals many of the characteristic mechanisms in the production of this *musica sacra* for the synagogue. For example, pieces were composed long beforehand to allow the choir and the musicians to rehearse the new compositions. Music by Giuseppe Palumbo for the evening service of Passover in 1890 is dated on January of the same year, some four months before its actual performance. The Padua collection incorporates materials from the repertoires of other Italian cities (Verona, Trieste, Rome), disclosing mutual ties that existed between the Jewish communities of the peninsula. Some music from the Padua collection was shared by the two Jewish choirs of the city, one Ashkenazi and the other Sephardi, while the same pieces were also used in Rovigo. In the Paduan sources, we also find synagogue music from beyond the Alps, for example, from Vienna (by the renowned Salomon Sulzer), Paris (by Samuel Naumbourg), London, and Berlin. Some pieces are copies from printed scores that circulated in small numbers. Small communities could never afford to commission new works and for this reason they relied on extant resources. For the opening of the synagogue in Soragna (Stato Parmense), choral music was borrowed from the Mantuan repertoire.²¹ The use of liturgical music borrowed from other communities was a compromise between the willingness to renovate the repertoire and the financial burden this created.

Despite this outburst of creativity with respect to liturgical music in late nineteenth-century Italy, one can state with certainty that the new music, whatever its sources, style, and setting, never substituted for the traditional performance of the liturgy in its entirety. In other words, unlike other Western European locations, in Italy there are almost no cases of musical settings covering complete liturgical orders.

There were, however, full musical settings for new, invented rituals. For example, pieces in the Paduan synagogue collection were designed for special events, such as the celebration of the introduction of instrumental music into the synagogue of Rovigo on 17 November 1861 or for the celebration of the birth of the heir to the throne of Italy, Francesco Giuseppe, on 26 May 1856. The great Sephardi synagogue of Livorno marked the death of Vittorio Emanuelle II in 1878 with a solemn ceremony that included instrumental music performed by non-Jews.²² New musical pieces were even composed for special rituals of thanksgiving. A composition by Maestro Treves, for example, was performed in the synagogue of Vercelli to celebrate the end of a cholera epidemic.²³

A final point relates to the Italian Jews' changing and ambivalent attitudes to their own liturgical musical past. As the new *musica sacra* became established in Italian synagogues, the longing for 'old' traditions became a player in the arena of liturgical music. Motivated by nostalgia or by the concern of losing older modes of ethnic or local identity to a more neutral new music, this 'ethnography of the past' led to diverse consequences, ranging from the methodic compilation of traditional tunes to the modern choral settings of old items.

The apparently clashing tendencies of modernization versus allegiance to the past can be detected in the rich documentation related to one of the most 'musical' nineteenth-century Italian synagogues, the Sephardi synagogue in Livorno.²⁴ The legacy of liturgical music of this major Jewish centre – conserved mostly in the Birnbaum Collection of Jewish Music at the Hebrew Union College in Cincinnati and at the Jacob Michael Collection of the Department of Music at the Jewish National and University Library in Jerusalem – testifies to the creation of new choral music for specific sections of various liturgical occasions, especially for the processions of the Torah scrolls during special Sabbaths and festivals. This choral musical tradition, sometimes accompanied by instruments, goes back at least as far as the late eighteenth century. For this reason, the Livornese rabbis were, as we have seen, one of the main targets recruited by reformers from Berlin and Hamburg to support their liberal agenda.[25]

The new choral music by synagogue composers such as Michele Bolaffi (1768–1842) and David Garzia (Bolaffi's contemporary) and new pieces from the synagogue repertoires of other Italian cities (such as Venice) and of Paris coexisted in Livorno with traditional repertoires. The traditional repertoires were chanted by a traditional cantor in styles that originated from the ancient Spanish-Portuguese tradition common to the synagogues of Amsterdam, London, and Hamburg, as well as from the traditions of Morocco, Tunisia, and Salonika.[26]

Yet, at the height of the original musical creativity at the synagogue of Livorno in the last quarter of the nineteenth century, one of the most ambitious projects of Jewish musical archeology in Italy was launched precisely there. The *Libro di canti d'Israele. Antichi canti del rito degli ebrei Spagnoli* (Florence 1892), a printed collection of the oral traditions from Livorno compiled by Federico Consolo, was carried out in the same city where the modern choral repertoire served as an inspiration for the partisans of synagogue musical innovations within and outside of Italy.

The 'triumph' of modern music over the venerable traditions of Livorno was vividly lamented, in retrospect, by Ernesto Ventura in one of his letters to Abraham Z. Idelsohn: 'Rabbi [Elia] Benamozegh [Chief Rabbi of Livorno] was right and ... I myself am guilty [of substituting traditional music with new music]. In fact, one could compose magnificent pieces by harmonizing and, in a certain manner, developing the traditional melodies and modes of our tradition. It is necessary, however, to have in mind that *today* the mentality is different and diverse and, let's face it, healthier than that of old times. In the synagogues of Bolaffi, the so-called intellectuals ... had little appreciation for the traditional chants then in use.'[27] This statement by Ventura recalls, once again, the ambivalent postures that characterized his predecessors in the second half of the nineteenth century. While they still celebrated 'tradition' over the music proposed by the 'so-called intellectuals,' they were interested in the creation of new 'magnificent pieces,' that is, arranged according to the new aesthetic sensibilities.

On the surface, the liturgical musical innovations in Italian synagogues in the second half of the nineteenth century were cherished as a desirable and inevitable reflection of the process of modernization, the adoption of norms of civility towards the Jews, and their full integration into Gentile society. The following note from Vercelli (1856) expresses the sentiment that modernized liturgical performances were a key element in the shaping of a new Italian Jewish identity.

> The last Passover in our synagogue [*tempio* in the original, E.S.] was cherished with various sacred choral pieces with instrumental accompaniment composed by our colleague and fellow citizen *signor* Bonaiut Treves, distinguished disciple of Mercadante. The profound philosophy of the pieces, the sincerity of their musical expression, the concordance between music and the meaning of the text were judged by the learned individuals worthy of praise. The various arrangements of *Min-Amezar*, of *Odú*, and *Lechà dodi* moved us profoundly by the [musical] notes that illuminated the text so well.
>
> No less worthy of praise are the gentlemen, all volunteers, who composed the choir, some adults, others adolescents, among whom prevailed by their skill and beautiful voice *sig.* D. Daniel Levi (tenore), *sig.* Elia Levi di Daniel (baritono) and *sig.* Ezechiel Levi (basso) who performed with mastery the duets and tercets. The satisfaction experienced in these events is due in great part to the diligence and industriousness of *sig.* Samuel Levi, who for a long time has trained our choir with indefatigable zeal even before the musical school was established, creating the nucleus [of the choir], and now he continues to pour out his care [for the choir] with skill and admirable dedication.
>
> It is expected that the desire, found in every one, to contribute to the restoration of the sacred temple [i.e., the local synagogue], will bear one day the expected results, and [the new building] will match the decorum and the skill with which the choir is now organized.[28]

In his important pamphlet *L'israelitismo moderno* (Venezia 1865), the Venetian rabbi and scholar Mose Soáve restates this enthusiasm and faith that the new music will help to strengthen Judaism in Italy in the face of assimilation:

> The harmonious and serious chant and the organ have become essential in our synagogues, which at the present, with rare exceptions, can be called conversation salons or places for friendly gatherings ... When the children of habit who murmur the prayers either incomprehensibly or without devotion will see the improvements of the recitation with concentration and sincere humility of shorter prayers, and thereafter leave the synagogue, we nurture the firm hope that they will support a logical reform ... We do not wish the reform to destroy the religious sentiment, but rather to reanimate it, purify it and render it worthy of the light of contemporary progress.

Yet, this enthusiasm for the new forms of religious musical expression was not shared by all, in all places, and at all periods. The diversity of Italian Jewry, as opposed to the uniformity of German Jewry did not favour the creation of a unitary consciousness and contributed to the preservation of the particular sentiments of distinct regional groups. In other words, each community adopted its own way of musicalizing its liturgy.

The following note regarding the Simhat Torah service in Modena in the early 1850s is an example of 'reactionary' positions against the changes in liturgical music:

> The observants [*religiosi* in the original] will have the satisfaction of knowing that although here in Modena the modern innovations were not yet introduced in the synagogue of Sephardi rite, the Evening and Morning [services] of *Simchà Torà*, and in particular the seven usual *Acafod*, functioned with commendable order and through a concert of voices (as customary) for the repetition of the *Piutim* sung with the old [*antiche* in the original], mostly pleasant tunes so much appreciated even by the large audience of Catholics of every social class, age and gender who were delighted. Praising the order and observing the decorations and ornaments, they sincerely declared that they would never have imagined that they will see and feel such an experience among us.[29]

This text also shows that, while the anxiety to gain the approval of the Gentile civil society was latent, the 'price' of attaining such a goal was not necessarily the abolition of older customs.

Changes in liturgical music in late nineteenth-century Italian synagogues reflect other social processes as well. Urbanization – that is, the decay of the small scattered communities and the ingathering of the Jews in major cities – led to the obliteration of local repertoires or to their absorption into larger frameworks, as well as their being substituted with new music commissioned by multi-ethnic centres. The liturgical music of the new, sumptuous synagogues of Turin and Florence and the unification of the ethnic communities of Venice into one entity are examples of this process. Also, the professionalizing of the musical staff of the Jewish community had economic consequences. Maintaining a musical director, a cantor, and a choir (mixed or male, depending on the community's approach) placed a burden on the public funds; the maintenance of a permanent music staff and the commission of new music were quite expensive.[30]

Finally, we can point out that, in nineteenth-century Italy, embellishing the services was occasionally designed to attract the constituency and was not entirely a move to create a new liturgy. Italian Jews were living in a situation of cultural, if not social and juridical, integration even before the emancipation. Thus, while there was a rebuttal of the official forms of reform characteristic of the English, French, German, and American Jewries, by the second half of the nineteenth century, Italian Jews lived in a contradictory situation: the rabbis lived as orthodox Jews, while the vast majority of their flock experienced a non-observant form of Judaism, removed from Orthodoxy.[31] The impressive investment in the beautification of the musical aspect of the liturgical services could hardly ameliorate the problem of synagogue attendance.

The outpouring of synagogue musical creativity, the establishment of choirs and the use of instrumental music, and the hiring of Jewish and non-Jewish professional musicians in nineteenth-century Italian Jewish communities were not at all detached from the changes occurring in the major European centres of Central and Western Europe such as Vienna and Paris. Yet the Italian process was unique, just as Italian Jewry's emancipation differed from parallel processes that occurred at the same time in other European Jewish communities. Unlike the solemn and sober musical styles of the modern synagogues of England, Germany, and the Austro-Hungarian Empire, the new repertoires of Italian synagogues disclose the documented passion of Italian Jews for opera, reminiscent only of some Parisian synagogue music.

Future research endeavours can certainly throw more specific light on the local repertoires of synagogue music and the circumstances of their development, on the relationship between repertoires (processes of borrowing, adaptation, and arrangement), on the individuals involved in music making in the synagogues (performers and composers), on the aesthetic and religious ideals of these individuals and of the communities that maintained their art, and on how this music represented the identities of Italian Jews in different geographical areas.

In all these undertakings, we must bear in mind that late nineteenth-century synagogue music in Italy stems from ambivalent and contradictory tendencies that characterize the confrontation of Italian Jewry with the predicaments of modernity. The reconciliation of old liturgical traditions with the public display of modern civility, and the struggle to maintain continuity with an imagined past while heeding the aesthetic sensibilities of contemporary congregations, especially their passion for opera, are facets of this predicament. Given that music is an ambiguous medium of communication itself and yet a powerful tool for displaying identity, we can conclude that the musical choices of the Italian Jews in their synagogues are among the clearest signifiers of their quandaries in facing the challenges of modernity.

Notes

1 While this essay is based on my own incursions in the field of the liturgical music of the Italian Jews, I benefited greatly from the research carried out on this topic by my doctoral student at the Hebrew University of Jerusalem, Francesco Spagnolo. His dissertation 'The Musical Traditions of the Jews in Piedmont (Italy)' was approved in 2008. Two of his papers contributed to the refinement of the present article: 'La stampa periodica ebraica come fonte per la vita sinagogale nell'Italia dell'emancipazione,' *Materia Giudaica* 9:1–2 (2004), 281–9, and 'Sounds of Emancipation: Shaping Jewish Identity through music in 19th-Century Italy' (the latter read at the conference of the Boston Association of Jewish Studies, Dec. 2003). I am thankful to Dr Spagnolo for allowing me access to these papers and for his insightful observations on this article.

2 On the abolition of the ghetto and its consequences see Donatella Calabi, 'Gli ebrei veneziani dopo l'apertura delle porte del ghetto: Le dinamiche insediate,' *Le metamorfosi di Venezia da capitale di stato a città del Mondo*, ed. Gino Benzoni (Florence 2001), 147–71; Gadi Luzzato Voghera, 'Gli ebrei,' *Storia di Venezia: L'Ottocento e il Novecento*, a cura di Mario Isnenghi e Stuart Woolf, *L'Ottocento 1797–1918*, a cura di Stuart Woolf (Rome 2002), 619–48, esp., the detailed literature on Venetian Jews in the late eighteenth and early nineteenth century in n4); Adolfo Ottolenghi, 'Il governo democratico di Venezia e l'abolizione del ghetto,' *Rassegna mensile di Israel* 2 (1930), 88–104.

3 The diary of Rabbi Abraham Jona is found at the New York Public Library, *P 80–573. For a detailed description of this manuscript, see Abraham Berger, 'The Diary of Abraham Jona, Last Rabbi of the Venetian Ghetto, 1797–1814,' *Bulletin of the New York Public Library* 66 (1962), 623–9. The English translations from the Hebrew original are mine.

4 These arguments were expounded especially in Robert Bonfil, *Jewish Life in Renaissance Italy* (Berkeley and Los Angeles 1984). For a summary, see David B. Ruderman, 'The Cultural Significance of the Ghetto in Jewish History,' *From Ghetto to Emancipation: Historical and Contemporary Reconsiderations of the Jewish Community*, ed. David M. Myers and William V. Rowe (Scranton, PA 1997), 1–16, esp. 7–9

5 See esp. Don Harrán, 'Tradition and Innovation in Jewish Music of the Later Renaissance,' *Journal of Musicology* 7 (1989), 107–30, and by the same author,

'Dum Recordaremum Sion: Music as Practiced and Theorized by the Venetian Rabbi Leon Modena (1571–1648),' *AJS Review* 23:1 (1998), 17–62.

6 Israel Adler, *La pratique musicale savante dans quelques communautés juives en Europe aux XVIIe–XVIIIe siècles*, vol. 1 (Paris and The Hague 1966), 237–8. Adler further discusses pre-modern Italian synagogue music, in 'The Rise of Art Music in the Italian Ghetto,' *Jewish Medieval and Renaissance Studies*, ed. A. Altmann (Cambridge MA 1967), 321–65, and 'La penetration de la musique savante dans les synagogues italiennes au XVIIe siécle: le cas particulier de Venise,' *Gli ebrei a Venezia, secoli XIV–XVIII* (Milan 1987), 527–35. For the overall musical activities of Italian Jews during the same period, see also Hayyim Schirmann, 'Ha-teatron ve-ha-musika be-shkhunot ha-yehudim be-Italiya' (Theatre and Music in the Jewish Quarters in Italy), *Studies in the History of Hebrew Poetry and Drama*, vol. 2, ed. Hayyim Schirmann (Jerusalem 1979), 44–94.

7 Jacob Katz, ed., 'Introduction,' *Toward Modernity: The European Jewish Model* (New Brunswick and Oxford 1987), 3.

8 See G. Goldberg, 'Jewish Liturgical Music in the Wake of Nineteenth-Century Reform,' *Sacred Sound and Social Change: Liturgical Music in Jewish and Christian Experience*, ed. L.A. Hoffman and J.R. Walton (Notre Dame IN 1992), 59–83.

9 This issue has been treated extensively by various authors. For the most detailed and updated discussion, see Lois Dubin, 'The Rise and Fall of the Italian Jewish Model in Germany: From Haskalah to Reform, 1780–1820,' *Jewish History and Jewish Memory, Essays in Honor of Yosef Hayim Yerushalmi*, ed. Elisheva Carlebach, John M. Efrom, and David N. Myers (Hanover and London 1998), 271–95, and see the bibliography in n3 there. For texts regarding the controversy on the use of the organ, Meir Benayahu's 'Da'at hakhme Italyah 'al ha-neginah be'ugav ba-tefillah,' (Opinions of Italian Rabbis on the Playing of the Organ in Prayer), *Assufot* 1 (1987–8), 265–318, is indispensable. Also valuable are the observations of Gadi Luzzato Voghera, in 'Cenni storici per una ricostruzione del dibattito sulla riforma religiosa nell'Italia ebraica,' *Rassegna mensile di Israel* 60 (1993), 47–70.

10 Dubin, 'Italian Model,' 284.

11 See, e.g., the strong differences of class in nineteenth-century Venetian Jewry and its effects on religious practices discussed in Luzzato Voghera, 'Gli ebrei,' 638ff.

12 For critical surveys of these important periodical sources, see, Israele Zolli, 'Il giornalismo israelitico in Italia,' *Rassegna Nazionale* 12 (Nov., 1924), 115–24; A. Milano, 'Un secolo di stampa periodica in Italia,' *Rassegna mensile di Israel* 12 (1938) (*Scritti in onore di Dante Lattes*), 96–133; Bruno di Porto, 'La stampa

ebraica a Livorno,' *Nuovi Studi Livornesi* 1 (1993), 173–98; idem, 'Il giornalismo ebraico in Italia "L'educatore israelita" (1953–1874),' *Materia Giudaica* 6 (2000), 60–90; idem, 'Il giornalismo ebraico in Italia. Un primo sguardo d'insieme al "Vessillo Israelitico,"' *Materia Giudaica* 6:1 (2001), 104–9.

13 For an overall appreciation of the early reactions of Italian Jews to the emancipation and the Reform movement, see Gadi Luzzatto Voghera, *Il prezzo dell'eguaglianza. Il dibattito sull'emancipazione degli ebrei d'Italia (1781–1848)* (Milan 1998).

14 Massimo Acanfora Torrefranca, 'Sulle musiche degli ebrei in Italia,' *Storia d'Italia*, Annali 11: *Gli ebrei in Italia* a cura di Corranco Vivantini, vol. 1 (Turin 1996), 478–93; quote appears on 492–3, my translation.

15 Marco Iona, 'Musica sinagogale in Veneto nell'800.' Unpublished manuscript.

16 See, C. Crestani, 'La biblioteca della comunità Ebraica di Verona,' *La biblioteca della comunità Ebraica di Verona, Il fondo ebraico*, a cura di D. Bramanti, F. Calabrese, C. Crestani, E.S. Israel; sotto la direzione scientifica di Crescenzo Piattelli, Giuliano Tamani (Verona 1999), 17–81, esp. 56, and bibliography in n193. On Giuseppe Consolo, see Maddalena Del Bianco Cotrozzi, '"Con zelo operosissimo e con illuminata sapienza." Il contributo di Giuseppe Consolo all'Ebraismo italiano dell'Ottocento fra tradizione e modernismo,' *Rassegna mensile di Israel* 67 (2001), 215–42.

17 Luzzatto Voghera, 'Cenni storici,' 55ff.

18 Luzzatto Voghera, 'Gli ebrei,' 643.

19 See Spagnolo, 'La stampa periodica ebraica,' 285–6.

20 *Regolamento della Corporazione dei Cantori del Templo Maggiore di Verona*, in *Regolamento organico della Comunione israelitica di Verona* (Verona 1855).

21 *L'educatore israelita* 3 (1855), 340–1.

22 Letter of Ernesto Venture to Abraham Z. Idelsohn, 14 Jan. 1933. See n26 below.

23 *L'educatore israelita* 2 (1854), 395.

24 Edwin Seroussi, 'Livorno: A Crossroads in the History of Sephardic Religious Music,' *The Mediterranean and the Jews*, vol. 2, *Society, Culture and Economy in Early Modern Times*, ed. Elliott Horowitz and Moises Orfali (Ramat-Gan 2002), 131–54.

25 D. Goldschmidt, 'Il rabbinato livornese e la riforma del 1818,' *Scritti sull'ebraismo in memoria di Guido Bedarida* (Florence 1966), 77–86.

26 Important sources for the music of the synagogue in Livorno are letters sent by the choir master and cantor Ernesto Ventura to Abraham Zvi Idelsohn in the mid-1930s. The letters are part of the A.Z. Idelsohn archive at JNUL, Music Department, Mus. 7, nos. 42, 114, 623, 634.

27 From 14 Jan. 1933 letter by Ventura to Idelsohn, 1933, my translation.
28 'Notizie diverse di Vercelli,' *L'educatore israelita*, vol. 1 (May 1853), 153.
29 *L'educatore israelita* 1 (Nov. 1853), 346. Quoted also in Spagnolo, 'La stampa periodica ebraica,' 287.
30 In one of the scores of the Padua collection, there is a note by a music copyist addressed to the administration of the community in which he complains about the delay in the payments due for copying music by composers from Verona and Mantua. See Marco Iona, *Musica sinagogale*.
31 Luzzatto Voghera, 'Cenni storici,' 60ff.

chapter eight

'Their *True* Tongue':
History, Memory, Language,
and the Jews of Italy[1]

SIMON LEVIS SULLAM

> They both talked in the same way: slowly, as a rule, underlining particular
> and quite unimportant words, the real meaning and weight of which they
> alone seemed to know, and slurring oddly over others, which you might
> have thought much more important. This they considered their *true*
> tongue: their own special, inimitable, wholly private deformation of Italian.
> Giorgio Bassani, *The Garden of the Finzi-Continis* (1962)

'It is not true that we all speak the same language. Every tribe has its own, a language that belongs to us and to us only, that makes us recognizable among everyone else and that divides us from everybody else.' Despite its 'tribal' reference, this quote by the critic Cesare Garboli, captures one of the essences of a masterpiece of twentieth-century Italian literature: Natalia Ginzburg's *Lessico famigliare* (*Family Sayings* or *The Things We Used to Say*, in the English and American translations), published by Einaudi over forty years ago.[2] The quotation also brings us straight to the core of one of the central aspects of the Italian Jewish experience between the nineteenth and the twentieth century upon which I would like to reflect here.

Lessico famigliare by Ginzburg is the story of an Italian Jewish family living in Turin in the 1920s and 1930s. It features the family of Professor Giuseppe Levi and his friends Terni, Lopez, Colombo, Coen, Olivetti, and Foa. Like that of the author herself, all are Jewish and half-Jewish families that are marked by a lively intellectual life, often a decisive anti-Fascist militancy, and a strongly assimilated Jewish identity. It is a story reconstructed through the recollection of the family sayings of this group: the passing of time, the episodes, the protagonists, and their deeds are all evoked on Ginzburg's pages through the remembrance of words, modes of speaking, word games, and recurring phrases. These are culturally marked by the reference to a Jewish belonging and to a Jewish past which has become a weak legacy but is still surviving as a distinct element of the group's life. The story of the Levi 'tribe,' as Garboli would put it, can be seen as a kind of sociological treatise on Italian Jewish assimilation in literary forms (in this way, similar to *Der Weg ins Freie* by Arthur Schnitzler in the German Jewish context, or *La Récherche du temps perdu* by Proust, in the French case). In Ginzburg's case, it is a sociological treatise on the life of a group at the centre of which lies – or, more accurately, which is in many ways still kept together by – a peculiar language.

The language of the Jews of Italy and the representation and memory of it are highly relevant aspects of the modern Italian Jewish experience, and I suggest that this language can be studied as the site of residual identification for the assimilated Jewish community. In so doing, I wish to make a contribution – especially in terms of method – to the historical interpretation and representation of the process of Jewish *assimilation*. I use this term not in the derogatory sense which has more or less prevailed in Jewish historiography, but both in its general anthropological/sociological meaning and, historically, as a dialectical process which is inherent in Jewish history throughout time.[3] Language allows the historian to study the ongoing transformation of the community: through notions of, for example, exchange, hybridity, self-fashioning, dissimulation, and memory – all of which contribute to critique and better determine the extremely problematic notion of 'identity.' It is also a site upon which we can document and historically reconstruct the elements of an Italian Jewish subculture (a term first used by David Sorkin to describe the German-Jewish experience[4]). In many cases, the role of language in this subculture has become merely an aspect of daily conversation; nonetheless, it is still one that structures and nourishes the changing identity, memory, and self-image of the Italian Jewish community.

With the publication in 1963 of *Lessico famigliare* we are near the end of the approximately century-long historical path that I will sketch through the use of different sources, such as literary representations of the Jews of Italy; scientific studies on Italian Jewish jargon; autobiographical testimonies by Jewish intellectuals and writers; and theories on the transformation of language by Jewish linguists. I will begin with the last source, and thus go back, albeit by brief references to the beginning of my historical itinerary – 1861.

The year 1861 is a central date in modern Italian history: it is the year of national unification, but also the year of the great linguist Graziadio

Isaia Ascoli's inaugural lecture of his course on *Oriental Grammar and Language* at the University of Milan. Ascoli, who can be considered the founder of modern Italian linguistics,[5] was born and raised in Friuli, a region of northeastern Italy where at least three languages were usually spoken at the time: Italian, German (because of the Austrian presence and influence), and *Friulano* (the regional dialect). Ascoli himself was nourished by a private, congenital bilingualism, Italian and Hebrew. Thus, in his opening lecture of 1861, he announced that despite belonging to the 'number of those called *unfaithful*,' he benefited in the study and teaching of linguistics from the fact he had 'in his blood since his childhood the word of Moses, David and Isaiah.'[6] The reference to Ascoli is not aimed so much at his linguistic studies devoted to the 'influence of the ghetto' on the Italian vernacular, but more at recalling one of his important linguistic theories which casts a broader light on the conception of language at the time: Ascoli's theory of the 'linguistic substratum.' By linguistic substratum, Ascoli meant the 'traces of the original language maintained by an ethnic group in adopting a more prestigious language.' This 'substratum' was the consequence of a 'linguistic change, when this takes place through a slow convergence and fusion of the two cultures represented by the languages which come into contact, and one of them finds itself in a position of subordination analogous to that which causes a dialect to dissolve into a national language.'[7]

Despite the fact that Ascoli did not refer explicitly to either Hebrew or Italian, and that he derived this theory from linguistic and ethnographic studies (in particular those by the philosopher and economist Carlo Cattaneo),[8] I think it is reasonable to suggest that this interpretation was also based on Ascoli's own bilingual experience which offered hints to, and possible confirmations of, his scientific meditation. This theory allows us to recall the relationship established in the nineteenth century between language and ethnic groups, or, to use the terms of the times, between 'language' and 'race.'[9] It was a relationship that affirmed 'racial' determinism in languages (particularly in the Jewish case). For example, according to a conception going back, among others, to Luther, connections were alleged between criminal jargon and Jewish jargon – a connection that was reaffirmed in the late nineteenth century by the Italian Jewish sociologist Cesare Lombroso.[10] Beyond the complex and thorny intertwining of linguistic, anthropological and racist theories, these conceptions were later developed also in the field of ethnolinguistics and the sociology of languages.[11]

The definition I offer of Ascoli's substratum theory was taken from an essay written exactly one century after Ascoli's inaugural lecture by the renowned historian of language, and perhaps Ascoli's major follower in the twentieth century, Benvenuto Terracini. Also of Italian Jewish origin, Terracini, faithful to his Crocean education, still wrote in the 1960s of a 'Jewish spirit' that he found in the language of Italian Jews. He provides us with a theoretical reflection on the conflicts of languages and cultures (also the title of one of his best-known volumes, where he refers to 'giudeo-piemontese,' Jewish-Piedmontese jargon, in the essay 'How a Language Dies'), as well as an autobiographical testimony showing the personal resonances of his scientific enquiry, and his sensitivity to reciprocal reflexes and interchange between the Jewish and Italian languages. I will focus particularly on this testimonial aspect, drawing it from Terracini's essay in the memorial volume of another student of Italian Jewish jargon and a poet in the Jewish-Leghornese jargon, Guido Bedarida. In this essay Terracini wrote:

> It is usually said that this jargon is something of a mixture of dialect and Hebrew words; but, if we look carefully, we notice that this is not precisely the case, and that if we were to make a distinction between dialect and Hebrew words, it would not be as easy as we could have thought. It is certainly mostly a dialect, but when I say for example '*scuola*' [*shul*], I am uncertain whether I am speaking Hebrew or Italian ... We are in the presence, in general, of words with an unmistakable sentimental value ... like '*hassid*' [sage] as I heard it as a child, full of affection, on my father's lips.[12]

Particularly during the 1950s and early 1960s, Terracini devoted various scientific articles to Italian Jewish jargon which appeared in Italy's major Jewish journal *La rassegna mensile di Israel*. Contained in these articles, apart from technicalities, were remarks that referred to the language of assimilated Italian Jews. Terracini wrote, for example, of an 'unconscious fusion' between Hebrew and the vernacular; he paused on the 'emphatic expression of a very intense emotional concentration' that was revealed by certain terms or formulas; he underlined the 'allusive' character of many expressions which referred, Terracini wrote, 'to traditional customs or festivities,' but also reflected 'very particular states of mind, circumstances and relationships which establish among the initiates ... an atmosphere of immediate understanding.'[13] Beyond the clear elements of idealization and aestheticization that we perceive today in Terracini's remarks, enlivened as they are by what he himself called his 'philological piety,' it is this 'atmosphere of immediate understanding' recorded autobiographically by Terracini that testifies to the persistence of a cohesive, residual sense of linguistic identification in assimilated Jewish contexts such as Terracini's Piedmont of the first decades of the past century. It is a linguistic identification with all its cultural, sentimental, and even psychological components and factors.

Through his articles, Benvenuto Terracini was partly accomplishing a much older project initiated around 1920 in the cultural circles of the Italian Jewish communities by, among others, Terracini himself and the economist Riccardo Bachi (the father of the Jewish demographer Roberto Bachi). It was a project aimed at rescuing linguistic testimonies, memories, and uses of Italian Jewish jargon, launched in the context of a more extensive research on the religious and traditional customs of the Jews of Italy.[14] The interest in Italian Jewish jargon, in fact, witnessed a revival in the first years of the twentieth century. This was due to two cultural developments: first, the increase in Italian regional folklore studies and, second, the cultural renaissance and rediscovery of Jewish history and tradition in Italy, which was stimulated by the Zionist movement.[15] This interest is well documented by a number of articles in the Italian Jewish press, among which, for example, are those in 1909 and 1910 by the chief rabbi of Modena Cammeo in the *Vessillo Israelitico*. It was also in 1909 that the Florentine rabbi and historian Umberto Cassuto published an article on the *parlata ebraica* ('The Jewish Way of Speaking' or 'The Hebrew Dialect') in the *Vessillo Israelitico*, in which he announced the start of a 'most complete collection of words, ways of saying, [and] proverbs used by Florentine Jews.' Cassuto defined the 'Hebrew dialect' in these terms: 'It is not different in essence from the Italian language or from the various dialects of the Italian provinces. Its major difference from Italian and the other dialects is the presence of some foreign elements, mostly Hebrew, in minor part Spanish, and most infrequently of other European origin.'[16]

The Florentine rabbi underlined the interest in this 'characteristic and almost ignored phenomenon, by which a small portion of the Italian population has linguistic proprieties of its own, which it does not share even with those parts of the population with which it lives more frequently in contact.' Despite his accusation that these dialects were in a decline close to oblivion, Cassuto noticed that 'some detached word [or isolated word: *qualche parola staccata*], some proverbs or modes of speaking could still be heard even on the lips of those who do not speak usually any longer in the Jewish way.' It is to these detached words, *parole staccate*, noticed by Cassuto that our attention now turns. I am not interested here in documenting and discussing the characteristics and diffusion of the *parlate*, the Italian Jewish jargons. Rather, it is the studies devoted to them that, beyond demonstrating the interest in these phenomena and their role in Italian Jewish collective memory, show the possible analogies between certain forms and mechanisms of the jargons and what I call the language of assimilated Italian Jewry. The survival and transformation of Hebrew lexical and semantic elements in the jargons – like the presence of isolated elements ('detached words') of biblical or liturgical Hebrew in the language of the Jews of Italy – still contribute to the ongoing formation of a linguistic community, or what we might call an Italian Jewish subculture.[17] Thanks to these linguistic peculiarities, even those who do not recognize themselves as belonging to the official and traditional Jewish community, nevertheless, may be said to belong – inadvertently – to this subculture.

The lexical and semantic elements that survive in the conversations of nineteenth- and twentieth-century assimilated Jews are primarily concerned with religion and traditions such as feasts, customs, rules, and dishes. However, they have often survived as a familial habit or remembrance, and are frequently no longer recognized as part of a religious practice. The existence of these traditional elements has become, paradoxically, in many cases, only 'linguistic,' and belongs mostly, through language, to personal and familial memories (sometime this may even entail an incomplete or uncertain understanding by the speakers of the terms themselves – and certainly of the origins of many of the terms – that they are using or simply recalling). This Jewish linguistic life does not, in any case, concern only the realm of religious or family tradition. Hebrew words or words of the local Jewish jargon may still appear with prohibitive functions, such as references to something one does not want to name precisely (e.g., illnesses, troubles, and deaths). This is also the case with taboos, that is, words 'forbidden,' 'dangerous' or 'indecent' for social and political reasons: for example, Mussolini was apparently referred to as the *rosh* (the boss) from time to time in the Fascist period. More generally, Jewish jargons in Italy – as, I suspect, in all the Jewish diaspora (and perhaps in all national diasporas) – may represent cover-languages that guarantee incomprehensibility for, and from, those who do not belong to the Jewish or the originary group.[18] Jewish signs or symbols can appear through language, for example in a conversation: this can be not only via specific references to religion or the particular uses I have just mentioned, but also through direct or indirect references, allusions, citations, and metaphors. The French critic Gérard

Genette studied, for example, Proust's use of 'indirect language' in *Récherche du temps perdu*, such as when the French novelist refers to his unnamable vices, among which was Judaism.[19] Sigmund Freud, at the beginning of the twentieth century, documented and testified to the emergence of Jewish identity through language in many pages and examples of his *Psychopathology of Everyday Life*. But I will just mention here two examples of 'direct language' concerning Jewish identity. These are examples in which language names Jews explicitly, as in the titles of two very different literary sources, neither of which belongs to the Jewish world per se.

The first example alludes to the semantic and symbolic tensions provoked by the sign /*ebreo*/ (/Jew/) and its alternative versions (with their different meanings and nuances): *giudeo* and *israelita*. In a novel by Rosetta Loy, the title of which is *La parola ebreo* (literally, the word Jew),[20] the author and protagonist recalls her discovery of the word 'Jew' as a child in a Catholic family living in Rome, during the time of Mussolini's 'racial laws.' The second example refers to the supposed contrast of the word /Jew/ with the word /*goj*/ (non-Jew), a term that defines symbolically and linguistically, from the Jewish perspective, who belongs and who does not belong to the community. This, however, is also a word that has found its way into non-Jewish Italian literature: *Un goj* (a goy) is, in fact, the title of a short story by Luigi Pirandello, in which the Sicilian writer tells the story of a converted Jew, Daniele Catellani, who, in his new ultra-Catholic family, paradoxically feels 'a *goj*, a foreigner.'[21]

We have come, then, again to literary sources.[22] Thanks to their ability to interpret and reproduce language and its specific features, they offer the best access to the historical reality I am trying to grasp, that is, the cultural and social implications of linguistic interaction.[23] After mentioning only two autobiographical accounts from Piedmont in which one can find the presence and use of jargon to evoke the atmosphere of times-gone-by,[24] we must turn to one of the capitals of Italian Jewish or, perhaps, European Jewish, literature of the twentieth century: Trieste.[25]

We will scarcely find, however, in the pages of Italo Svevo (Ettore Aron Schmitz), one of Italy's best-known novelists,[26] traces of a peculiar Jewish language on the lips of his characters. As the well-known critic, also Jewish, Giacomo Debenedetti, noted in a 1929 essay on the 'Svevo case,'[27] the novelist had, in fact, never made the protagonists of his novels Jewish, despite the Jewishness of their traits and their environment. Debenedetti suggested the existence of a kind of censorship by Svevo, which, we may notice, also worked from the linguistic aspect.[28] Schmitz had received a Jewish education within his family and at the local Jewish elementary school, and thus he could, for example, still refer to his family in his letters (despite his non-Jewish wife, and his own conversion to Catholicism) as the *mispacha* (family).[29] His use of the Hebrew word, probably indicates how the language of the fathers was still resonant for him and his most private affections.

We now turn to another name of the Triestine pantheon, the poet Umberto Saba,[30] and consider not his well-known collection of autobiographical lyrics, the *Canzoniere*, nor his posthumous novel *Ernesto*. Instead, we examine his lesser known collection of short stories and recollections: *Ricordi-Racconti, 1910–1947*, which includes a section by the title *Gli ebrei* (the Jews), which was written in Trieste in 1910–13 and published over forty years later in 1956.[31] These five stories were written, as the poet explained in his preface, 'when anti-Semitism seemed a joke; when I was able, without remorse, to yield to a benign irony, tinged with hidden affection for people and things ... I knew and saw, or ... of whom I'd heard talk during my childhood.'[32] Entitled, for example, *A Hebrew Scholar* or *Trieste's Ghetto in 1860*, the stories are mostly sketches in which Saba depicted, with quick brushwork, the Italian Jewish environment of the Friuli region or of Trieste in the second half of the nineteenth century. The narrative is continuously enlivened by the appearance of typical characters, imagined or remembered by the poet, and the linguistic fabric of the story is held together by Hebrew or Triestine Jewish or Venetian Jewish words. In the dialogue between the young Samuele Davide Luzzatto (*ShaDaL*) with his teacher and with other students, we find the epithets *haham* (sage or master), and *hamor* (dunce), the remembrance of the *Schèmagn Israel* (*Shma Ysrael*, the most important Jewish prayer) and the menace of the *reschmud* (the anti-Semitism, according to Saba) of the Slovene guards. ShaDaL spoke with his master 'half in Hebrew, half in Italian,'[33] while in the shops of the Trieste ghetto 'language, dialect, smiles changed according to the age, sex and nationality of the customer' – 'During the purchase,' Saba writes, 'mother and daughter spoke, between owners, a jargon of a sugary Triestine, intermingled with baser Hebrew words, incomprehensible to the uninitiated.'[34]

A note by Saba at the end of the story on the ghetto explains the meaning of the term '*Goi*: not *iudi*, not Jewish.' However, other notes following the stories translate the expressions mentioned, such as '*Reschmud*: anti-Semitism. The word comes from *raschagn*, which means evil,' or '*Haham*: wise, or educated (particularly in the Law).' 'A *haham*, a real *haham* said my good old religion teacher about me,' recalls Saba, 'going from one classroom to the other.' Other terms are explained as well: *Magnod* (money), *Taled* (the tallith), *Cascer* (kosher).[35] As his school memories and episodes tell us, Saba, the son of a Jewish mother and Catholic father who had converted to Judaism and whom the poet never met, had learned a peculiar Italian mixed with Triestine dialect and Hebrew or Italian Jewish words: a language that would now and then, perhaps, still resound during the poet's conversations at a cafe or in the bookshop he owned and ran in Trieste, and that Saba used to recall the world of his childhood, to trace its peculiar traits, and to draw its essential characteristics.[36]

Saba published his stories due to the insistence of another Jewish writer and friend, Carlo Levi (the well-known author of *Christ Stopped at Eboli*).[37] A few years later, another writer particularly close to Levi, and like Svevo and Saba also of Triestine Jewish origin on her father's side, came out with a novel that had language – and a partly Jewish language – at its core. And so we return to Natalia Ginzburg.[38] 'One of those phrases or words would make us recognise each other in the darkness of a cave or among a million people,' writes Ginzburg in a kind of statement of poetics of her *Family Sayings*:[39]

> These phrases are our Latin, the vocabulary of our days gone by, our Egyptian hieroglyphics or Babylonian symbols. They are the evidence of a vital nucleus which has ceased to exist, but which survives in its texts salvaged from the fury of the waters and the corrosion of time. These phrases are the foundation of our family unity, which will persist as long as we are in this world, and which is recreated and resuscitates in the most diverse places on earth.[40]

As we noted in the beginning, part of Ginzburg's 'family sayings,' part of those 'hieroglyphics,' was of Hebrew or Jewish origin or referred to the Jewish world, to certain habits, or to certain conceptions. Another of Ginzburg's pages introduces us to one of her family scenes in a Jewish bourgeois setting of 1920s or 1930s Turin:

> A stage worse than silly men were 'negri.'[41] A 'negro' for my father was one whose manners were gauche and lacking in assurance; one who dressed inappropriately, who was no good at mountaineering, and was ignorant of foreign languages. Any act or gesture of ours which he thought out of place was classified by him as a 'negrigura.' 'Don't be "negri," don't do those "negrigure,"' he shouted at us endlessly.

In these scenes there were Levi family's remarks and ways of saying about 'Aschkenazis' and 'Sephardis,' on 'good-looking' and 'ugly' Jews, on the 'half-blood' (i.e., the 'half Jewish'), and the word games that came from, and mocked, a peculiar way of dividing and classifying the world:

> My father always spoke rather favourably of the Ashkenazic Jews. Adriano on the other hand always praised people of mixed blood, who were, he said, the best people. Among these he liked best the children of a Jewish father and Protestant mother, as he was himself.
>
> In those days we had a game at home ... The game consisted of dividing the people we knew into animal, vegetable and mineral. Adriano was a mineral-vegetable and Paola an animal-vegetable. Gino was a mineral-vegetable ... My father was animal-vegetable and so was my mother.
>
> 'Nonsense!' said my father, catching a few words in the passage. 'Always that nonsense of yours.'
>
> As for the pure vegetables, imaginary pure, there were very few in the world.[42]

Sometimes, as with the last quotation, the question of the Jewish origin, or of identity in general, was evoked by indirect reference, by allusion. For example, through what we can call, using a term taken from rhetorics, a *hyperbolic synecdoche*. This happens, for example, in the episode that deals with the arrests by the Fascists in the mid-1930s of a group of anti-Fascists in Turin, many of whom were close to the Levi family. On this occasion, Fascist newspapers immediately spoke of a Jewish conspiracy against the regime, and Ginzburg's mother ran around the apartment screaming, 'It's like the Dreyfus affair! It's like the Dreyfus affair!'[43]: a hyperbolic synecdoche.[44]

Cesare Garboli has suggested a close relationship between Ginzburg's novel and another well-known fictional description of Italian Jewish assimilation during the Fascist period. It is the story of an *haute-bourgeoisie* Jewish family and its world – Giorgio Bassani's *Il giardino dei Finzi-Contini* (The Garden of the Finzi-Continis). The relationship between Ginzburg and Bassani's book has been suggested not based on the mere fact that Bassani's book preceded Ginzburg's by just one year, nor on the general affinities of the milieus described, but because of their mutual attention to language. Garboli comments that the *Finzi-Continis* may be at the origin of 'the strong relationships established *ex-silentio* by Ginzburg between her Jewish origins and the family use of a jargon understandable only to initiates.'[45] Moreover, he recalls the secret and made-up language used by Alberto and Micol, the Finzi-Contini brother and sister. Bassani writes:

> They both talked in the same way: slowly, as a rule, underlining particular and quite unimportant words, the real meaning and weight of which they alone seemed to know, and slurring oddly over others, which you might have thought much more important. This they considered their *true* tongue: their own special, inimitable, wholly private deformation of Italian. They even gave it a name: Finzi-Continian.[46]

Like Ginzburg, Bassani introduces us to family scenes[47] in which traditional ways of speaking, specific words, and modes of speaking contribute to evoke and keep alive an entire world that has disappeared – but is still linguistically productive or, at least, linguistically active.

Reviewing Ginzburg's *Family Sayings* in the pages of the Jewish journal *La Rassegna mensile di Israel*, an Italian Jewish intellectual who lived most of his life in Israel, Giorgio Romano, noted:

> We not only recognize people and facts, but the 'lexicon' (the language, *il lessico*) is well known to us in many of its expressions which are common to our families and to those of our friends; analogue to the one we know well in such way that sentimental, regional and personal memories influence our impressions and our opinion.
>
> It is a lively and human picture of the domestic life of a bourgeois family, which is, moreover, a precious document of the Italian Jewish world, assimilated and intellectual, at a turning point of Italian history.[48]

Another contemporary reader probably identified with Bassani's, and especially Ginzburg's, picture and the linguistic world they resuscitated. Later, this writer elaborated and freely recreated for himself this same world in the pages of a novel also based on personal memories. His novel, however, was not set in bourgeois Turin or Ferrara but, in its first chapter, in small Piedmontese villages between the nineteenth and the twentieth centuries.

This itinerary in the linguistic life of the Jews of Italy thus ends recalling the name of Primo Levi and the opening chapter 'Argon' of his novel *The Periodic Table*. It is a novel in which Levi evokes and revives the small and ancient world of shops, pubs, family businesses, and homes of his ancestors, and particularly their mythical and now largely forgotten language – a mixture of Italian, Hebrew, Piedmontese, and French.[49] 'Since my childhood,' wrote Levi in 1984, in a lecture devoted to the 'Itinerary of a Jewish Writer,' 'I was intrigued and moved by the pathetic survival of biblical language in family jargon and dialects.' In many other writings, Levi showed his interest in language, not only of Jewish origin, and particularly in what he called 'fossil words' (*parole fossili*).[50] This expression in itself tells us that Jewish language and the words of the Italian Jewish jargon have at this stage become overtly a 'structure of memory' more than a 'structure of life': a true *lieu de mémoire* in and of itself. We have moved, then, not only and explicitly to the 'age of memory' but, to quote Pierre Nora, into the 'age of commemoration' (*'l'ère de la commémoration'*).[51]

With the 'age of commemoration' this fast-paced literary and historical itinerary comes to an end. Personal testimonies, folklore studies, scientific theories and literary pages all indicate how, in the nineteenth and twentieth centuries, notions of persistence, exchange, mutual influence, and transformation infuse the question of language in the process of acculturation of the Jews of Italy[52] – and, we may perhaps assume, of the Jews of Europe more generally.[53] And thus the language of the Jews, *their true tongue*, deserves the attention of the historian as a central site of residual identification, transformation of religious and cultural identity, memory, and self-representation of the individual and of the community: all the tortuous dynamics of the 'dialectics of assimilation.'

Notes

1 This essay appeared in a previous version as '"La loro vera lingua." Storia e memoria linguistica degli ebrei in Italia tra Ottocento e Novecento,' *La rassegna mensile di Israel* (quoted hereafter as *RMI*) 69:1 (2003), special issue: *Saggi sull'ebraismo italiano del Novecento in onore di Luisella Mortara Ottolenghi*, a cura di Liliana Picciotto, 49–72.

2 See Cesare Garboli, 'Introduzione' to Natalia Ginzburg, *Lessico famigliare* [1963], (Turin 1999), v–xvii.

3 See Amos Funkenstein, 'The Dialectics of Assimilation,' *Jewish Social Studies* 1:2 (1995), 1–14, who considers assimilation as a dialectical process inherent to all Jewish history. In this sense, also the phenomenon of the Jewish group's linguistic assimilation is ancient and has been, so to speak, always present, since there do not exist historically 'pure' languages (or groups).

4 I applied it to the Italian case in my *Una comunità immaginata. Gli ebrei a Venezia 1900–1938* (Milan 2001), 12–17, where I referred to David Sorkin, *The Transformation of German Jewry 1780–1840* (New York and Oxford 1987). The definition of subculture I used there was based, however, on Luciano Gallino,

'Subcultura,' in *Dizionario di sociologia* (Turin 1978), 703–5, which gives also Italian Jews among its examples.
5 On Ascoli see, as a starting point, the entry by T. Bolelli in *Dizionario biografico degli italiani*, vol. 4 (Rome 1962), 380–4. See also the recent publication by Antonio Casella and Guido Lucchini, *Graziadio e Moisé Ascoli. Scienza, cultura e politica nell'Italia liberale* (Pavia 2002).
6 Cited in Benvenuto Terracini, 'Nel cinquantenario della morte di Graziadio Ascoli,' *RMI* (Jan. 1958), 11. See also, by the same author, 'L'opera e il pensiero di Graziadio Isaia Ascoli,' *RMI* (June 1930), 67–81.
7 See Benvenuto Terracini, 'Sostrato,' in *Enciclopedia Italiana* (Rome 1961), Appendix III, 1949–1960: 780–1.
8 On Ascoli's linguistic theories see Sebastiano Timpanaro, 'Carlo Cattaneo e Graziadio Ascoli,' in *Classicismo e illuminismo nell'Ottocento Italiano* (Pisa 1965), 229–357.
9 See, for the following, Sander Gilman, *Jewish Self-Hatred: Anti-Semitism and the Hidden Language of the Jews* (Baltimore and London 1986), 68–9. I owe to this study the first hint to the relevance of the question of language in Jewish assimilation, despite the fact that it is devoted to the German experience, in which Yiddish (and *Mauscheln*, i.e., German pronounced with a Yiddish accent) were phenomena of much greater cultural relevance than Italian Jewish jargons. The question of language could be studied within the European (and non-European) Jewish experience more in general, looking in particular at important figures of assimilated Jewish intellectuals, who, in different ways, made of language a relevant or even central aspect of their thought and work. In the twentieth century, e.g., Sigmund Freud (already studied by Gilman, for the indirect relationships in his theories between the role of language and the Jewish experience), or, among others, Ludwig Wittgenstein, or Jacques Derrida.
10 Reference to Lombroso (but not to his lingustic theories) is made also in ibid., 290–1. For Lombroso's linguistic theories, and particularly for his vision of jargons, not only criminal but, e.g., professional, and – what is more relevant to us – family jargons, see the pages of *L'uomo delinquente* (1878), now collected in Cesare Lombroso, *Delitto, genio, follia. Scritti scelti*, ed. Delia Frigessi, Francesco Giacanelli, and Luisa Mangoni (Turin 2000), 430–6. On the relationships between criminal and Jewish jargons, see ibid., 432, and a few hints in Lombroso, 'Gerghi nuovi,' *Archivio di Psichiatria* [no editorial notes], 125–33. Finally, on the traces in Jewish language of Jews' 'special tendency to industries and commerce,' see Lombroso, *L'antisemitismo e le scienze moderne* (Turin-Rome 1894), 88.
11 I am thinking in particular about the work of Joshua A. Fishman, among

which his edited volumes *The Rise and Fall of Ethnic Revival: Perspectives on Language and Ethnicity* (Berlin, New York, Amsterdam 1985), and, more specifically, *Readings in the Sociology of Jewish Languages* (Leiden 1985). These references show at the same time that the phenomena described here for the Jews can be recorded also among other groups, particularly minorities, e.g., among immigrant communities, in colonial contexts, and in the confrontation of different 'subcultures' within the same society.

12 See Benvenuto Terracini, 'La grande illusione,' *Scritti sull'ebraismo in memoria di Guido Bedarida* (Florence 1966), 213. On the same page Terracini uses the expression 'Jewish spirit,' which I referred to above.

13 I quote from Benvenuto Terracini, 'Residui di parlate giudeo-italiane raccolte a Pitigliano, Roma e Ferrara,' *RMI* (Jan., Feb., March 1951), 3–11, 63–72, 113–21 (quotations refer to 7–9). See also his earlier 'Due composizioni in versi giudeo-piemontesi del sec. XIX,' *RMI* (April–June 1938), special issue: *Scritti in onore di Dante Lattes*, 164–83, and the more recent 'La poesia giudeo-romanesca di Crescenzo Del Monte,' *RMI* (Dec. 1955), 499–506, and 'Le parlate giudaico-italiane negli appunti di Raffaele Giacomelli,' *RMI* (March–April 1962), special issue: *Volume speciale in memoria di Federico Luzzatto*, 260–95.

14 Riccardo Bachi presented this project in his article, 'Ricerche folkloristiche e linguistiche degli Ebrei d'Italia,' *RMI* (Oct. 1926), 362–7.

15 Previously, the ideology of emancipation and the ideals of 'regeneration' and 'self-civilization' of the Jews of Italy would cause denial of the fact that Jewish jargons different from the Italian and the various dialects had ever developed. See, e.g., Lelio Della Torre, 'In qual lingua si predicò in Italia nei tempi passati,' *Corriere Israelitico*, 1862–63, in his *Scritti sparsi*, vol. 2 (Padua 1908), 238–45 (cited by Attilio Milano, *Storia degli ebrei in Italia* [Turin 1963], 575). The rabbi Della Torre wrote: 'Italian Jews always spoke the common dialect, and they never used, as in the northern countries, a particular jargon, made of Italian and Hebrew, that they only would understand and not be understandable to anybody else. Segregation only provoked in their language a slightly different accent, that is disappearing with integration and no trace of which will soon remain. I actually wonder if anybody noticed the peculiar fact that where dialect is the most remote from the written language, the language of the Jews is closer to the written form' (ibid., 238–9). To the contrary, on the 'trilingualism' of a noted contemporary of Della Torre, see Cyril Aslanov, 'Elia Benamozegh scrittore trilingue: il fattore della lingua nelle sue opere,' *RMI* (Sept.–Dec. 1997), 29–41.

16 See *Vessillo Israelitico* (June 1909), 254–60.

17 In many ways it would certainly be more appropriate here to speak of the 'lan-

guages' and 'subcultures' of the Italian Jewish communities, because of the relevant linguistic differences among them, and of the different cultural, and even socioeconomic differences, that characterized these communities. It would suffice to just mention such diverse contexts and experiences as those of Turin (or Northern Italy more generally) and, e.g., Rome. Together with the different regional contexts, so typical of Italian geography and history, the different path to and pace of integration of these Jewish populations should be taken into account. Because I am working mainly on questions of method, I try to make here broader suggestions, hoping that they may be considered applicable (and perhaps useful) on a more general level.

18 See Maria Mayer Modena, 'Osservazioni sul tabù linguistico in giudeo-livornese,' *Scritti in memoria di Umberto Nahon. Saggi sull'ebraismo italiano* (Jerusalem 1978), 166–79, where the reference to Mussolini is also found; and by the same author, 'Le parlate giudeo-italiane,' *Storia d'Italia. Annali* 11. *Gli ebrei in Italia* II. *Dall'emancipazione a oggi*, ed. Corrado Vivanti (Turin 1997), 939–63, esp. 947, for a survey of the debate on Italian Jewish jargons and an updated bibliography on the subject.

19 See Gérard Genette, 'Proust and Indirect Language' (1969), in *Figures of Literary Discourse*, trans. by Alan Sheridan (New York 1982), 229–95, and the use I make of this approach in my own *Una comunità immaginata*, 19–21.

20 See Rosetta Loy, *La parola ebreo* (Turin 1997). See also the American translation: *First words: A Memoir*, trans. Gregory Conti (New York 2000).

21 See Luigi Pirandello, 'Un "goj"' (1922), *Novelle per un anno*, ed. Pietro Gibellini, vol. 1 (Florence 1994), 465–71; an English version entitled 'Goy' appears in Pirandello, *Horse on the Moon: Twelve Short Stories*, trans. Samuel Putnam (New York 1932), 147–57. For an interpretation of this short story and particularly of its context, see Alberto Cavaglion, 'Una feracità da Terra promessa. Siciliani ed ebrei nella cultura italiana fra Otto e Novecento,' *Ebrei e Sicilia*, ed. Nicolò Bucaria, Michele Luzzati, and Angela Tarantino (Palermo 2002), 265–70.

22 On this see, in English: H. Stuart Hughes, *Prisoners of Hope: The Silver Age of the Italian Jews, 1924–1974* (Cambridge, MA 1983) and, esp. Lynn M. Gunzberg, *Strangers at Home: Jews in the Italian Literary Imagination* (Berkeley 1992).

23 I hint here to the fact that historians may try to use fictional literature both (and in some cases at the same time) as a heuristic and epistemological tool *and* as a historical source. I will only mention here, among those who have tested and thought about these possibilities, the work of Carlo Ginzburg. Beyond his own historiography and its relations to literature, I think of his reflections on the distinctions between history and fiction (see his *History, Rhetoric and Proof* (Hanover, NH 1999), but most esp. now of his thoughts on

the challenges of fiction for the historian (which represent, in my view, a further development and self-reflective move of his own practice). See *L'aspra verità: una sfida di Stendhal agli storici*, in Carlo Ginzburg, *Il filo e le tracce: vero falso finto* (Milan 2006), 167–84, in which Ginzburg discusses the challenge represented for historians by Stendhal's use of 'free direct discourse.' I feel this discussion as analogous to the direction I am going towards by highlighting the possible suggestions offered by Genette's analysis of Proust's 'indirect language,' which I briefly mention above and return to below.

24 I will only quote two examples from the not so rich Italian Jewish autobiographical tradition of the past two centuries which show a presence of, or an interest in, Italian Jewish jargons. See Alberto Cavaglion, 'L'autobiografia ebraica in Italia fra Otto e Novecento. Memoria di sé e memoria della famiglia: osservazioni preliminari,' *Zakhor. Rivista di storia degli ebrei d'Italia*, III (1999), 171–7. They are the slim *Autobiografia di un rabbino italiano* (Palermo 1991), by the chief rabbi of Bologna, Marco Momigliano (an uncle of the noted historian of antiquity, Arnaldo), and the *Memorie di vita ebraica. Casale Monferrato-Roma-Gerusalemme, 1918–1960* (Rome 1979), by the Jewish activist and scholar Augusto Segre. Some pages of these autobiographies display the use of the jargons: in the first case with reference to rituals, festivities, aspects of religious life, but also well-wishing words or quotations (which use the typical spoken Italian Jewish pronunciation of Hebrew or the form of the jargons). In the case of Segre, the visit to his neighbourhood in the little city of Casale Monferrato is evoked also through the recollection of the use of jargons, e.g., in shops to avoid being understood by Gentiles.

25 On which one may see, e.g., for a general literary overview, Angelo Ara and Claudio Magris, *Trieste. Un'identità di frontiera* (Turin 1982), but also, Giorgio Voghera, *Gli anni della psicanalisi* (Pordenone 1980).

26 He is particularly known for his *La coscienza di Zeno* (1923). On Svevo, see as a starting point, Alberto Cavaglion, *Italo Svevo* (Milan 2000).

27 See Giacomo Debenedetti, 'Svevo e Schmitz' (1929), now collected also in Debenedetti, *Italiani del Novecento* (Florence 1995), 47–90. But on the genesis of this essay and its significance in the biography of the Piedmontese critic, particularly for his personal, ambivalent relationship with Judaism, see Alberto Cavaglion, *La filosofia del pressapoco. Weininger, sesso, carattere e la cultura del Novecento* (Naples 2001), 115–22.

28 Debenedetti was maybe thinking about this kind of self-censorship when he wrote (perhaps involountairily speaking also of himself): 'If Svevo had incarnated in his characters that certain moment of the Jewish consciousness, which has appeared to us in the final analysis as the only and most certain explanation laying behind them, their *expressions*, their *words* and their

frames of mind would have acquired another significance ... Below Svevo's clarity, hide involountary reticences, *unconfessed words*, which forbid abandon' (see Debendetti, *Svevo e Schmitz*, 89, my emphasis). Reference to this page, although in a different perspective, is made also by Stuart Hughes, *Prisoners of Hope*, 42. On Svevo's language and writing, but with particular reference to the relationships between Italian and German, see also Giorgio Voghera, 'Considerazioni eretiche sulla "scrittura" di Italo Svevo,' in Debenedetti, *Gli anni della psicanalisi*, 45–51.

29 See the entries 'Ebraismo,' I and II, and 'Dialetto,' in Cavaglion, *Italo Svevo*, 69–78, 55–9.

30 For Saba's complex relationship with Judaism see, e.g., 'Carteggio con Joachim Fleischer' in Umberto Saba, *Lettere sulla psicoanalisi*, ed. Arrigo Stara (Milan 1991), esp. 39–41. See also Giorgio Voghera, 'Gli estri di Saba,' in *Gli anni della psicanalisi*, 53–86; Alberto Cavaglion, *Saba e Weininger*, published in *Umberto Saba, Trieste e la cultura mitteleuropea*, Atti del Convegno, Rome, 29–30 March 1984, ed. Rosita Tordi (Milan 1986), 269–77; Cavaglion *La filosofia del pressapoco*, 122–6.

31 See Umberto Saba, *Ricordi-Racconti (1910–1947)* (Milan 1956), 15–85 – and the English version, *The Stories and Recollections of Umberto Saba*, ed. Estelle Gislon (Riverdale-on-Hudson NY 1993), 3–44. The section 'Gli ebrei (Trieste, 1910–1912),' opens with a testimony by Carlo Levi, 'On an Early Manuscript by Saba.' This collection – which I quote from the first edition – appears also in Umberto Saba, *Tutte le prose*, ed. Arrigo Stara (Milan 2001). In the introduction to this edition, 'L'altro Saba,' Mario Lavagetto now insists for the first time on the importance of *Ricordi-Racconti* (see ibid., xi–xlvi). I owe to Alberto Cavaglion the idea of using this text by Saba for the present investigation.

32 Saba, *Stories and Recollections*, 9.

33 Ibid., 12–19.

34 Ibid., 21–2 (I have changed the translation of the second quote).

35 Ibid., 18–19 and *passim*. I have changed some of the English translation and preserved the original Italian translitteration of the Hebrew jargon words; the note explaining the word '*goj*' does not appear in the published translation.

36 In a letter to his friend Nello Stock, dated 22 Nov. 1952, Saba wrote of his work, a few years before the publication of *Ricordi-Racconti*: 'Let me tell you that it seems to me marvelous today, to have been able to reconstruct the language etc. of those strange characters which lived in Trieste in 1823' (cited in 'Note ai testi' in Saba, *Tutte le prose*, 1248). On some literary and linguistic aspects of Judaism in Saba, see also Mario Lavagetto, *La gallina di Saba* (Turin 1989), and particularly the essay 'Nascere a Trieste nel 1883' (1972), where

Lavagetto asks 'if, and to what degree, the linguistic conservativism of the Jewish communities had an influence on Saba.' See also his final pages, 'Fra gli stessi ebrei' (1986), ibid., 239–51.
37 See Carlo Levi, 'Su un vecchio manoscritto di Umberto Saba,' in Saba, *Ricordi-Racconti*, 16, where Levi writes: 'I was able to convince Saba ... to publish a part [of these short stories], the one which carries here the title "Gli Ebrei" and which is a collection of novellas and short stories on the same topic: the lovely description of a world far away in memory, but still our own and present in our heartbeat.' But on the origins and the editorial fortunes of the work see actually 'Note ai testi' in Saba, *Tutte le prose*, 1247–51.
38 See Ginzburg's portrait of Carlo Levi at the time of his death, published in *Corriere della Sera*, 8 Jan. 1975, and now collected in Natalia Ginzburg, *Non possiamo saperlo* (Turin 2001), 19–25.
39 On this work see, beyond the above-mentioned introduction by Garboli, and with particular reference to the question of language: Anna Nozzoli, '*Lessico famigliare* e altre storie torinesi (in appendice la novella "Settembre"),' and Carlo Prosperi, 'Il linguaggio della tribù: una lettura di *Lessico famigliare* di Natalia Ginzburg,' Atti del convegno internazionale di San Salvatore Monferrato, 14–15 May 1993, published in *Natalia Ginzburg: la casa, la città, la storia*, ed. Giovanna Ioli (San Salvatore Monferrato [Cuneo] 1995), 43–58, 59–74.
40 See Natalia Ginzburg, *Family Sayings*, trans. D.M. Low (New York 1989), 24. I have slightly changed the translation: see the original Ginzburg, *Lessico famigliare*, 22.
41 The racist or xenophobic undertones of this expression, apparently of Sephardic origin, have not been sufficiently explored yet by linguists and historians of Italian Jewish languages.
42 See Ginzburg, *Family Sayings*, 82, and Ginzburg, *Lessico famigliare*, 94; other references to *minerali* and *vegetali*, ibid., 112 and 123.
43 See Ginzburg, *Family Sayings*, 87.
44 I refer with this expression again to Genette's reading of the role of language in the *Récherche du temps perdu*, concerning which, one should not overlook Ginzburg's debt towards Proust also for the rendering of linguisitic phenomena. Ginzburg was not only an avid reader but also a translator into Italian of Proust, who often appears among the favourite authors of the Levi family and of the *Lessico famigliare* in general. See Prosperi, 'Il linguaggio della tribù'; and the afterword by Ginzburg to her translation of Marcel Proust, which dates back to the years up to the Second World War: *La strada di Swann* (Turin 1990), 559–64.
45 See Garboli, 'Introduzione' in Ginzburg, *Lessico famigliare*, xi–xii and xv.
46 See Giorgio Bassani, *The Garden of the Finzi-Continis*, trans. Isabel Quigly (Har-

mondsworth, UK, and Victoria, Australia 1969), 40. I have slightly changed the translation, which has 'their *real* language' in place of 'their *true* tongue.' See also Giorgio Bassani, *Il giardino dei Finzi-Contini* (1962) (Turin 1999), 42.

47 See Bassani, *Il giardino*, 37–44, 72, 74, 99.
48 See Giorgio Romano, review of Natalia Ginzburg, *Lessico famigliare*, *RMI* (June 1963), 277–8. But the non-Jewish reception of the *Lessico* should also be studied, with particular reference to the question of language. The success of the novel (fifty-four editions up to 1998; over half a milion copies sold) shows that many readers and their families, of the most diverse origins, identified with the Levi family, their friends, their 'family sayings' (on the standing of the *Lessico*, see Domenico Scarpa, 'Cronistoria di *Lessico famigliare*,' in Ginzburg, *Lessico famigliare*, 215–61). This is certainly due to the fact that all families (Jewish and not-Jewish) have 'family sayings' – Ginzburg's sayings, however, are in good part, if not mostly, Jewish or, better, Italian Jewish sayings.
49 See Primo Levi, *Il sistema periodico* (1975), in *Opere*, vol. 1, ed. Marco Belpoliti (Turin 1997), 741–6, and the English version, *The Periodic Table*, trans. Raymond Rosenthal (New York 1984), 3–20. On the origins and composition of the novel, see now the 'Note ai testi' of Levi's collected writings: *Opere*, vol. 1. See also Einaudi's school edition of the *Sistema*, with footnotes by the same Levi and an introduction by Ginzburg, and her review of the novel in *Corriere della sera*, 25 May 1975, now collected in *Primo Levi*, ed. Marco Belpoliti, special issue of *Riga*, 13 (Milan 1997), 125–7. On 'Argon' and its context, see also the already mentioned Cavaglion, 'Argon e la cultura ebraica piemontese' (which contains also the first version of the chapter). Cavaglion also alluded to a possible relationship among the 'Jewish pages' of Saba, Ginzburg and Levi: see Cavaglion, *La filosofia del pressapoco*, 126–7; and on the same line, Scarpa, 'Cronistoria di *Lessico famigliare*,' 247–50. It may actually be that, e.g., in Levi's 'curiosity' and 'tenderness' as a 'Jewish writer,' for the 'pathetic survival of the Biblical tongue in the family and vernacular language,' one may also find a far echo of Saba's above mentioned 'irony,' and 'hidden tenderness' towards his own *Ebrei*.
50 See, now in Primo Levi, *Opere*, vol. 2, the articles from Levi's collection of 1985, *L'altrui mestiere*: 'La miglior merce,' 'Il fondaco del nonno,' in English, respectively, 'The Best Goods' and 'Grandfather's Store,' in Levi, *Other People's Trades*, trans. Raymond Rosenthal (New York 1989) and, in particular, 'Le parole fossili,' which does not appear in the English translation of this collection, possibly for the difficulty in translating most of its language and jargon. See also Levi's prefaces to *Gli ebrei a Torino* and to *Gli ebrei dell'Europa orientale*, and his 'Itinerario di uno scrittore ebreo' (1984), from which I quoted (ibid.,

1214). On Levi's lingustic interests, see in particular Stefano Bartezzaghi, 'Cosmichimiche,' *Primo Levi*, ed. Belpoliti, 267–314.

51 See Pierre Nora, 'L'ère de la commémoration' in *Les lieux de mémoire*, III. *Les France*, vol. 3, *De l'archive à l'emblème* (Paris 1992), 977–1012.

52 On the role of language in the life and 'cultural memory' of groups, on the lines of Maurice Halwachs' sociology of memory, but referring also to aspects of Wittgenstein's thought on language, see also Jan Assmann, *La memoria culturale. Scrittura, ricordo e identità nelle grandi civiltà antiche* (Turin 1997; orig. ed. Munich 1992), esp. 107–9. Assmann sees the 'word' as 'the principal organ for the constitution of a group,' and 'language' as the means through which the 'cultural meaning' of a group is codified and articulated in a common knowledge and memory, i.e., its 'symbolic universe' or 'vision of the world' ('shared values, experiences, expectations, interpretations').

53 Beyond Sander Gilman's work on the German case, among the most recent remarks on the European dimension and relevance of this experience are those made (also through references to literary sources, and even personal recollections) by Eric Hobsbawm, 'Benefits of Diaspora,' *London Review of Books* 27:20 (20 Oct. 2005). See also Yuri Slezkine, *The Jewish Century* (Princeton NJ 2004), in reference to which I would like to emphasize (as also Slezkine does for many aspects of the modern Jewish experience) that the centrality of linguistic processes and their relationships to 'identity' are true for all 'identities' (individual and collective), although they are possibly more visible in the experience of minorities, and they perhaps create particularly evident tensions in the Jewish case.

chapter nine

Growing Up Jewish in Ferrara: The Fiction of Giorgio Bassani

GUIDO FINK

This essay, first and foremost, concerns the transition from historiography to such fields as literary arts, that is, from reconstructions of the 'real' world to the reconstruction of artistic or personal interpretations of particular events connected with that world. Such a transition – which is easier today thanks to the stimulating interchanges between culture and society, or works of art and other non-artistic texts, carried out by recent critical trends such as the new historicism in America – proves almost automatic in the case I will discuss. Giorgio Bassani's Ferrara may be, as an American critic has called it, a 'semiotic labyrinth,' but it is no doubt a faithful representation of this city, its history and topography. The success of his works, especially *Giardino dei Finzi Contini* (The Garden of the Finzi-Continis), a novel that remained for years at the top of the bestseller list and was adapted into an Oscar-winning movie directed by Vittorio De Sica – although Bassani was never happy with it – did succeed in putting Ferrara on the map. Thousands of international tourists eagerly flocked to Ferrara to view the city's medieval walls, the ghetto district, and the seventeenth-century Jewish cemetery, but often expressed regret at not finding the luscious garden of the title that Bassani had mentally transported there from Rome (it was based, unbeknownst to the hapless tourists, on the garden of the Palazzo Torlonia).

Even if Ferrara was still an anonymous *città di provincia*, a provincial town, the first collection of stories that Bassani published in 1940 under an assumed Catholic surname has been justly defined by André Sempoux as 'a monument of urban psychosociology,' where streets, houses, restaurants, clubs, theatres, and so on, are just named or quoted, never *described*, as a non-citizen would have to do.[1] This holds, no doubt, for the Ferrara in which he lived, after his birth in nearby Bologna, from childhood to the 1940s. Following his arrest and detention by the Fascist police, Bassani moved to Naples and later to Rome after the temporary fall of Fascism in July 1943. Rome became his favourite city, although he often returned to Ferrara to visit his mother and the family home. But even the older Ferrara, the Ferrara of a distant past, which he obviously had not seen, was easily reconstructed and revisited, as in the opening lines of such Ferrarese stories as *La passeggiata prima di cena* (A Walk before Dinner) or *Gli occhiali d' oro* (The Gold-Rimmed Spectacles). All the narrator needs is an old picture postcard, which soon comes alive and teeming with real people, or a verbal flashback that reminds us of the two or three thousand indifferent screenplays Bassani wrote or contributed to and that he always claimed were just business to him: 'Time has begun to thin their ranks, but still you cannot say they are few, the people in Ferrara who remember Doctor Fadigati ... It was in 1919, just after the other war. Because of my age, I myself can give only a rather vague, confused picture of the period. The cafés swarmed with officers still in uniform ... trucks went by constantly with flags flapping; on the scaffolding that covered the façade of the Insurance building then under construction an enormous scarlet banner ... invited friends and enemies of socialism to drink in harmony the Lenin aperitif.'[2]

Athos Fadigati, the ear, nose, and throat specialist who is the protagonist of *Gli occhiali d' oro* (not so short a story, its length being that of the classic Jamesian novella), is one of the few Bassani characters who is not Jewish and not a Ferrarese, having moved there from nearby Veneto. But what happens to him towards the end of the 1930 – a sudden ostracism, the complete banishment from Ferrarese society because of a scandal deriving from what we would today politely call his sexual orientation – is similar to what happens to the Jewish Ferrarese narrator of the story. The narrator, a student in his early twenties, presents what is obviously one of the first autobiographical representations of the author, a process that Marilyn Schneider calls self-inscription.

Gli occhiali d' oro was soon followed by the worldwide success of the *Giardino dei Finzi Contini* (a very touching and well-crafted novel that some readers, including myself, find artistically less perfect than *Gli occhiali d' oro* and some of the earlier *Storie ferraresi*). The year is 1938: the Ferrarese papers announce the imminent proclamation of new regulations concerning Jews, issued by the Great Council of the ruling Fascist party. The narrator, a student belonging to an upper-middle class family who has never given much thought about his own and his family's Jewishness, suddenly feels outraged and furious at his non-Jewish fellow citizens, whom he mentally calls *goyim* for the first time. But he is also shocked by the idea of being considered similar to those *other* Jews, those who never moved out of the ghetto: 'Goy, goyim! How shameful, how humiliating, what repugnance at expressing myself in this way! And yet I could do it ... like any Jew from Eastern Europe, who had never left the ghetto. In a more or less distant future they, the goyim, would force us again to live there, in the medieval quarter, from which after all we had emerged only seventy or eighty years ago. Huddled one against the other, behind the gates, like so many frightened animals, we would never escape it again.'[3]

The narrator's father is a well-established professional man who has been reassured by Fascist acquaintances that nothing serious will ever happen to Italian Jews, while his best friend, a left-wing Catholic law student from a prominent family, decides that he had better join the Fascist party, not so much for the sake of his career but to prevent the party from going too much to the right. Feeling suddenly estranged, the narrator discovers he can only talk to another outcast, a homosexual physician abandoned by all his friends and patients; his own timid solidarity, however, is unable to save the lonely, lost, middle-aged man from committing suicide. If in nearby Modena the first victim of the anti-Fascist regulations is the well-known Jewish publisher Formiggini, who jumped from the city's famous La Ghirlandina tower, hoping to stir some public reaction (in vain, as Italian newspapers during the Fascist regime were not permitted to print news of suicides), in Bassani's Ferrara the first casualty is the non-Jewish and fictional Athos Fadigati.

Curiously enough, the feeling of being an outcast, of not belonging any longer to one's former world or society – something that is so bitterly resented by Bassani's autobiographical narrators, both in *Gli occhiali d'oro* and in *Giardino dei Finzi Contini* – is strongest in the earliest *Storie ferraresi*. This is the case with characters like Fadigati, who are *not* Jewish, and Jewish characters who, in these early stories, appear to withdraw into a world of their own, unwilling to share it with people close to them. In the very first of the *Storie*, which appeared in the 1940 edition, the protagonist is a Catholic working-class Ferrarese girl, whose name, Debora, sounds Jewish (in later editions she is renamed Lida to avoid possible confusion). She has an affair with a nervous, restless, ambitious young Jewish man, David, and vainly dreams not so much of being married by him, or introduced to his affluent Jewish family. Instead, she imagines herself walking openly with him in the main streets of the town or being taken to Ferrara's elegant cafés rather than to second-run movie theatres and the park near the city walls for some rapid, violent sexual encounters. 'Who was David? What was he looking for? Why?' Such questions, for Debora/Lida, do not have an answer: she bears David's child, but the young man, who is insensitive enough to tell her how much he loves another beautiful girl belonging to his own social class, soon abandons her. Finally, she is lucky enough to find a good-natured middle-aged man who marries her and takes care of the child.

Elia Corcos, the protagonist of *La passeggiata prima di cena*, is a Jewish surgeon of modest extraction who, at the end of the nineteenth century, notices young Gemma, one of the Catholic nurses working in the hospital. Unlike David, Elia respectfully asks permission to walk home with her and to have an official meeting with her parents in order to express his honest intention of proposing marriage. They do marry and have children – whom Elia, a free-thinker who refuses to be a member of the Jewish community, wants for some reason to be raised as Jews. Yet, the doctor, while a good and kind husband until Gemma's untimely death, remains committed to his profession, to scientific research, and to his love for music and opera, completely apart from the daily domestic life of his wife and his wife's sister, Ausilia. After Gemma's death Ausilia becomes part of the household, secretly adoring her silent, mysterious Jewish brother-in-law, but never daring to say one word to him. Perhaps, in such early attempts to represent Jewish characters, David may bear some autobiographical significance, while Elia is none other than the mythical grandfather who appears like a sacred and benevolent figure in much of Bassani's later fiction and poetry. The writer confronts them, so to speak, from a distance, trying to figure out how they would appear in the context, or in the eyes, of their fellow citizens. Only in later texts do they become protagonists, often narrators, especially when, as in *Gli occhiali d'oro* and *Giardino dei Finzi Contini*, they belong to the same generation as the author.

Three different generations of Ferrarese Jews are mirrored in the body of Bassani's work. He often expressed some vague intentions of going back in his literary projects to early modern times or to the Renaissance – maybe to explore the ghetto of nearby Venice or evoke the arrival of the twenty affluent families of Spanish Jews invited to settle in Ferrara after the Expulsion. But he never went back so far in time, to the mythical 'little Jerusalem' that apparently bloomed in Ferrara under Estensi rule, or to the following centuries, when the government of the Pope's envoys, the so-called *Cardinali Legati*, made things more difficult for the Jews. He never wrote of the Jews closed within the ghetto walls, compelled to listen to sermons urging them to convert to the true faith, and condemned to bury their dead during darkness only, without any marker or stone.[4] Despite his intent to explore such projects, he never carried them out and his work remained concentrated within the twentieth century, a period in which the number of Ferrarese Jews decreased to seven hundred by 1938 and to little more than a hundred after the Second World War. Yet, the first generation, like the much quoted but never seen Moisé Finzi Contini or Dr Elia Corcos, was not affected by the 1938 anti-Semitic regulations or by the Nazi occupation. The fictional Moisé had been dead for a long time, while Cesare Minerbi, Bassani's maternal grandfather and the real-life counterpart of Elia Corcos, was never arrested or bothered by the Germans, since he was almost ninety at the time, although he was still a practising physician. As a child, in the late 1940s and early 1950s, I remember spotting his horse-drawn carriage – the last one in a town full of bicycles, motorcycles, and small Fiat cars – bringing him to his office every day, which was one block from my mother's home.

Then we meet the fathers, the first generation born after the emancipation. They were the ones who had been allowed to leave the ghetto and become respected citizens, refusing to believe until the last moment that Italy would issue anti-Semitic regulations: after all, some of them, like Geremia Tabet, had joined the Fascists and become prominent members of the party. Even after being deprived of their rights and of their jobs, many among them still hoped that all this was a passing mood just to keep the German allies quiet, and that soon things would go back to normal (such are the feelings and the obstinate hopes of the father of the autobiographical narrator in both *Gli occhiali d'oro* and *Giardino dei Finzi Contini*, even though he is strongly anti-Fascist). Finally we meet their sons, the ones who, like their author, suffer a persecution that threatens to destroy them just as they are preparing to leave school and live their lives. The painful confrontations the sons encounter with their loving but pathetically optimistic fathers are often the most touching scenes in Bassani's oeuvre.

At the end of a 1972 collection called *L'odore del fieno* (The Smell of Hay), Bassani describes the slow process that led him to become the real and only protagonist of his stories. He writes that he tried to keep apart from his early works. This was not for lack of personal interest; on the contrary, Bassani wanted to avoid a possible excess of emotional involvement. But after the first three chapters of *Gli occhiali d'oro*, he felt the moral necessity of directing the spotlight upon himself, a radical change that would lead to *Giardino dei Finzi Contini* and to the embarrassing adolescent confessions of *Dietro la porta* (Behind a Closed Door, 1964). Significantly enough, at the same time he introduced a fictional double for himself, a dark-haired Ferrarese Jew whose name is Bruno Lattes. Both in their early twenties, both excellent tennis players expelled from the town's tennis courts because of anti-Semitic regulations and therefore admitted to the secret mysteries of the private tennis court hidden inside the Finzi Contini garden, Bruno and the protagonist (who speaks in the first person but, unless I am wrong, is never called Giorgio) meet at the gate of that garden, together with their Catholic friends, and silently exchange 'the inevitable flicker of Jewish understanding ... as, half anxious and half revolted, I had foreseen we would.'[5] They will both suffer unrequited love, the protagonist for the elusive Micol, the other for a fickle and vain Catholic girl, Adriana Trentini. But we had already met Bruno Lattes, as the protagonist in one of the *Storie Ferraresi*. In 'The last years of Clelia Trotti,' he served as teacher in the Hebrew school after the expulsion of Jewish pupils from the city institutions (as Bassani himself did), and where he met, and perhaps later disappointed, an old, respectable, pathetic Socialist woman also persecuted by the government (as, perhaps, Bassani himself feared he might have done). Soon Bruno is back again, among the stories of *L'odore del fieno*, in the Jewish cemetery for the burial of an uncle, by now totally estranged, not a Lattes but a Marchi (the name of his – and also Bassani's – Catholic paternal grandmother). Later again, we find that he had moved to the United States, hoping to make a career for himself as a lecturer in Italian, maybe one day a professor, in an American university.

Clearly, Bruno Lattes takes upon himself the task of embodying the feelings of estrangement and detachment that, to Bassani and to his first person narrator, are somehow embarrassing. But it also evident that Bassani himself was not as interested in modern, postwar Ferrara as he had been in the town of his childhood and adolescence, the town he wants to lovingly preserve frozen in time. Perhaps it was different; perhaps it was not different *enough*. Yes, in the *new* Ferrara, Fascists monuments are removed, a few streets revert to their original names after having been renamed to honour heroes of the Fascist government, but the lazy rhythms of provincial life do not seem to change. *Una notte del '43* (One Night in 1943) is the dramatic description of a tragic pogrom carried out by Italian Fascists (and not approved, as it was later revealed, by the recently arrived German occupiers). The last sections of the story relate the vain, sleepy, unsuccessful attempts to find the culprits, to shed light upon the horrible events of that bloody night that nobody wants to be reminded of, while the unseen but audible chorus of the average citizens expresses the city's desire to forget, to delete those bad recollections that only upset and compromise the need to bury the past. Geo Josz, the protagonist of another story, *Una lapide in via Mazzini* (A Memorial Stone in Via Mazzini), returns unexpectedly from Buchenwald to find that his name has been erroneously included in the list of the victims on the walls of the synagogue; he is a ghost, a scary, unpleasant reminder to his fellow citizens of a not-so-distant past that they are happy to obliterate. He meets someone who had been a well-known informer, notorious for reporting Jews to the Nazis; he is still there, quietly sipping his cappuccino in the same coffee shop he used to patronize during the war. It is perhaps significant that Bassani's only novel set in Ferrara in the late 1950s, *L'airone* (The Heron, 1968), written as a polemical response to the French experimental *école du regard*, describes the allure of death and immobility for a man in late middle age who has been twice unpopular and criticized – first, before the war as a Jew and then, after the war, as a landlord and capitalist.

Survivors, like Geo Josz, are bound to remain such forever. In a short story that appeared in a Milanese paper on 25 December 1969, with the title *Fiaba* (A Fairy Tale) – later to be included with another title in *L'odore del fieno* – Bassani described a sort of Jewish version of the miracle of the Nativity. The story tells of a thirtyish Ferrarese woman who belongs to a well-established Sephardic family and who suddenly decides that she wants a son. For this reason only she marries, below her station, a blue-eyed Russian refugee, Yuri Rotstein, who, together with his father, mother, and sisters, is killed in Auschwitz. The miracle happens and the woman has a wonderful blue-eyed baby, also called Yuri Rotstein. After the war, among the ruins of the synagogue, Yuri, the son, is a symbol of survival, bound to live forever with his loving mother, isolated and never marrying, in the big house in Ferrara.

Clearly inspired by the marriage of my own parents, this story moved but somehow embarrassed me: after all, my eyes weren't blue, I didn't live in Ferrara with my mother as the archetypal emblem of survival. I was married, I was connected to American universities like the somehow disagreeable Bruno Lattes, and Bassani knew it very well. As for Bassani himself, having described my mother, whom he dearly loved as *né bella né brutta* (not a beautiful girl, but not entirely plain), he was a little afraid of her reactions. My mother was enough of a Jewish Momma to be pleased, and to feel puzzled but somehow flattered when I told her that in the Marilyn Schneider book she was described as a 'mythopoetic figure of fertility.'[6] The only real criticism came from my aunt, my mother's elder sister, who, being very much a lady and the widow of a Latin professor, wanted at least a footnote in new editions of the story to correct a misimpression: my mother, from the *matroneo*, smiled at this young man, and at the beginning of the following paragraph I was already born, without any mention of the proper marriage ceremony performed in the synagogue. In any case, it was only a matter of time before that short story inspired a theatrical and musical adaptation, whose protagonist, an Italian boy with the name of Rotstein, reconstructs the story of his Russian grandfather and of his great-grandfather who was a cantor in the Ferrara German *shul*. The author and performer was born a couple of months before the story was first published and, even if this may have more to do with my wife than with my 'Rotstein' ancestors, his eyes are blue.

Notes

1 André Sempoux, *La città di Bruno Lattes* (Brussels 1984), 7. Bassani remained unidentified, or just identified with a capital F followed by a dot, until the 1956 award-winning edition of what was finally called *Cinque Storie Ferraresi*.
2 Giorgio Bassani, *The Gold-Rimmed Eyeglasses*, trans. William Weaver, in *The Smell of Hay* (London 1996), 83–4.
3 Ibid., 168.
4 Some of the preceding grave markers were removed and used for other purposes, like, for instance, in the *colonna di Borso d'Este* when it was restored at the beginning of the eighteenth century.
5 Giorgio Bassani, *The Garden of the Finzi-Continis*, trans. Isabel Quigly (London 1965), 80.
6 Marilyn Schneider, *Vengeance of the Victim: History and Symbol in Giorgio Bassani's Fiction* (Minneapolis 1986), 187.

Index

acculturation: after emancipation, 11, 105, 106, 160; complexity of, 10; defined, 7; compared with assimilation, 7; 'discontents' of, 7; dynamics of, 7; Gordon and, 7; and identity, 165; in music, 167; problematic of, 5; in Rome, 57, 58, 60, 67; process of, 7, 8, 12, 13, 167, 194, 202n53; products of, 60; public mechanisms of, 67; ruptures of, 8; vehicles of, 58. *See also under* assimilation; Cohen, Gerson; Endelman, Todd; exchange (Jewish-Christian); identity; Katz, Jacob; subculture; Ruderman, David; Veltri, Giuseppe; Zimmerman, Joshua
Adler, Israel, 166, 170
Aguilar, d' Lady, 122
Alessandria, 170
Allgemeines Gesetzbuch (*Allgemeine Bürgerliche Gesetzbuch*), 119, 121, 129, 130. *See also* Habsburg (state); Jews: and civil regulation of marriage/divorce
alterity, 72, 73, 96n67. *See also* Otherness

Amfiparnaso (Vecchi): portrayal of Jews, 77–8, 79, 82, 89, 91n7; 'Tich, tach, toch,' 77–8, 82, 91n7, 94n37. *See also ebraiche*
Amsterdam, 40, 175
Ancona, 43, 156
Andreini, G.B.: *Lo schiavetto*, 72 (epigraph), 94n32, 96–7n67
Arendt, Hannah, 86
Arezzo: 'Viva Maria' insurgency, 158, 159, 162n33
armatura dei forti, L' (Bonet), 155
Ascoli, Graziadio Isaia, 12; theory of the 'linguistic substratum,' 185; Terracini on, 185–6
'aspra verità: una sfida di Stendhal agli storici, L' (Carlo Ginzburg), 197–8n23
assimilation, 5; Arendt on, 86; Cohen on, 7; dialectics of, 12, 169, 194, 194n4; distinguished from acculturation, 7; fictional description, 192; language and, 184, 195n9; liturgical music and, 176; processes, 184
Assmann, Jan: on language and 'cultural memory,' 202n52

Asti, 170
Austria, 134, 148, 149, 150, 158, 159, 162n22. *See also* Habsburg (state); Mantua
Austro-Hungarian Empire, 178
Autobiografia di un rabbino italiano (Momigliano): Italian Jewish jargon in, 198n24

Bachi, Riccardo: father of Roberto Rossi, 187; project on jargons, 187, 196n14
Bacon, Francis, 101
Banchieri, Adriano, works: *Barca di Venetia per Padova*, 88, 91n7, 97nn70–1; 'Latrai nai,' 79, 80–1, 81, 91n5, 94n37; 'Samuel, Samuel,' 90–1n5. *See also ebraiche*; Vecchi, Orazio
Barbieri, Nicolò, 89
Barca di Venetia per Padova (Banchieri), 88; 'Latrai nai,' 81, 91n5, 94n37, 97nn70–1; 'Samuel, Samuel,' 90–1n5. *See also ebraiche*
Baron, Salo, 4
Bassani, Giorgio, 12, 13; autobiographical characters, 204, 205, 207, 208; biography, 203–4; compared with Ginzburg (Natalia), 193; evokes Ferrara, 203, 204, 208; portrays 'outsiders,' 204, 205–6, 208, 209; portrays 'survivors,' 209–10
Bassani, Giorgio, works: *Cinque Storie Ferraresi*, 203, 204, 205, 208, 210n1; *Dietro la porta*, 207; *Gli occhiali d'oro* [The Gold-Rimmed Spectacles (Eyeglasses)], 204, 205, 207; *Il giardino dei Finzi-Contini* [Garden of the Finzi Continis], 13, 183, 193–4, 204, 205, 206, 207; *La passeggiata prima di cena* [A Walk before Dinner], 204, 206; *L'odoro del fieno* [The Smell of the Hay], 207, 208; 'The Last Years of Clelia Trotti,' 207
Bedarida, Guido: Terracini on, 186
Be'er Hetev, 129
Benedict XIV (pope): and Jews, 153, 161n13
Berardelli, Allesandro: and Coppio Sullam, 30
Berengo, Marino: on toleration in Venice, 28
Berlin, 146n78, 173, 175
Bertinoro, Obadiah (rabbi): commentary on Mishna, 105, 107
Boccaccio, Giovanni: parable of the three rings, 53n80
Bolaffi, Michele, 175
Bologna, 156, 203. *See also* Papal States; Jews (Italian)
Bonaparte, Napoleon: and Enlightenment ideals, 155–6; and Paris Sanhedrin of 1807, 11, 166; emancipates ghetto of Venice, 165; invasion of Italy, 148–9, 150, 155–6, 159
Bonet, Francesco Rovira: director of the Roman Casa dei Catecumeni, 155; *L'armatura dei forti*, 155; *Life* (of the boy-saint Simon), 155, 161–2n21
Bonfil, Robert: on boundaries, 9; on ghettoization, 5, 6, 166; on Roman law and Jewish arbitration, 138n7; on Roth, 5
Bonifaccio, Baldassare: and Coppio Sullam, 29
boundaries: and identity, 74; blurring of (*débordement*), 74, 76; dialectics of, 73. *See also* Derrida, Jacques
Britain, 149, 158

Brugnalesco (Brunalesco), Valeria, 39. *See also* Venice, Inquisition
Bucharest, 173
Burney, Charles, 81

Calabria, 150, 158. *See* Santa Fede, La; Italy, *Sanfedisti* movement; Ruffo, Fabrizio (cardinal)
Cammeo (chief rabbi of Modena), 187
'Canzona de' giudei' (dell'Ottonaio), 78, 92n17
canzoni villaneschi, 91nn5–6
Capponni, Giovanni Battista, 40. *See also* Venice, Inquisition
Carraton, Francisco, 40. *See also* Venice, Inquisition
Casale Monferrato, 170, 198n24
Case dei Catecumeni, 154, 155, 161n16
Cassuto, Umberto (rabbi of Florence), 187
Castaigne, Gabriel de, 112n5
Castiglione, Samuel, 57
Catholic Church: and Jansenist reform, 153–4, 155; anti-Semitism in, 153, 155; Counter Reformation and Jews, 6, 22, 35, 75, 154, 161n16; forced baptism, 25, 153, 154, 161n3; reaction against Enlightenment, 155; under Fascism, 15n12. *See* Bonet, Francesco Rovira; Benedict XIV; Case dei Catecumeni; Clement XIV; Gregory I; Innocent III; Inquisition; Paul IV; Pius VI; Priuli, Lorenzo; Ruffo, Fabrizio; Sarpi, Paolo
Cattaneo, Carlo,185
Cavaglion, Alberto: on Italian Jewish autobiographical tradition, 198n24; on 'Jewish' pages of Saba, Ginzburg, and Levi (Primo), 201n49; on Svevo, 198n27, 199n31
Cazes, Moses ben Samuel, 111n1
Cebà, Ansaldo: and Coppio Sullam, 28–9; *L'Ester*, 28
Charles III (of Naples), 153
Cisalpine Republic, 149, 150, 158
Cispadane Republic, 162n24
città bella, La (Coppini), 81–4, 90n4, 95nn41–6
Clement XIV (pope): and Jews, 44, 153, 155. *See also* Ganganelli, Cardinal
Clenche, John, 30
Cocceji, Samuel, 130
Codice Civile Universale. *See Allgemeines Gesetzbuch*
Cohen, Gerson, 7
community: diversity, 168; corporate organization, 20, 56, 61, 151; emancipation and, 120, 136, 152; 'emotional,' 61; Italian, 3, 4, 13; language and, 184, 189, 194; 'linguistic,' 188; role of 'masque' in, 56; self-governance in, 151; status of converts, 76; synagogues and, 171–2, 177; Università degli Ebrei, 20, 151. *See also under* boundaries; ghettos; ghettoization; identity
Consolo, Federico, *Libro di canti d'Israele: Antichi canti del rito degli ebrei Spagnoli*, 175
Consolo, Giuseppe, 170–1
Coppini, Alessandro: 'La città bella,' 81–5, 91n5, 95nn41–6; depicts Florentine Jews, 81–5; setting of 'Canzona de' giudei,' 92n17
Coppio Sullam, Sara [Copio Sullam]: and Berardelli, 30; and Paluzzi, 29–30; contacts with Christian men of

letters, 28–30; corresponds with Cebà, 28–9; friend of Modena; *Manifesto*, 29; polemic with Bonifaccio, 29; wife of Jacob Sullam, 28
Correggio, 154, 155
Coryate, Thomas, 79
Counter Reformation, 6, 35
Cozzi, Gaetano, 31
Cracovia, Jacob Emanuel (rabbi), 166
Crescimbeni, Giovanni Mario de,' 73
Cum Nimis Absurdum of 1555 (papal bull), 24, 35
Cultural Intermediaries: Jewish Intellectuals in Early Modern Italy (Ruderman and Veltri), 7

d'Argento, Ferdinando, 144n62
Davis, Natalie Zemon, 67, 141–2n36
De Auro dialogi tres (Portaleone), 10, 112n3–4, 114n23: alchemic medicine, 102; compared with *Shilte ha-Giborim*, 107, 108; empiricism and religious belief, 102; metaphor of enclosed space, 101; on epistemology, 100–2; on medical powers of gold, 10, 100; on properties of precious stones, 107, 108; on 'quintessence,' 102, 112n4; purpose of, 112n3
De Fano, Menahem Azaria, 111n1
De Felice, Renzo, 154
de' Ricci, Scipio de' (bishop), 155
de' Rossi, Azaria [Azariah]: *Me'or 'enayim*, 107, 111n1, 114n25
Debenedetti, Giacomo, 198n 27, 198–9n28; on the 'Svevo case,' 189–90
Declaration of the Rights of Man, 156
dell' Ottanaio, Giovambattista: 'Canzona dei giudei,' 78, 92n17
Della Pergola, Alberto, 173

Della Torre, Lelio (rabbi), 196n15
Derrida, Jacques, 195n9; *débordement* of boundaries, 74; theme of exclusion, 91n9
Descartes, René, 101
Discorso sopra il stato degl'Hebrei et in particolar dimoranti nel'inclita città di Venetia (Simone Luzzatto): apology for Jews, 8, 31, 44, 50n36, 52–3n68
Dubin, Lois, 10–11, 167–8

ebraiche, 9, 88; composers, 90–1nn4, 5; Hebrew and Hebrew vocables in, 79, 93–4nn27–30; in musicological studies, 90–1n5; interpretation of, 85–9; portrayals of Jews, 72–3, 76–9, 86; roots, 73. See *Amfiparnaso*; Banchieri, Adriano; *Barca di Venetia per Padova*; Coppini, Alessandro; Vecchi, Orazio; *Veglie di Siena*
Edict of Emancipation (1848), 166. See also emancipation
educatore israelita, L', 169
emancipation, 120, 136; Edict of (1848), 166; 'first,' 135, 148, 149, 150, 151, 152, 156, 159–60, 168; nineteenth-century, 166, 169, 178, 181n13, 196n15, 120, 135, 136, 207; of ghettos, 11, 12, 148, 151, 156, 159, 165
emotion. See *under* community; language; Rome, Jews of
Endelman, Todd, 7
England, 167
Enlightenment, 4, 130–1, 144n62, 152, 155–6
Ernesto (Saba), 190
Ester (Modena), 29
Ester, L' (Cebà), 28
estro poetico armonico, L' (Marcello), 32

Europe, 13, 19, 26; acculturation, 7, 194; Central, 167, 178; Eastern, 205; Western, 164, 178
Evelyn, John, 75
exchange (Jewish-Christian); boundaries and, 9, 73, characteristics of, 5, 9, 11, 74, 166; cultural, 6, 7, 8, 9; economic, 8, 35–6, 38, 40; in inquisitorial processes, 34, 38–41; legal, 9, 15n4; sexual, 23, 41–2, 44, 48n13; social, 8, 15n4. *See also under* Coppio Sullam, Sara; Cozzi, Gaetano; ghettoization; Gradenigo, Pietro; Inquisition; Jews (Italian); language; Marcello, Benedetto; Misson, Maximilien; Modena, Leon; Morosini, Giulio; Rome; Saint-Didier, Alexandre-Toussaint Limojon de; Sanuto, Marino; synagogues; toleration/tolerance; Venice

Falavolti, Laura, 94n32
Farissol, Abraham, 111n1
Ferrara: Jewish community of, 13, 152–3, 156, 172, 206–7. *See also* Bassani, Giorgio
Fishman, Joshua A., 195–6n11
Flavius, Josephus, 107
Florence: French occupation, 149; ghetto, 159; Jewish communities, 4, 151, 170; synagogues of, 177; 'Viva Maria' insurgency and Martini, 159
Florence (Jews of): Christian conversions, 85, 171, 177; conditions of return, 81, 85; emancipation, 149; expelled, 81; liturgy and liturgical music, 167, 168, 171, 177; Medici and, 95n47; portrayed, 78–9, 81–4, 90n4, 95nn41–6; Savonarola and,

95n47; synagogue, 177. *See also* Cassuto, Umberto; Della Pergola, Alberto
France: and emancipation, 148, armistice with Piedmont, 149; regulation of marriage/divorce, 121–2, 130, 135, 136; synagogue music, 167
Francés, Immanuel, 111n1
Francés, Yaa'kov, 111n1
Francis II (Habsburg emperor), 162n22
Freeze, ChaeRan, 134
Freud, Sigmund: Gilman on, 195n9; *Psychopathology of Everyday Life*, 189
Friuli, 185, 190
Frizzi, Benedetto [Ben Zion ha-Kohen; Ben Zion Rafael ha-Kohen]: and Morschene, 125, 126, 130, 135, 146n82; physician, 141n20
Funkenstein, Amos: 'dialectics of assimilation,' 12, 194, 194n4

Galileo (Galileo Galilei), 101, 104, 105
Galizisches Gesetzbuch, 129, 130
Gallino, Luciano, 194n3
Ganganelli, Cardinal, 44. *See* Clement XIV
Garboli, Cesare, 183, 184; on *Lessico famigliare* and *Il giardino dei Finzi-Contini*, 192
Garden of the Finzi Continis, The. See giardino dei Finzi-Contini, Il
Garzia, David, 175
Garzoni, Tommaso, 89
Genette, Gérard: on Proust's use of 'indirect language,' 188–9, 198n23, 200n44
Genoa, 148, 149, 150; and Jews, 162n29
Germany, 9; Jewish identity in, 164;

Jewish Reform movement in, 12, 166, 171; synagogues, 167, 178. *See also* Berlin; Hamburg; Jews, German
Gershom, Rabbenu, 123
ghettos, 5, 6, 42; and Jewish identity, 12, 43; emancipation, 11, 12, 148, 151, 156, 159, 165; Jewish perceptions of, 6, 58; purpose, 43, 44; as 'urban condom,' 43–4; in Corregio, 154–5; in Ferrara, 203; in Florence, 159; in Mantua, 151; in Trieste, 155, 190; Turin; 151. *See also under* ghettoization; identity; Rome; Venice
ghettoization: and cultural identity, 6–7, 166; Bonfil on, 5, 6; effects, 6, 8, 166; extent in Italy, 151; process, 154; purpose, 43; responses to, 56–8. *See also under* exchange (Jewish-Christian); ghettos; Rome, Jews of; Venice, Jews of
giardino dei Finzi-Contini, Il (Bassani), 13, 183, 203, 204; language in, 192–3; narrator, 205, 206, 207
Gilman, Sander, 96n67, 195n9
Ginzburg, Carlo: 'L'aspra verità,' 197–8n23; on fiction and historiography, 197–8n23; *Rhetoric and Proof,* 197n23
Ginzburg, Natalia, 12; and Proust, 200n44; Cavaglion on, 201n49; *Lessico famigliare* [Family Sayings], 183, 184, 191–2, 193, 200n44, 201n48; on Levi (Carlo), 200n38
giudíata, 73, 94n32
Gli ebrei (Saba), 190–1, 200n37; Levi (Carlo) and, 199n31, 200n37
Gonzaga, Ferdinando (duke of Mantua), 86

Gonzaga, Guglielmo I (duke of Mantua and Monferrato), 112n3, 114n23
Gordon, Milton, 7
Gradenigo, Pietro, 32
Gregory I (pope), 45
Guetta, Alessandro, 6, 10
Guide for the Perplexed (Maimonides), 112n3

Habsburg (monarchy). See Habsburg (state)
Habsburg (state): *Allgemeines Gesetzbuch,* 119, 121, 129, 130; and Jewish emancipation, 136; and Jewish religious law (rabbinic law), 120, 121, 128, 131–2, 133, 134, 136; and women, 122, 133, 147n87; civil regulation of marriage, 120–1, 133, 134, 136, 142n3; edicts on Jewish marriage/divorce, 121, 132; *Ehepatent,* 119, 120–1, 129, 134, 146n84; *Galizisches Gesetzbuch,* 129, 130; *Josephinisches Gesetzbuch,* 119, 121, 129; offensive against Church power, 154; religious toleration in, 120, 136; Toleration Patents (1781–82), 151; 136. *See also* Austria; Francis II; Joseph II; Holy Roman Empire; Trieste; Zinzendorf, Karl von
Halwachs, Maurice, 202n52
Hamburg, 122, 135, 167, 175
Harmat, Ulrike, 136
Harrán, Don, 9, 11
Harré, Rom, 62, 69–70n17
Hebraorum Gens (papal bull), 43
Hebrew Scholar, A (Saba) 190
Hebrew Union College: Jewish liturgical music collection, 174

history (Italian Jewish). *See* experience (Italian Jewish)
Hofstadter, Richard, 67
Holy Roman Empire, 122. *See also* Habsburg (state)
Holland, 122
Hughes, H. Stuart: on Svevo, 199n28; *Prisoners of Hope*, 197n22 199n28

Idelsohn, Abraham Zvi, 175, 181n26
identity: acculturation and, 165; and alterity, 96n67; and assimilation, 7; and Italian national unity, 168; defined by exclusion, 72, 74; disintegration of, 169; emancipation and, 152; ethnic variants of, 168, 170, 174; formal, 164; Freud on, 189; German Jewish reform, and 167; ghettoization and, 166; in *Lessico famigliare*, 183–4, 192; language and, 184, 192, 194; linguistic processes and, 194, 202n53; modern, 170; modes of, 174; music and, 169, 176, 179; redefined, 168; religious component of, 152, 164; role of the synagogue, 164; symbolic poles of, 6–7. *See also under* acculturation; assimilation; Assmann, Jan; community; *ebraiche*; ghettoization; language; music (Jewish liturgical); Otherness; Rome, Jews of; subculture; synagogues; Venice, Jews of
Innocent III (pope), 68n2
Inquisition, 53n80, 76; Venetian Jewish cases, 34–5, 38–42
Iona, Marco, 170
Israel (state), 3, 13
Israel, Menasseh ben, 45
israelitismo moderno, L' (Soáve), 176

Italy, 6, 8, 9, 13, 72, 89; and Enlightenment, 152, 153, 155, 156, 157; anti-Semitism, 153, 155, 157, 190; Bonaparte in, 148, 149, 155–6; Case dei Catecumeni, 154, 155, 161n16; *commedia dell'arte* of, 73, 88, 89, 96n62; cultural mimesis in, 9; ethnic song types, 73; Fascist, 13, 15n12; French in, 148, 150, 152, 156, 157, 158; Jacobin republics (regimes), 148, 149–50, 152, 156, 157, 158, 159, 162n24; Jewish communities, 150–1, 152–4, 168; Jewish law and Roman law (*jus commune*) in, 58, 59, 138n7; *Judenrein* regions, 150; Old Regime restoration, 160; *Sanfedisti* movement, 150, 157, 158; secular music, 73, 93n21; 'throne' and 'altar' uprisings, 155; synagogues, 170, 173, 174, 175; Università degli Ebrei (Nazione Ebrea), 20, 58, 151, 153; 'Viva Maria' insurgency, 149, 150, 157, 158, 159, 162n33. *See also* Catholic Church; emancipation; Inquisition
Italy, Jews of: *See* Jews (Italian)

Jacobin republics (regimes). *See under* Italy
jargons (Italian Jewish): and assimilation, 195n9; and familial (personal) memory, 188; as cover-languages, 188–9; Commeo and, 187; Cassuto and, 187; cultural functions of, 188–9, 195n9; Della Torre on, 196n15; in Bassani, 192–3; in Ginzburg (Natalia), 191; in Levi (Primo), 193–4; in Loy, 189; in Pirandello, 189; in Saba, 190–1; in Svevo, 189–90; *parole staccate* in,

187; of Piedmont, 187, 189, 193; preservation projects, 187; prohibitive functions of, 188; Terracini on, 186–7. *See also* language; *Rassegna mensile di Israel; Vessillo Israelitico*

Jerusalem: Jewish National and University Library Jewish liturgical music collections, 170, 174; Temple, 104

Jewry (Jewries). *See* Jews; Jews (Italian)

Jewry, Roman. *See* Rome, Jews of

Jews: and civil regulation of marriage/divorce, 11, 121–2, 134–6, 145n75, 146n84; and modernity, 7, 99, 164; and Josephinian reforms, 119–20, 121, 155; Ashkenazim, 3, 168; divorce law, 122–3; *Ehepatent*, 119, 120–1, 129, 134, 146n84; English, 178; expulsions, 43, 81, 162n29; French, 178; German, 7, 166, 167–8, 177, 178, 184; Gregory I and, 45; Iberian, 3; language and identity, 189; Levantine, 20; *maskilim*, 145n68; Middle Eastern, 3; musical portrayals of Christians, 86–8; Ponentine, 21; Sefardim, 3, 168; subculture formation, 188; synagogues, 8, 164, 166, 172, 173, 175, 178; Tedeschi, 20; women, 70n22, 121, 122–3, 128–9, 133–4, 146–7n87, 172. *See also* acculturation; alterity; assimilation; boundaries; community; identity; ghettos; ghettoization; Jews (Italian); Otherness; toleration/tolerance

Jews (Italian): and forced baptism, 25, 42, 153, 154, 161n13; and ghettoization, 12, 154, 166; and inclusion/exclusion dialectics, 8, 10, 13, 73, 74; and Italian nationalism, 166, 170–1; and liturgical change, 174–7; and modernity, 166, 178, 179; arbitration practices, 59, 60, 67, 70n18, 138n7; *Case dei Catecumeni* and, 154, 155, 161n16; clothing laws, 23, 68n2; coexistence with Christians, 74, 166; defined by exclusion, 72, 74; demographics, 3, 150–1; diversity, 3–4, 8, 168, 177, 196–7n17; emancipation, 148, 150, 151, 152, 156, 159, 160, 166, 169, 178, 181n13, 196n15, 120, 135, 136, 207; Enlightenment and, 4, 152; German Jewish Reform movement and, 166, 167, 168, 171, 177, 178; Habsburg law and, 120, 121, 122, 127, 128–9, 130, 131–3, 135–6, 144n64, 147n87, 156; in historiography, 4–6, 7, 13, 15n12, 90n2, 194; *minhag italki*, 4; modern experience, 183–4; *monti di pietà* and, 23, 95n47; openness towards Italian culture, 12; papal rulings on, 23, 45, 68n2; self-governance, 58, 61, 64, 67, 122, 123, 151; under Fascism, 8, 13, 15n12, 205, 208. *See also under* Catholic Church; *ebraiche*; *giudíata*; Habsburg (state); Inquisition; Italy; *under* individual Italian cities, regions, or states; and *under* various subject entries

Jews in Italy under Fascist and Nazi Rule (Zimmerman), 7, 15n10

Jona, Abraham (rabbi), 165–6; diary of, 179n3

Joseph II (Habsburg emperor): *Allgemeine Bürgerliche Gesetzbuch*, 119, 121, 129, 130; *Ehepatent*, 119, 120–1; emancipates Jews, 151, 155; *Josephinisches Gesetzbuch*, 119, 121, 129;

reforms, 119–21, 155; and toleration, 120, 151, 155, 156; Toleration Patents [Edicts], 151, 155
Josephinisches Gesetzbuch, 119, 121, 129

Kabbalah, 40, 75, 111n1
Karlsruhe, 129, 143n53
Katz, Jacob, 167
Kerman, Joseph, 72
Klagenfurt, 127
Klingenstein, Grete: and Zinzendorf journals, 144n62
Kuehn, Thomas: notarial acts in Renaissance Italy, 69n12

La Rue, François de. *See* Rueo, Franceso
Lagasius, Johann Georg Hasenöhrl von (court physician, Vienna), 125, 141n20
Lane, Frederick, 27, 28
language: and assimilation, 184, 186, 188, 195n9, 196n15; and identity; 74, 79, 189, 195–6n11, 202n52; and memory, 188, 195n9, 202n52; and processes of acculturation, 194; and subculture, 184, 188; Assmann on, 202n52; 'direct,' 189; Garboli on, 183; Hebrew vocables and, 79; indirect in Proust, 188–9; in *Lessico famigliare*, 183–4; in Roman notarial acts, 59; 'indirect,' 188; Italian Jewish, 184, 188–9, 196–7n17, 200n41; 'linguistic substratum' and, 185–6; of emotions, 9; relationship with 'race,' 185; representation and memory of, 184; transformation of, 184; use of Hebrew words, 189–90; vernacular in synagogues, 171

Lassels, Richard, 93n22
'Latrai nai.' See *Barca di Venetia per Padova; ebraiche*
Lavagetto, Mario: on Saba, 199n36; on *Ricordi-Racconti*, 199n31
Leone, Battista de, 38. *See also* Venice, Inquisition
Leone, Yehuda Messer [Yehiel, Yehuda ben], 111n1
Lessico famigliare [Family Sayings] (Natalia Ginzburg), 183, 184, 191–2, 193, 200n44, 201n48; Cavaglion on, 201n49; Garboli on, 192; hyperbolic synecdoche in, 192; jargon examples from, 191–2; Romano on, 193
Lessing, Gotthold Ephraim: parable of the three rings, 53n80; *Nathan the Wise* 53n80
Leti, Gregorio, 76
Levant, the 19, 21, 22
Levi, Carlo, 191, 200n37, 200n38
Levi, Isacco, 41. *See also* Venice, Inquisition
Levi, Primo, 12; Cavaglion on, 201n49; Ginzburg on, 201n49; interest in *parole fossili* [fossil words], 194, 201n50; 'Itinerary of a Jewish Writer,' 193; on jargon, 193–4; *The Periodic Table*, 193–4, 201n49
Leviim, Isaac min, 41
Levis Sullam, Simon, 12
Libro di canti d'Israele: Antichi canti del rito degl ebrei Spagnoli (Consolo), 175
Life [of the boy-saint Simon] (Bonet), 155, 161n21
Liguria, 157
Ligurian Republic, 149, 162n24
linguistics. *See* language

liturgical music. *See* music (Jewish liturgical); synagogues; synagogues (Italian)
Livorno, 170; and 'Viva Maria' rebels, 158; Jewish community, 4, 151, 152; reactions to reform in, 153, 167, 171; synagogue music in, 168, 174, 175
Lo schiavetto (Andreini), 94n32, 96–7n67
Lombardy, 149, 150, 158; expels Jews, 43; emancipates Jews, 156; 'Viva Maria' insurgency, 150; Jansenist reform in, 153, 155
Lombroso, Cesare, 185; on jargons, 195n10
London, 173
Lovisoni, Francesco Saverio, 123
Loy, Rosetta: *La parola ebreo*, 189
Loyola, Ignatius [of], 104
Luzzatto, Lucio: husband of Rachele Morschene 119; Morschene charges against, 124–5; responses to charges, 124, 125–6; charges against Frizzi, 125, 126
Luzzatto, Rachele (née Morschene). See Morschene, Rachele
Luzzatto, Samuel David (rabbi), 170
Luzzatto [Luzzato], Simone: Cozzi and, 31; *Discorso sopra il stato degl'Hebrei et in particolar dimoranti nel'inclita città di Venetia*, 8, 31, 44, 45, 50n36, 52–53n68

Maddalena, La, 86, 87; Rossi and, 86–8
Maimonides: *Guide for the Perplexed*, 112n3; *Mishneh Torah*, 26, 105
Manifesto (Coppio Sullam), 29
Mantua (city and duchy): 10, 33; dukes of, 86, 112n3, 114n23; emancipation, 156; ghetto, 151; Jewish community, 99, 111n1; Jewish liturgical repertoire, 173, 182n30; *La Maddalena*, 86; toleration and, 151, 155; under Austrian rule, 151, 155, 165
Marcello, Benedetto (composer): *L'estro poetico armonico*, 32
Marli, Samuel Raphael, 111n1
Martini, Antonio (archbishop), 159, 162–3n36
Martini, Karl Anton, 145n65
'masque.' *See under* Rome, Jews of
Medici, Caterina de', 86
Medici, Lorenzo de', 95n47
Melamed, Avraham, 104
memoria culturale: Scrittura, ricordoe indetità nelle grandi civiltà antiche, La (Assmann), 202n52
Memorie di vita ebraica: Casale Monferrato-Roma-Gerusalemme, 1918–1960 (Segre), 198n24
memory: historical, 164; language and, 184, 194; and forgetting, 208–9
Me'or 'enayim (de' Rossi), 107, 111n1, 114n26. *See also* Portaleone, Avraham; *Shilte ha-Giborim*
Mestre, 25
Milan (city), 149
Milan, Duchy of, 150
Milano, Attilio, 154, 161n14
minhag italki. See under Italy, Jews of
Mishna, 105, 106, 110
Mishneh Torah (Maimonides), 26, 105
Misson, Maximilien, 28, 30–1
Modena: Jewish community in, 4, 156, 177, 205
Modena, Leon (rabbi): and Coppio

Sullam, 29; autobiography, 28, 31; Christian opinions of, 51n51; on Christians at synagogue services, 31; and Isaac ha-Leviim, 41; on Rossi's Hebrew songs, 76

Momigliano, Marco (chief rabbi of Bologna): *Autobiografia di un rabbino italiano*, 198n24

Monferrato (Duchy of), 112n3, 114n23

Montaigne, Michel de, 80

Monte San Savino: and 'Viva Maria' insurgency, 158

Montepulciano: and 'Viva Maria' insurgency 158

Monteverdi, Claudio, 86, 87

Morley, Thomas, 86

Moretti, Giorgio, 39–40. *See also under* Venice, Inquisition

Morocco, 175

Morosini, Giulio (Venetian): and Carraton, 40; on Jewish-Christian exchange, 30, 31–2; *Via della fede*, 30, 31, 51n52

Morschene, Rachele, 137n1, 144n63; court rulings on petition, 127–9, 142n46; Frizzi and, 125, 126, 130, 135, 146n82; Lagasius and, 125; petition for divorce, 10–11, 119, 120, 121, 123–7; uses language of Enlightenment, 126–7. *See also* Lovisoni, Francesco Saverio; Tedesco, Raffael Natan; Trieste

Morschene, Rachele Luzzatto [Luzzato]. *See* Morschene, Rachele

Moscato, Yehuda, 111n1

music, 72, 73, 88; and identity, 169, 176, 179

music (Jewish liturgical), 164, 179, 180n6; acculturating tendencies, 10, 165, 168; associated with *desaccord*, 80; changes in, 12, 166, 170, 171–3; choral, 174, 175; German Reform and, 167, 168, 171; modernity and modernization, 164, 166, 168, 177, 178; *musica sacra*, 12, 173, 174; musicology of, 164, 165, 168; 'old,' 167, 174; practices, 171–3; pre-modern, 168, 171, 180n6; processes of acculturation and, 167, 169, 178; repertoire collections, 170, 174–5, 181n26, 182n30; traditional and non-Jewish sources in, 166, 168, 169–70; Spanish-Portuguese tradition of, 175; Temple norms, 10; uniqueness of Italian style, 166–7; variants, 167, 168, 174–5. *See also* Burney, Charles; Marcello, Benedetto; Naumbourg, Samuel; Palumbo, Giuseppe; Soáve, Mose; Sulzer, Salomon; synagogues; synagogues (Italian)

music, synagogue. *See under* synagogues; synagogues (Italian)

Naples (city), 4, 150, 158; Spanish expulsion of Jews, 43. *See also* Naples, Kingdom of

Naples, Kingdom of 149; and Jews, 153; Jacobin republics in, 150, 158; *Sanfedisti* in, 157

Napoleon. *See* Bonaparte, Napoleon

Nathan the Wise (Lessing), 53n80

Naumbourg, Samuel, 173

Netherlands, The, 167

New Christians, 21–2, 25, 34–5, 43

Nora, Pierre, 194

Norzi, Yedidiya Samuel, 111n1

notarial acts. *See* Castiligione, Samuel; Lovisoni, Francesco Saverio; Pia-

telli, Isaac; Piatelli, Judah; Rome, Jews of
Nussdorfer, Laurie, 59

Otherness (Jews as the Other), 19, 28; and toleration, 43; in historiography, 89–90n2; of Venetian Jews, 45–6. *See also* alterity

Padua: musical archive, 170, 173, 182n30; rabbinical seminary, 170
Palestine, 123
Palumbo, Giuseppe, 173
Paluzzi, Numidio, 29–30. *See also* Coppio Sullam, Sara
Papal States, 149; emancipation, 156; *Hebraorum Gens* and, 43; policies towards Jews, 43, 153, 154, 155; 'Viva Maria' insurgency, 158
Paracelsus, 112n4
Paris, 178; Sanhedrin of 1807, 11, 135, 166; synagogue repertoire, 173, 175
parola ebreo, La (Loy), 189
Parthenopean Republic, 158
Pas, David, 34. *See also* Venice, Inquisition
Pasquali, Prudenza, 40–1. *See also* Venice, Inquisition
Passeri, Mgr (titular bishop of Larissa), 162n33
Paul IV (pope), 35. See also *Cum Nimis Absurdum* (1555)
Pergola, Alberto Della, 173
Periodic Table, The (Primo Levi), 193–4, 201n49
Peter Leopold (grand duke of Tuscany): and Jewish community of Livorno, 151; and Martini, 163n36; reforms of, 155, 157

Piacenza, 156
Piattelli, Isaac (Isach): and arbitration, 70n18; and coded emotion, 60, 62; Hebrew notarial acts, 57, 59, 62, 63, 68n3; son of Judah Piatelli, 57. *See also* Rome, Jews of
Piatelli, Judah: and arbitration, 70n18; and coded emotion, 60, 62; father of Isaac Piatelli, 57; Hebrew notarial acts, 57, 59, 62, 63, 68n3. *See also* Rome, Jews of
Piedmont, 156, 158; and the 'Viva Maria' insurgency, 150, 157; church-state relations in, 150, 154; emancipation in, 156; Jewish communities, 4, 154, 156; Jewish jargon of, 187, 189, 193; Jewish liturgical music in, 168; in Primo Levi, 193
Pin, Emile, 56
Pirandello, Luigi: *Un goj*, 189, 197n21
Pitigliano: and 'Viva Maria' insurgency, 158
Pittoni, Pietro Antonio, 144n62
Pius VI (pope): and Martini, 163n36; deposed by Jacobins, 149, 156; restrictions on Papal State Jews, 153, 155, 161n20
Po (Italian river valley), 149, 152
Portaleone, Avraham [Abraham ben David Portaleone]; acculturated Jew, 10; ancient and modern authorities in works, 100, 103, 106, 107; changes intellectual course, 103–5; exemplary quality of works, 110–11; member of Mantuan Jewish intellectual elite, 99; on properties of precious stones in, 105, 107, 108, 109, 110, 111n1, 112n3, 113n10, 114n26, 114n30, 115n32. *See also* Portaleone, Avraham, works

Portaleone, Avraham, works: *De Auro dialogi tres*, 10, 100–2, 107, 108, 109, 112nn3–4, 114n23; *Shilte ha-Giborim*, 10, 99, 102–7, 108–9, 110, 114n26. See also Portaleone, Avraham

Portaleoni, Yehuda de'Sommi, 111n1

Priuli, Lorenzo (cardinal), 32

Prisoners of Hope: The Silver Age of the Italian Jews, 1924–1974 (Hughes), 197n22, 199n28

Proust, Marcel, 184; Genette on, 188–9, 198n23, 200n44; Ginzburg (Natalie) and, 200n44; 'indirect language' in, 188–9, 198n23; *Recherche du temps perdus*, 184, 188–9, 200n44

Provenzali, Avraham, 111n1

Provenzali, Moshe, 111n1

Prussia, 130, 147n87

Psychopathology of Everyday Life (Freud), 189

'publicity.' See under Rome, Jews of

Pullan, Brian, 8, 26, 39, 53n80

rassegna mensile di Israel, La, 186, 193. See also Romano, Giorgio; Terracini, Benvenuto

Ravid, Benjamin, 8, 166

Recherche du temps perdus (Proust), 184, 188–9, 200n44

relations (Jewish-Christian). See exchange (Jewish-Christian)

Renaissance, 10, 73, 166, 206; Italian Jewish experience in, 4, 5, 7, 12; Jews as the Other in, 89–90n2; in Mantua, 99; music, 72, 73, 88, 166, 167; theatre, 9, 88–9

Rhetoric and Proof (Carlo Ginzburg), 197n23

Ribeiro, Joao, 34. See also Venice, Inquisition

Ribera, Francisco, 114n32

Riccioli, Giovan Battista, 101

Ricordi-Racconti, 1910–1947 (Saba), 190, 199n31

Rodriga, Daniel, 20–1

Romanelli, Giuseppe: and the 'Viva Maria' insurgency, 162n33

Romano, Giorgio: on Ginzburg (Natalia), 193

Rome, 3, 5; arbitration in, 59, 70n18; Bassani and, 203, 204; Carnival, 78, 93n22; *Casa dei Catecumeni*, 154, 155, 161n16; Christian jurisdictions in, 61; Congrega, 58; conversion efforts in, 75, 154; Fattori, 58; French in, 158, 159; ghetto, 9, 11, 56, 57, 58, 61, 149, 151–2, 156, 159, 160n4; *Hebraorum Gens* and, 43; in Loy, 189; Jacobin republic in, 149–50, 156, 158; Jewish-Christian exchange in, 9, 15n4; Jewish community, 152, 197n17; Jewish liturgical manuscripts from, 170, 173; *jus commune* and Jewish arbitration, 59; Lassels on, 93n22; Montaigne on, 80; Morosini and, 40; Neapolitan army and, 149, 158, 159; papal vicar in, 59, 61, 62, 64, 66, 68n3; Ponte Sisto (Compagnia della Santissima Trinità), 75, 92n11; restrictions on Jewish loan banks, 154, 161n15; synagogues, 58, 61, 75. See also Bonet, Francesco Rovira; Catholic Church; Evelyn, John; Italy; Rome, Jews of

Rome, Jews of, 3, 9, 40; acculturation, 57, 58, 60, 67; adoption practices, 61; domestic conflict resolution,

64–7; during Carnival, 78, 93n22; emancipation, 159; language, 197n17; liturgical music, 80, 168, 170, 173; management of emotion, 61–2, 63, 64–7, 70n29, 71n36; 'masque' and, 56, 57, 63; papal vicar and, 59, 61, 62, 64, 66, 68n3; Piatellis and, 57, 59, 60, 62, 63, 68n3; political instinct of, 9; 'publicity' of, 58–9, 60–1, 63, 64; reactions to revolution, 153; responses to ghettoization, 56–8; 'Romanity' of, 57, 63, 67; self-governance, 57, 58, 61, 64; 'social theatre' of, 59–60, 63, 64, 65, 69n11, 70n20; status, 58; use of arbitration, 59, 60, 67, 70n18, 138n7; use of notarial acts, 57, 58, 59, 60, 61, 62, 70n29; 'virtual Jewish state' of, 9, 57, 67. *See also* Bassani, Giorgio; Benedict XIV; Castiglione, Samuel; Clement XIV; Gregory I; Piatelli, Judah; Piatelli, Isaac; Pius VI; Rome

Rosenwein, Barbara, 61

Rossi, Azaria de' [Azariah de']. *See* de' Rossi, Azaria

Rossi, Salamone, 86–8

Roth, Cecil, 4, 5, 9, 90n2

Rouen, 130

Rovigo, 170, 173; synagogue, 174

Ruderman, David, 5, 9, 166

Rueo, Francesco (François de la Rue), 107, 114n28

Ruffo, Fabrizio (cardinal): and the *Sanfedisti* movement, 150, 158

Ruggiero, Guido, 60

Russia, 149, 150, 158

Saba, Umberto, 12, 190, 199n36; and Levi (Carlo), 191, 199n31, 201n49; Cavaglion on, 201n49; Lavagetto on, 199n36; Triestine Jewish origins, 191; use of Triestine Jewish jargon, 190–1

Saba, Umberto, works: *A Hebrew Scholar*, 190; *Ernesto*, 190; *Gli ebrei*, 190–1, 200n37; *Ricordi-Racconti*, 190, 199n31; *Trieste's Ghetto*, 190. *See also* Cavaglion, Alberto; Lavagetto, Mario

Saint-Didier, Alexandre-Toussaint Limojon de, 30

Salonika, 175

'Samuel, Samuel.' *See Barca di Venetia per Padova; ebraiche*

Santa Fede, La (Army of the Holy Faith), 150. *See also* Italy, *Sanfedisti* movement

Sanuto, Marino, 32

Sardinia, 150

Sarpi, Paolo, 42

Savonarola, Girolamo, 95n47

Scaletta, Orazio, 80

Scazzocchio, Abramo ben Aron (rabbi), 64

Schenkelbach, Erwin, 56

Schmitz, Ettore Aron. *See* Svevo, Italo

Schnitzler, Arthur: *Weg ins Freie, Der*, 184

Segre, Augusto: *Memorie di vita ebraica*, 198n24

Senigallia: 'Viva Maria' insurgency, 158, 159; Jewish community, 172

Seroussi, Edwin, 11

Shilte ha-Giborim (Portaleone), 10, 99, 102–7, 114n26; compared with *De Auro dialogi tres*, 107–8; dissimulation in, 106–9; dual nature of, 103; example of acculturation, 105, 106; function of Temple imagery in,

104; modern disciplines in, 105, 106; non-Jewish sources in, 106; on ancient authorities and truth, 104–5; on experience and knowledge, 109; on limits of human knowledge, 102–3; synthesis of past and present in, 105–6; work of atonement, 103–4. *See also* de' Rossi, Azaria; Flavius, Joseph; *Spiritual Exercises*
Shomrim la-boker, 172
Shulhan Arukh (Karo), 26, 129
Sicily, 3, 150
Siegmund, Stefanie, 138n7
Siena: Jewish community of, 4, 151, 159; 'Viva Maria' insurgency, 159
'social theatre.' *See under* Rome, Jews of
Soáve, Mose: *israelitismo moderno, L'*, 176
Soragna, 173
Sorkin, David, 9, 184
Spain, 6, 21, 43
Spiritual Exercises (Loyola), 104
Stock, Nello,199n36
Stow, Kenneth, 8–9, 15, 138n7
Struever, Nancy, 58
subculture, 195–6n11; definitions, 9, 194n3; Gallino and, 194n3; Italian Jewish, 184, 188, 196–7n17; language and, 184; Sorkin on, 9, 184
Sullam, Jacob, 28. *See also* Coppio Sullam, Sara
Sullam, Sara Coppio. *See under* Coppio Sullam, Sara
Sullam, Simon Levis. *See* Levis Sullam, Simon
Sulzer, Salomon, 173
Svevo, Italo (pseud. for Ettore Aron Schmitz): Debenedetti on, 198–9n28; Hughes on, 199n28; Triestine Jewish origins, 191; use of Hebrew words, 189–90; Voghera on, 199n28
Sweden, 130
synagogue music. *See under* music (Jewish liturgical); synagogues; synagogues (Italian)
synagogues, 8, 172, 173, 175, 178; and Jewish identity, 164; cantor, 172; music, 164–5, 178; music repertoires, 172, 173, 175; participation of women in, 172. *See also* music (Jewish liturgical); synagogues (Italian)
synagogues (Italian): architectural innovations, 171; community participation in, 171–2; liturgical musical reform, 171–3; local repertoires, 178; music, 11, 80, 81, 166, 167, 168, 169, 171, 173–4, 175, 178, 179, 180n6; *musica sacra* in, 12, 173, 174; of Florence, 177; of Livorno, 174, 175; of Padua, 170, 173; of Rome, 58, 61, 75; of Rovigo, 174; of Soragna, 173; of Turin, 175, 177; of Venice, 24, 25, 26, 27, 31–2, 48n19, 79, 166; of Vercelli, 174, 175; practises, 168, 171, 172, 173, 174; role of the cantor, 172; role of the music director; role of women, 172. *See also* music (Jewish liturgical)

Talmud, 6, 13, 26, 65, 105, 106, 146n84, 161n20
Tam, Rabbenu, 123
Tedesco, Raffael Natan (chief rabbi of Trieste), 124, 125
Terracini, Benvenuto, 12; concept of 'Jewish' spirit, 186, 196n12; 'How a

Language Dies,' 186; 'La Grande Illusione,' 186, 196n12; on Ascoli's 'linguistic substratum,' 185, 186; on Italian Jewish jargon, 186–7

'Tich, tach, toch.' See *Amfiparnaso*

Toland, John, 45

toleration/tolerance: cultural exchange and, 5; Jewish history and, 6, 43; in the Renaissance, 8; in Venice, 26–8; Josephinian, 120, 151, 155, 156. *See also under* alterity; Habsburg (state); Otherness

Torah, 106

Torrefranca, Massimo, 169

Tourrete, Alexandre de la, 112–13n10

Trento, 155

Treves, Maestro, 174

Trieste, 135; civil court, 119, 144n62; Enlightenment proponents in, 130–1, 144n62; French occupation, 156; ghetto, 155, 190; Jewish community, 3, 151, 152, 156; Jewish literary culture, 189, 190, 191; Jewish liturgical repertoire, 173; Josephinian reforms in, 119–20; Luzzatto family in, 119, 124, 137n2; Morschene family in, 119; rabbinical authority and civil courts, 11, 132; Saba and, 190, 191, 199n36. *See also* Martini, Karl Anton; Tedesco, Raffael

Trieste's Ghetto (Saba), 190

Trissino, Giovan Giorgio, 88

Tunisia, 175

Turin, 170, 183, 197n17; ghetto, 151; Jewish community, 152; Jewish conversions in, 154; Jewish liturgical music, 175; synagogue, 175, 177

Turner, Victor, 69n11

Tuscany, 152, 155, 156; emancipation, 149; 'Viva Maria' insurgency, 157, 158

Vecchi, Orazio, 86; Banchieri and, 91n7; Hebrew vocables and language in, 79, 93nn25–7, 94nn30–1. *See also* Vecchi, Orazio, works

Vecchi, Orazio, works: *Amfiparnaso*, 77–8, 79, 82, 89, 91n7; 'Tich tach toch,' 77–8, 82, 94n37; *Veglie di Siena*, 78, 86, 93n20. See also *ebraiche*; Vecchi, Orazio

Veglie di Siena (Vecchi), 78, 86, 93n20

Veltri, Giuseppe: *Cultural Intermediaries: Jewish Intellectuals in Early Modern Italy*, 7

Venetian Republic (Most Serene Republic), 21, 22, 45

Venetian Terrafirma, 156

Veneto, 156, 165

Venice (city), 5, 170; adjudication practises and Jews, 26; and Counter Reformation, 6, 35; and Levantine Jews, 20, 21, 23, 35; and New Christians, 21–2, 25; and non-Jewish foreigners, 20, 26–7, 28, 46; and papal policies, 21–2; and Ponentine Jews, 21–2, 23, 35; and Tedeschi Jews, 20, 22–3, 32, 42; Avogadari di Comune, 25; Cattaveri, 32–3, 36, 37–8, 42; ceded to Austria, 162n22; charters on Jews, 20, 21, 22, 24–6, 35, 38, 41–2; Christian interest in Judaism in, 24, 26, 31–2, 38–41; Cinque Savii alla Mercanzia, 22, 35–6; citizenship laws, 19–20, 22, 47n6; conversions to Judaism, 40–1; Council of Ten, 26, 32; Essecutori contro la Bestemmia, 36–7, 42;

ethnic unification, 177; ghetto (Ghetto Vecchio), 5, 6, 8, 13, 24, 25, 27, 32, 34, 35–6, 42, 151, 162n22, 165, 168, 206; Inquisition, 33–5, 38–41; Interprete della Ligua ebrea in, 26; Jewish community of, 52n67, 152; Jewish-Christian exchanges in, 8, 28, 32–41, 53n83; Levant trade, 19, 21, 22, 47n6; policies towards non-Catholic religions, 26–8, 34, 42, 46; print culture, 6, 24, 48n15; restrictions on Christian presence in the ghetto, 36, 37–8; Rodriga and, 20–1; Senate (*Maggior Conseglio*), 33, 42; Serrata, 46n2; synagogue repertoire, 175; synagogues, 24, 25, 26, 27, 31–2, 48n19, 79, 166; Talmud published in, 6, 13. See also Berengo, Marino; Garzoni, Tommaso; Lane, Frederick; Luzzatto, Simone; Misson, Maximilien; Vecchi, Orazio; Venetian Republic; Venetian Terrafirma; Veneto; Venice, Jews of
Venice, Jews of: allowed synagogues, 24; and Austrian rule, 165, 168; and forced baptism, 25, 42; and ghettoization, 6–7, 8, 21, 23, 166, 168; and Inquisition, 34–5, 38–42; and Otherness, 45–6; Avogadari di Comune and, 25; Cattaveri and, 32–3, 36, 37–8, 41, 42; charters, 20–2, 24, 25, 26, 35, 38, 41–2, 47n10; Clenche on, 30; clothing regulations, 23, 37; community fissures, 152; Coryate on, 79; conditions of residence, 23; *Cum Nimis Absurdum*, 24, 35; economic exchanges with Christians, 33–4, 35–7, 38, 52–3n68; economic restrictions on, 23–4, 35–7; emancipation, 156, 162n22, 165, 168; ethnic communities unified, 177; Fourth Lateran Council and, 23; Garzoni on, 89; Italian national unity and, 168; legal status of, 8, 19–20, 22, 28, 50n36; liturgical repertoire from, 170, 175; Luzzatto (Simone) on, 45, 50n36, 52n68; Misson on, 30–1; Morosini on, 30; population, 52n67; practise of Jewish rites and customs, 24–6; relations with Venetian nobility, 30–1; restrictions on, 154, 168; Saint-Didier on, 30; Sanuto on, 32; sexual relations with Christians, 41–2, 48n13; Shomrim la-boker, 172. See also Coppio Sullam, Sara; Jews (Italian); music (Jewish liturgical); ghettoization; Jona, Abraham; Modena, Leon; Venice (city)
Ventura, Ernesto: letters to Idelsohn, 175, 181n26
Venturi, Franco, 153
Vercelli: *L'educatore israelita* established, 169; synagogue, 174, 175; synagogue music, 170
Verona: Jewish liturgical repertoire, 173; reform in, 10–1, 167
vessillo israelitico, Il. See *Vessillo Israelitico*
Vessillo Israelitico, 169, 187
Via della fede (Morosini), 30, 31, 51n52
Vienna, 128, 131, 173, 178. See also Habsburg (state); Lagasius, Johann; Martini, Karl Anton
'Viva Maria' insurgency. See under Italy
Voghera, Giorgio, 199n28

Washington, Booker T., 160, 163n40
Weg ins Freie, Der (Schnitzler), 184
Weill, Yedidiah Tiah (rabbi), 129, 143n53
Wittgenstein, Ludwig, 195n9, 202n52
Württemberg, 130

Zakut (Zacuto), Moshe, 111n1
Zimmerman, Joshua: *Jews in Italy under Fascist and Nazi Rule*, 7, 15n10
Zinzendorf, Karl von, 144n62
Zorattini, Pier Cesare Ioly, 34

www.ingramcontent.com/pod-product-compliance
Lightning Source LLC
Chambersburg PA
CBHW030316080526
44584CB00012B/580